THE
PERMANENT
COUP

Also by Lee Smith

THE PLOT AGAINST THE PRESIDENT
The True Story of How Congressman Devin Nunes
Uncovered the Biggest Scandal in US History

THE PERMANENT COUP

HOW ENEMIES FOREIGN AND DOMESTIC
TARGETED THE AMERICAN PRESIDENT

LEE SMITH

CENTER
STREET®

NEW YORK   NASHVILLE

Center Street
Hachette Book Group
1290 Avenue of the Americas, New York, NY 10104
centerstreet.com
twitter.com/centerstreet

First Edition: August 2020

Center Street is a division of Hachette Book Group, Inc. The Center Street name
and logo are trademarks of Hachette Book Group, Inc.

The publisher is not responsible for websites (or their content)
that are not owned by the publisher.

The Hachette Speakers Bureau provides a wide range of authors for speaking events.
To find out more, go to www.HachetteSpeakersBureau.com or call (866) 376-6591.

Print book interior design by Timothy Shaner, NightandDayDesign.biz

Library of Congress Cataloging-in-Publication Data has been applied for.

ISBNs: 978-1-5460-5955-4 (hardcover), 978-1-5460-5954-7 (ebook)

Printed in the United States of America

LSC-C

10   9   8   7   6   5   4   3   2   1

To Augustus, my son

And to the Flynn family, fighters

- Donald Trump announces his candidacy for president on June 16.
- On July 14, the Obama administration strikes a nuclear agreement with Iran.
- In the summer, CIA analyst Eric Ciaramella is detailed to the White House and works with Biden.
- In October, Washington, DC–based opposition research firm Fusion GPS hires CIA contractor Nellie Ohr for research on alleged Trump ties to Russian organized crime figures.
- On December 7, a *New York Times* article reports on Hunter Biden's work for Ukrainian firm Burisma.
- On December 9, Joe Biden first publicly calls for the Ukrainian government to clean out the prosecutor's office investigating the company that is paying his son.

2016

- In mid-January, the Obama White House invites Ukrainian officials to Washington and asks them to drop the investigation of the company paying Hunter Biden. US officials also ask for information on a Republican strategist who worked with Ukrainian officials, Paul Manafort. Biden aide and Ukraine specialist Ciaramella is in attendance.
- Former MI6 agent Christopher Steele, senior Department of Justice official Bruce Ohr, and Fusion GPS founder Glenn Simpson begin to correspond regarding Trump and Russia issues.
- Trump names his foreign policy team in March 21 interview with the *Washington Post*.
- A smear campaign tying Trump officials to Russian interests begins to appear in the US press at the end of March.
- Paul Manafort is named Trump campaign convention manager on March 29.

CHRONOLOGY OF
THE PERMANENT COUP

2013

- The Maidan Revolution is born as protestors take to the streets in Kiev, Ukraine, on November 21.

- Between November and February, Vice President Joe Biden makes nine phone calls to Ukrainian president Victor Yanukovych.

- In December, State Department official Victoria Nuland is in Kiev meeting with Yanukovych, opposition, and protestors in effort to shape foreign government.

2014

- After Ukrainian president Yanukovych flees to Russia in February, Biden visits Kiev in April to warn Ukrainian officials against corruption.

- In May Biden's son Hunter is appointed to the board of Bursima, an energy company owned by an ally of the exiled Yanukovych.

- In August, a Ukrainian prosecutor opens investigation of Burisma. By end of year, owner of company paying Biden's son $80,000 a month has fled Ukraine and is on the most wanted list.

2015

- Through the spring and summer, Biden is in regular contact with the new Ukrainian president, Poroshenko.

CONTENTS

- On March 29, the Ukrainian parliament dismisses the prosecutor investigating the company paying Biden's son.

- In April, Fusion GPS is hired by the Hillary Clinton campaign and the Democratic National Committee.

- Rome-based academic Joseph Mifsud tells Trump aide George Papadopoulos on April 24 that Russia possesses the Hillary Clinton emails.

- Papadopoulos meets in early May with Alexander Downer. In late July, the Australian diplomat tells US counterpart Elizabeth Dibble that the Trump aide suggested Russia may have damaging information on Clinton.

- In May, Fusion GPS hires Steele to investigate Trump's ties to Russia.

- Donald Trump Jr. agrees to a June 9 meeting at Trump Tower with a Russian lawyer, Natalia Veselnitskaya. She has Clinton-funded Fusion GPS under contract to push pro-Putin, anti-US information campaign.

- On June 12 Julian Assange announces that Wikileaks will publish Clinton-related emails.

- The first memo, dated June 20, from the dossier attributed to Steele, alleges that Trump is supported by Russian government.

- Steele meets FBI agent Michael Gaeta in London on July 5.

- The same day, FBI director James Comey clears Clinton regarding the private computer server investigation.

- Carter Page delivers a speech in Moscow on July 7.

- Halper meets Carter Page at a Cambridge University symposium on July 11.

- A July 19 Steele memo alleges that prior to visiting Cambridge, Page had met with Russian officials in Moscow.

- Wikileaks posts stolen Democratic National Committee emails on July 22.

- On July 24, Clinton campaign manager Robby Mook claims that Russia hacked the DNC emails to assist Trump. Dossier memo from late July makes same allegation.

- Steele meets with Bruce and Nellie Ohr in Washington, DC, on July 30.

- On July 31, the FBI opens an umbrella investigation of the Trump team based on the information regarding Papadopoulos that the Australian diplomat gave to the US embassy in London. The investigation is called Crossfire Hurricane.

- On August 10, the FBI begins separate investigations of Manafort, Page, and Papadopoulos.

- On August 11 and 12, Crossfire Hurricane agents meet with FBI informant Stefan Halper, who claims an acquaintance with Page, Manafort, and Flynn.

- FBI agent Peter Strzok sends the "insurance policy" text to FBI lawyer Lisa Page on August 15.

- On August 16, the FBI opens an investigation of Flynn, called "Crossfire Razor."

- August 20, Halper meets with Page and asks if the Trump campaign is planning an October surprise to spring on the Clinton campaign. He records Page.

- CIA director John Brennan briefs Senate minority leader Harry Reid on Trump-Russia claims on August 25.

- Reid sends an open letter on August 29 to Comey regarding Carter Page and demands that he come forth with information he is holding.

- On September 15, Halper meets twice with Papadopoulos and records him.

- Yahoo News publishes a story sourced anonymously to Steele that implicates Page as a Russian spy on September 23. The article by Michael Isikoff is later used to obtain a spy warrant on Carter Page.

- On September 28, FBI deputy director Andrew McCabe is notified of Clinton emails found on a Clinton aide's laptop.

- The Foreign Intelligence Surveillance Court grants the FBI a warrant to monitor Page's communications on October 21.

- The FBI reopens the Clinton email investigation on October 28.

- On October 30, Harry Reid sends a second letter to Comey.

- News stories in several outlets dealing with false allegations about Trump's ties to Russia publish in the *Financial Times*, *Mother Jones*, the *New York Times*, and *Slate* on October 31.

- Donald J. Trump is elected forty-fifth president of the United States on November 8.

- No later than November 30, Obama officials commence surveillance of incoming Trump officials. Flynn's identity is unmasked from transcripts of classified intercepts no less than fifty-three times by thirty-nine Obama aides.

- On December 9, Obama directs CIA chief John Brennan to conduct an Intelligence Community Assessment that determines Russian president Vladimir Putin interfered with the election to help Trump win.

- On December 29, Obama imposes sanctions on Russia for interfering in the 2016 elections.

- Flynn's December 29 call with the Russian ambassador becomes a weapon for Obama officials to get rid of Flynn.

2017

- On January 4, FBI agent Peter Strzok is told by FBI leadership to see if the investigation of Flynn is still open.

- On January 5, Obama meets with Biden, Comey, national security advisor Susan Rice, and deputy attorney general Sally Yates. Strzok's notes show that Obama tells FBI director, "Make sure you look at things and have the right people on it." Rice writes an email to herself January 20 claiming that she and Joe Biden heard Obama tell Comey at the January 5 meeting to go "by the book."

- The declassified version of the Intelligence Community Assessment is released on January 6. The same day President-elect Trump is briefed on the ICA and the Steele dossier.

- CNN's story on Trump being briefed posts on January 10. Hours later, BuzzFeed publishes the dossier.

- David Ignatius writes a January 12 *Washington Post* column sourced to a leaked transcript of the conversation between Flynn and Kislyak.

- Crossfire Hurricane interviews Steele's primary subsource in January as part of a massive cover-up to hide abuses and crimes committed during the Trump probe.

- Trump is inaugurated as the forty-fifth president of the United States on January 20.

- In late January, the Crossfire Hurricane team discusses how to entrap Flynn in forthcoming interview.

- On January 24, Flynn is interviewed by FBI agents, who tell FBI leadership that he didn't lie.

- George Papadopoulos is interviewed for the first time January 27, six months after the FBI opened Crossfire Hurricane, based on allegations regarding his connections to Russians.

- On February 9, the *Washington Post* publishes a story sourced to the transcript of the Flynn-Kislyak call.

- Flynn leaves the White House on February 13.

- On March 2, Trump tweets that Obama had him wiretapped.

- The same day, Attorney General Jeff Sessions recused himself from the Russia investigations after a *Washington Post* story sourced to intercepts reports that he failed to declare meetings with the Russian ambassador.

- Comey's March 20 testimony before the House Permanent Select Committee on Intelligence (HPSCI) reveals the FBI's investigation of Trump.

- On March 22, the HPSCI chairman, Representative Devin Nunes, reveals the Obama administration's unmasking of Trump officials.

- Kashyap "Kash" Patel joins the HPSCI staff in April, and Objective Medusa, their investigation of abuses and possible crimes committed during FBI Russia probe, commences.

- Trump fires Comey on May 9.

- In May, deputy attorney general Rod Rosenstein reportedly suggests to FBI and DOJ officials that they record Trump.

- FBI acting director Andrew McCabe opens an investigation of Trump.

- In a bid to orchestrate the appointment of a special counsel, Comey leaks memos of meetings and conversations with Trump to the *New York Times* for a May 16 story.

- Robert Mueller is appointed special counsel on May 17.

- On May 23, John Brennan testifies in front of HPSCI that he initiated the Trump-Russia investigation.

- On June 14, the CIA's reported Russian asset Oleg Smolenkov leaves Moscow.

- The *Washington Post*'s June 23 story reports the existence of a CIA mole deep inside the Kremlin.

- The *New York Times* publishes stories on four consecutive days (July 9–12) about a Trump Tower meeting the year before between Donald Trump Jr. and a Russian lawyer.

- On July 12, the FBI interviews another attendee at the Trump Tower meeting, who corroborates Trump Jr.'s account and says that nothing nefarious happened.

- Rosenstein writes an August 2 memo outlining the scope of the special counsel investigation, parameters that are based on allegations made in the dossier.

- In October Objective Medusa uncovers that Clinton campaign paid for the dossier; the role of senior DOJ official Bruce Ohr and wife, Nellie, in the Crossfire Hurricane investigation; and that FBI agent Peter Strzok was dismissed from the Mueller team.

- After the special counsel leaks that Flynn's son may be indicted, on December 1 the former Trump confidant pleads guilty to making false statements to the FBI.

2018

- On January 23, former vice president Joe Biden gives a talk at the Council on Foreign Relations in which he boasts of a 2016 quid pro quo with the Ukrainian government. He tells the audience that he used $1 billion in US taxpayer money as leverage to get the Ukrainians to fire the prosecutor who was investigating the company paying his son Hunter.

- On February 2, the HPSCI majority releases the Nunes memo, showing that the FBI used the Clinton-funded dossier to obtain a FISA warrant on Page.

- The House Intelligence Committee releases its "Report on Russian Active Measures" on March 22.

- In April, the *New York Times* and the *Washington Post* are jointly awarded a Pulitzer Prize for pushing the collusion conspiracy theory with stories based on leaks of classified intelligence.

2019

- On February 14, William Barr is confirmed as attorney general.

- On March 22, Mueller files his final report on the special counsel investigation.

- On May 13, Barr appoints the US attorney from Connecticut John Durham to investigate the origins of Crossfire Hurricane.

- On July 24, Mueller testifies before House Judiciary and Intelligence Committees as Russia investigation concludes.

- Trump's July 25 phone call with Ukrainian president Zelensky is overheard by National Security Council staffer Lieutenant Colonel Alexander Vindman, who discusses it with colleague Eric Ciaramella.

- On August 12, Ciaramella files a whistleblower's complaint based on hearsay with intelligence community inspector general Michael Atkinson.

- After the Department of Justice finds that the report does not meet the statutory requirements to qualify as a whistleblower's complaint, Atkinson notifies the House and Senate Intelligence Committees on September 12 that he has a whistleblower's complaint.

- On September 13, California congressman Adam Schiff subpoenas the complaint.

- On September 24, Trump releases a transcript of the call. The same day House Speaker Nancy Pelosi announces a formal impeachment inquiry.

- Throughout October, Schiff conducts dozens of interviews to vet and rehearse witnesses before the public hearings begin.

- On December 9, 2019, the DOJ's inspector general Michael Horowitz releases his long-awaited report detailing evidence of crimes and abuses the FBI committed during the Crossfire Hurricane investigation.

- After public hearings conclude in early December, Pelosi waits until January 15 to pass two articles of impeachment to the Senate.

2020

- A week after Senate proceedings begin, Trump is warned about the approaching coronavirus and shuts down travel from China on January 31.

- On February 5, the Senate acquits the president, and the next day he celebrates with allies in the White House.

- In February, Kash Patel is detailed to the Office of the Director of National Intelligence as Ambassador Richard Grenell's deputy. The documents they declassify give more evidence of government crimes and abuses committed during the Trump investigation.

- In order to better allocate federal resources to manage the pandemic, Trump declares a national emergency on March 13.

- On March 29, the president extends stay-at-home guidelines through April.

- Barack Obama makes an unprecedented appearance on social media on April 10 to remind his supporters of his political presence.

- On May 7, the Justice Department withdraws its case against Flynn.

- On May 8, Obama leaks a conversation in which he suggests Flynn might yet be prosecuted for perjury.

- On May 25, a Minneapolis man dies when a police officer kneels on the back of his neck for nearly nine minutes. The ensuing protests spread throughout America, leaving a wake of death and destruction.

- On May 31, rioters massing at the White House set fire to a historic church.

- On June 1, Trump leads senior cabinet members on a walk across Pennsylvania Avenue to visit the church. The president holds a Bible in his hands and says, "This is a great country."

- Former defense secretary James Mattis publishes a statement on June 3 that encourages senior Pentagon officials to put distance between themselves and the president, thereby destabilizing the government of the United States.

- The same day, June 3, Obama holds a video town hall in which he says the protests that ravaged America offer an opportunity for change.

- The coup continues.

ONE

CLOUD OF DUST

"We've all been through a lot together," said the president.

It was February 6, 2020, and Donald Trump was addressing the allies he'd brought together at the White House. The Senate had just acquitted him of impeachment charges, and it appeared that the plot that had begun even before Trump became president was finally over.

The country had been through a lot ever since he was elected to lead it. And there would be more only a few months ahead, epochal events that no one could have imagined, a global pandemic, and then nationwide riots that convulsed the country. Even these shared traumas that should've united America were seen by Trump's opponents as instruments to undo him. It was by that time the normal course of things.

Almost immediately after he'd won the presidency, a vocal and privileged minority led by government bureaucrats and the media convinced millions of Americans to turn on their neighbors, families, and fellow citizens just because they voted for Trump. They called the rancor they used to divide the country "Resistance." The instability they provoked was meant to impede the president's agenda with the ultimate goal of forcing Trump from the White House.

But in February, the president was just relieved to have been acquitted. He talked about his 2016 opponent, whose political warfare operation tasked a former British spy to invent a story about him and imaginary ties to Russia. "Hillary Clinton and the DNC paid millions of dollars for a fake dossier," said Trump, "and now Christopher Steele admits that it's fake."

The FBI used the dossier to get a warrant to spy on Trump and his associates. He described his interactions with the former director of the Bureau, who'd managed the coup until May 2017. "Had I not fired James Comey," said Trump, "it's possible I wouldn't even be standing here right now. We caught him in the act. Dirty cops. Bad people."

In May 2017, control of the operation was passed to a special counsel, Comey's predecessor at the FBI, Robert Mueller. He conducted a nearly two-year investigation based on the Clinton campaign's fake dossier. "We then went through the Mueller report," said the president, referring to the more than four-hundred-page document that found no evidence of the collusion story the Clinton campaign had invented to destroy Trump. "They should have come back one day later," he said, referring to the two years and $40 million that Mueller wasted chasing a vulgar fairy tale—and that came after the FBI had already investigated the case for a year.

The effort to impeach the president followed within hours after the curtain came down on Mueller. The impeachment charges were tailored to the precise pattern of the Russia collusion narrative. Clinton's campaign had alleged that Trump had made promises to Russia in exchange for help defeating her in 2016. And now at the start of 2020, career bureaucrats and House Democrats accused Trump of offering a quid pro quo to the president of Ukraine for help against the man they planned to run against him, Joe Biden.

"They made up facts," said Trump. "A corrupt politician named Adam Schiff made up my statement to the Ukrainian president. He brought it out of thin air. Just made it up." He was referring to a bizarre, fake rendition of Trump's phone call with the Ukrainian president that Schiff had read out during a public hearing of the House Intelligence Committee.

Trump was comfortable among his Republican allies that afternoon. He let on that he wasn't really holding a news conference, nor was he was giving a speech. The media didn't know what to make of it. Trump was having fun. He knew how to hold an audience. "It's a celebration," he said. He wanted to thank friends. "I call them friends because," he said, "you develop friendships and relationships when you're in battle and war much more so than in a normal situation."

He singled out Devin Nunes for praise. "He's the most legitimate human being. He's the hardest worker. He's unbelievable. He took tremendous abuse."

The California Congressman was the first, as the president said, to step forward to say he'd seen evidence of an espionage operation within the U.S. government targeting Trump. Nunes had few allies at first. Even many of the people in the room where the president had gathered his friends had initially shied away. It wasn't because they distrusted the 45-year-old nine-term representative. They'd just been scared off. They had seen how the press destroyed its opponents. They'd seen how activists drained their targets of money, threatened their jobs, and used their media partners to portray their opponents as extremists, racists, and Russian stooges. They'd watched as the intelligence community picked apart Trump appointees. Who wanted to be part of that? So Nunes had been on his own.

"They wanted to destroy him. They tried. They got close, but he wouldn't let it happen," said Trump. "He came out of nowhere. He's saying, 'These people are corrupt.' He's still saying it. He was unbelievable."

Recognized by the president, Nunes stood for a second and clapped. When everyone else stood to applaud their colleague, Nunes sat down. It looked like he wanted the moment over quickly.

I ask Nunes if he was uncomfortable with the attention. No, he says. "It's just not time for a victory lap, no reason to celebrate yet, there's a lot more to do. No reason to celebrate until these freaks are locked up."

It's late winter 2020, a few weeks after the acquittal, and we're driving out of Tulare, California, Nunes's hometown, and headed north. He's scheduled to deliver the keynote speech for a Bay Area Republican group's Lincoln dinner. Nunes is still surprised that so many in his audiences know the details of his investigation and those he was investigating.

"Everyone knows all the names and what they did—all the dirty cops at the FBI, from Comey on down, Andrew McCabe, Peter Strzok, Lisa Page." That so many people know is evidence that Americans recognize the plot represents a large rupture in US political life. It's now a part of American history, like the Civil War. It was Nunes who fired the first shot against the coup plotters.

The team he assembled as chairman of the House Permanent Select Committee on Intelligence (HPSCI) and the investigation he'd initiated in the early spring of 2017 had found evidence that the FBI had abused the resources of the federal government to spy on Trump and his associates. Clinton operatives and prestige press organizations worked to smear Trump as a Russian asset, as Obama appointees across the administration spied on him and his team as Trump was candidate, president-elect, and then president.

"Everyone asks if the people who did this are going to pay," says Nunes. "Believe me, after the president, there's no one who wants these bastards to go down more than I do. I want to see the job finished."

Nunes's lead investigator for HPSCI's inquiry into FBI crimes and abuses was Kashyap "Kash" Patel, a former Department of Justice prosecutor. He'd previously worked with the senior FBI officials involved in the plot and warned his colleagues they'd find irregularities. Patel had warned them that Comey, McCabe, and the rest were driven by agendas. He had told Nunes there were so many elements to their inquiry that they'd have to cut it off at the head. It was Patel who named the investigation Objective Medusa.

After leaving Nunes's committee in the fall of 2018, Patel went to the White House. He was the National Security Council staff's senior director for counterterrorism when US special forces took down master terrorist Abu Bakr Al-Baghdadi.

"We couldn't have done what we did without Kash," says Nunes. The congressman sees everything significant in terms of his first calling, farming. He compares meeting Patel and their work together to how the California pistachio industry started.

"One night these two guys, Corky Anderson and Ken Puryear, wind up meeting in a bar," says Nunes. "They didn't know each other before, but they get to talking. Ken was a dentist, and Corky persuaded him to go into farming. It must have sounded promising, because he agreed. They went into business together, then struggled to keep it going, until one day Ken finds a tree stock going all the way back to the nineteenth century. They know it's survived the Central Valley climate that long, so now they have their foundation. And that's how they started the pistachio industry. It created thousands of jobs. What they made supported not just families but an entire region. It all came from a chance meeting."

It was chance that Nunes rather than someone else was in charge of HPSCI when the coup unfolded, and it was chance that he and Patel met. Their character determined their actions, without which it's unlikely the anti-Trump operation would have been discovered. If not, no one would have been there to stop the plot.

Now, after three years on defense, Trump was unbound and eager to get the country back to work. The economy was already at full steam. The unemployment rate was the lowest it had been since 1969. Americans across the political spectrum, African Americans, Latinos, Asians, and women were all working in numbers and producing at a pace no one had ever seen before. "The best is yet to come," Trump liked to say. Now he would have the time and room to implement the agenda for which he was elected—build America and protect Americans.

Nunes also had work to do. There were important things he wanted to accomplish with the Intelligence Committee. He was finally going to turn his attention to China. "When Trump was elected, we were optimistic because we were going to be able to focus on China," Nunes had said frequently. "All the time we spent on Trump-Russia collusion was a waste of important time."

He was sent to Washington to represent the interests of the residents of the San Joaquin Valley, whose ability to make a living depended on the steady flow of water coming off the Sierra Nevada snowpack, which makes California's 22nd district, as Nunes likes to say, the breadbasket of the solar system.

We're on Highway 99 with the Sierra Nevadas to our east with Mount Whitney, the tallest spot in the continental US, hidden in the mist. "The pioneers knew that if you could capture that snow before it went to the Pacific Ocean," says Nunes, "you'd create the most valuable land in the history of planet Earth."

That water is also what keeps California's major population centers, Los Angeles and San Francisco, from becoming deserts. "If you live where Nancy Pelosi lives," Nunes says of the Speaker of the House, "they'd run out of water in a few days. Without the snowpack, she'd be drinking saltwater."

In the early 1900s Congress rerouted water destined for the San Joaquin valley and sent it to San Francisco. It soon became one of most powerful cities in the world and, with the advent of Silicon Valley in the 1970s, the capital of global technology.

Up ahead is where the Sacramento and the San Joaquin Rivers meet to form the California Delta. "That's where it started," says Nunes. "It's the reason I got into politics."

The delta is ground zero for California's water wars, a struggle between urban activists and the Central Valley's working middle class. The melting snow fills the delta with more than enough water for all of California's 40 million residents several times over. But due to environmental regulations, nearly 80 percent of the water is flushed into the ocean. Environmental groups explain it's to save wildlife species, like the Delta smelt.

"That shows you how hypocritical our opponents are," says Nunes. "The smelts' main problem isn't farmers; it's the striped bass, a nonnative species that preys on the smelts."

Nunes says most of the early environmentalists really were serious about saving species. "But that changed in the 1970s when left-wing politicians saw it as a way to co-opt the environmentalist movement to gain political power. The irony is that the people who work the land are closest to the natural environment. They're at the intersection of soil and weather and the surroundings. We're the last ones who'd want to destroy the environment—we're the people who make a living from it. We farmers are the closest to nature."

The water wars were part of a larger progressive offensive that zeroed in on the timber industry as well as agriculture. At that point it was no longer about preserving wildlife but controlling people, their use of land, and their ability to make a living. The left saw it as war—they were laying siege to the economic base of the Americans they saw as enemies.

The water wars drove Nunes into the political arena. If he hadn't, he says, "the progressives would've crushed the hopes and dreams of every family in the Valley, the Okies who moved here from the Dust Bowl, foreign immigrants like my family who came here looking for economic freedom, everyone."

Fighting that campaign taught Nunes to recognize the conflict he engaged in when he stepped up in March 2017 to say he found evidence the president had been spied on. "The tactics were different, and it took a little while to realize exactly their game, but it was the same kinds of people, bureaucrats, media, left-wing activists," says Nunes. "It's the same fight."

And that's why Nunes says the three-year-long anti-Trump siege isn't really about the president.

"It's much bigger," he says. "And it's been going on for a long time. Look at Bush, McCain, Romney—it was all the same, they treated them just like Trump. Take Romney—successful, rich, good-looking, no scandals. He flip-flops, he's not my kind of guy, but he's smooth, and he didn't even come close to beating Obama, who was a total failure. The economy, Obamacare, Iraq, Al-Qaeda, the reset with Russia—Obama failed on everything. And still Romney got smoked. Why? Because of the slow takeover by the left. Now with Trump, it's all exposed because unlike those guys, he fights back. It's clear now the press is a state-owned leftist enterprise. They control everything—universities, nonprofits, bureaucracies, the Beltway corridor, all the mainstream media, and social media is controlled by billionaire tech oligarchs."

The left is furious they didn't win in 2016, says Nunes. "We got lucky. A figure like Trump doesn't come around very often. He's an outsider. He's a great communicator, he has abilities the swamp creatures don't. He spent his career in marketing, and thirteen years doing a successful TV show," Nunes pauses. They hate him because he's fighting, because before him the left got away with defaming, slandering, and libeling anyone who got in their way."

Trump was also fortunate to draw the opponent he did in 2016. "He happened to run against someone who was totally corrupt," says Nunes. "They're so corrupt that Trump didn't even know how bad it was—they turn the CIA and FBI against him. Why? They say it's because he went to a beauty pageant in Moscow once back in 2013? It's unreal."

Outside of Republicans, Trump gets little credit for what he's done the last three years, while fighting a coup. "He says he should have high approval ratings, and he should," says Nunes. "He has the highest approval ratings in Republican history. I've never seen polling among Republicans like this. So why is he stuck in the low forties? Because of the poison coming out of the press. He has zero Democrats and is struggling to keep independents. If you did a poll today, you'd find that at least 50 percent still think he's a Russian agent."

It's not about Trump, says Nunes. It's bigger. It's about the future of the country.

"We knew this," says the congressman. "It was right in front of our eyes. We got lucky in '16, because of Clinton's corruption and Trump's abilities. He's just in their face more, but they're not going after Trump. They're going after everything America has stood for, government that governs close to the people so the people can make decisions for themselves and not have their lives decided by the Washington bureaucracy. The leftists are like leftists around the globe in their bloodthirst for power—they want to make everyone else their slaves. The immigrants who are coming for the same reason my family came from the Azores want the American dream, but that's on the verge of extinction. They're walking into a trap— the most beautiful and powerful state in the Union is becoming like the places those immigrants left to find freedom here. And the whole country is going in the same direction as California."

He pauses for a second. "We're left with no choice but to fight." That's why the audience is here tonight—because Nunes fights.

Over the last month, I'd traveled California from Los Angeles to the Bay Area, sometimes with the congressman and other times on my own. I found that there are two questions people want answered.

First, will anyone be charged for plotting against Trump? Will law enforcement, intelligence, other US officials, or Clinton operatives pay for using extraconstitutional means to remove a duly elected president in an attempt to undo an election?

The question then isn't really about Trump. Rather, it's about those who voted to send him to the White House. They're asking about their future. Will people go to jail for trying to strip them of their right to choose who governs them, their voice in how they and their families, friends, and communities live? If not, and if those who see them as enemies can take away their home, their land, and their ability to make a living just because they exercised their right to participate in our political process, then we are moving into a different phase of American history.

The second question flows logically from the first: Who with the power to make a difference is defending us? Who's fighting? They see Trump fighting and Nunes, too. Who else?

It's a long fight, Nunes responds. He says that Objective Medusa's goal was to get the information to the American public so they could see for themselves what happened during the 2016 campaign and after. If they could convince a slim majority of the country to understand that Obama officials and Clinton operatives had undermined the American political process, they'd count it as a victory. Nunes is still fighting to get there.

In October 2017, Objective Medusa showed that the Clinton campaign had paid for the dossier. In February 2018 the Nunes team documented how the FBI had used the dossier to get a warrant to spy on Trump. In March 2019, the Mueller Report came up empty on Russia collusion. The December 2019 DOJ inspector general's report gave evidence of a massive FBI cover-up to hide the crimes and abuses committed during its investigation of Trump. In May 2020, transcripts of General Michael Flynn's phone calls with Russian ambassador Sergei Kislyak were released, showing that the incoming national security advisor never lied to the FBI, though he was blackmailed into pleading guilty to the charge.

And for all the evidence now available, the media continues to advance the most destructive conspiracy theory in US history—that the Trump campaign colluded with Russia. Nunes acknowledges that it's unlikely the left will ever admit that Russiagate was a sinister lie. The collusion narrative has torn what's likely an irreparable hole in America's social fabric.

The fight is a grind, says Nunes. "It's every day you wake up in the morning, knowing that because the media is against you you're probably going to lose and you still resolve to be a happy warrior. And some days you gain ground." He compares it to an unending football game and a punishing series of downs. "Every day, it's three yards and a cloud of dust."

This book is about that fight. The coup aimed at toppling Donald Trump will not end in November 2020, whether he is reelected or not. That's because it is aimed primarily at Americans, whether they support Trump or not. As Nunes says, the coup takes Trump as its immediate target, but it's weaponized to destroy anyone the left perceives as an enemy. The tyranny that so many fled for the promise of America has taken root here, and so the fight is ongoing. It is the permanent coup.

This book identifies the various instruments used to try to remove Trump. Readers of *The Plot Against the President* will find that the present book provides a much broader perspective on the coup, now in its third year.

For instance, the book explores how foreign actors—like a former British spy and top-level Ukrainian officials—were assigned roles in the ongoing campaign against the American public and subsequently their current commander in chief. Most significantly, the book describes how officials from both parties betrayed the ambitions of working Americans in order to enrich themselves by tying US interests to those of the Chinese Communist Party. Trump was elected in part to free America from this poisonous embrace. As COVID-19 started to take its toll on America, it was no accident that the media's anti-Trump messaging mirrored Chinese propaganda since both perceive Trump as a threat to their interests.

At other times, the left used the specter of foreign subterfuge to disguise its own active measures to destabilize America. For instance, as riots began to spread across the country at the end of May, former Obama deputies like Susan Rice and Democratic Party media outlets like CNN blamed Russia for the violence. It was a reminder that the Russia collusion narrative remains the key instrument in the anti-Trump plot. Those who had injected a poisonous conspiracy theory into the bloodstream of American life were not about to abandon it.

And yet at the same time, the nature of the plot became increasingly clear—thanks in part to Kash Patel. In February, he was assigned temporarily to the Office of the Director of National Intelligence, where he served as deputy to acting DNI Richard Grenell, the former ambassador to Germany and one of Trump's most effective appointees. Together Grenell and Patel declassified documents that Nunes had been trying to put before the American public for more than three years.

The newly available documents show that the anti-Trump operation drew on a much broader base than just the FBI and included officials from across the previous administration. But the deep state was misdirection, obscuring something much more dangerous than an entitled and entrenched bureaucracy.

CIA director John Brennan had directed surveillance of the Trump campaign. After the Republican candidate defeated Clinton, the "collusion" narrative was repurposed to keep the new president on the defensive and obscure the massive scale of the previous administration's illegal espionage campaign targeting US citizens, including Trump and his associates.

In Spring 2020, an unprecedented media event further illuminated the nature of the plot. Trump's predecessor broke more than two-hundred-year-old protocol preventing former presidents from meddling in the affairs of their successors. Barack Obama leaked a phone call to a reporter who had played a major part in pushing Russiagate. In the call, the forty-fourth president of the United States complained of the Justice Department's decision to drop its case against Michael Flynn. Trump's former national security advisor was the first casualty in the anti-Trump plot, a target designated by Obama himself.

Thus, he had not only claimed responsibility for the coup, but he'd also shed light on its ultimate goal. The rationale for destabilizing the country in the hope of removing Trump from office was to hold out until Obama's vision could be restored. As he put it a decade ago, that vision entailed the fundamental transformation of America. Thus, anything was permitted to complete the coup.

TWO

THE DIRECTOR

Attorney General William Barr said during his confirmation hearing that the Trump campaign was spied on. To find out whether the investigation the FBI opened in July 2016 was "adequately predicated," he appointed US attorney John Durham. The career prosecutor, according to Barr, was not just looking at the FBI, "he's looking at other agencies."

Durham was interested in what the former director of the Central Intelligence Agency might have done, so he asked for John Brennan's emails, call logs, and other documents. Barack Obama's fourth and longest-serving CIA director had virtually begged to be investigated.

Brennan couldn't stay off social media. He shared his thoughts about the state of the world and the American president as eagerly as a high school debate captain. He had a contract with NBC/MSNBC as a national security analyst. The network was happy to offer the twenty-five-year CIA veteran a platform to attack the president whom he said he had spied on. Since May 2017, Brennan had boasted that he had initiated the investigation into the Trump campaign's ties to Russia. He couldn't help himself.

Luke, a sixty-two-year-old former intelligence officer, worked for the CIA for nearly thirty years, retiring in 2018, is not surprised.

"To know who Brennan is, let's reason backwards from what we know about him," says Luke. "Look at his Twitter feed. It's a glimpse into his soul. His tweets are full of lies, bad judgment, and politics. He's not only unprofessional; he strongly implies he knows something, gives aid and comfort to our enemies, and to terrorists. He divides the country."

> It is in the interest of America's security if NATO leaders push back against the reckless behavior of Donald Trump, who is dangerously naive & grossly ignorant of how the world works. History inevitably will regard Trump as one of the most disastrous figures of the 21st century.

> Compare the words, tone, & spirit of any previous President with the undignified, divisive, & hate-filled invective spewed by Mr. Trump. Until so-called "Republicans" put nation above party & condemn his vile rants, this crisis will only get worse & more dangerous for all.

> What responsible & right-thinking adult can point to @ realDonaldTrump as a role model for our youth? Whenever he spews lies, insults, and polarizing hate speech against fellow Americans, think of its harmful impact on our young people and the way they talk, act, & treat others.

"His tweets are full of threats and insinuations that show he's vindictive and unprofessional," says Luke. "So, this compels you to ask, what kind of analyst was he? What sort of manager was he? Remember, as director, he was in charge of major operational decisions. We have a reckless analyst and a manager with a bad temper making stupid and highly partisan comments in public directed at the president. Bear in mind, the gold standard of an intelligence officer is objectivity and judgment—for ops officers, analysts, targeters, techies, and especially senior managers. You must separate fact from opinion. Embellishing, fabricating, insinuating, politicizing, involving your emotions—these get you reprimanded or fired," Luke explains.

"This is Brennan at his most mature and seasoned, on the internet, which is totally public and is forever, and he is unhinged. I hate to imagine a less grown-up Brennan holding enormous power and influence, protected by secrecy."

In January 2017, Brennan's handpicked team of analysts from the CIA, FBI, and National Security Agency assessed that Vladimir Putin had sought to assist Trump win the 2016 election. During Trump and Putin's July 2018 Helsinki summit, a reporter asked the commander in chief to corroborate Brennan's assessment and rebuke Putin to his face for helping him become president. Trump demurred. Brennan took to Twitter to defend his work product.

> Donald Trump's press conference performance in Helsinki rises to & exceeds the threshold of "high crimes & misdemeanors." It was nothing short of treasonous. Not only were Trump's comments imbecilic, he is wholly in the pocket of Putin. Republican Patriots: Where are you???

"Treason is a third rail," says Luke. "It's what gets you executed or put in a supermax. Among the charges you can make against an intelligence officer, stuff like embellishing or fabricating intelligence, these are mortal sins. But treason is something else. For a former CIA director to be accusing a sitting president of it is mind-boggling. And again, it offers a glimpse into the hubris and impunity Brennan seems to have enjoyed as CIA director."

It's late winter and we're sitting in a restaurant in Culver City. Los Angelenos are becoming steadily aware of a virus circulating across the Pacific and headed this way, but today the actors, writers, and executives who work in the neighborhood are looking for lunch tables outside in the sharp March light.

Luke—not his true name, but a throwaway alias he has used throughout his career—comes from a large and accomplished family. Like Brennan, Luke's roots are blue collar and Catholic, and only a short generation or two separate their generation from European immigrants to greater New York. Luke began working for the intelligence community as an Arabic linguist. Brennan, who reportedly served as station chief in Riyadh during the Clinton administration, claims to be fluent in Arabic. Luke says he and Brennan weren't friendly.

"Brennan grew up as an analyst in the Agency," says Luke, who also started in the Directorate of Intelligence. "We have the best analysts in the world. But in an espionage organization, the analyst is like the brother-in-law. Brennan was named station chief, and the Directorate of Operations did not like this. It's not that they don't like analysts, but that he had no background or training for it. Brennan did not understand operations. To that he added arrogance and a complete inability to build rapport and trust with the DO—skills that are foundational in ops, whether you are recruiting a spy network or building credibility with foreign liaison services."

Brennan was born in Bergen, New Jersey; attended Fordham University; and studied Arabic at the American University in

Cairo. When applying for the CIA, he told interviewers that he'd voted for Communist Party USA's presidential candidate Gus Hall in 1976. He said it was to register his "dissatisfaction with the system."

Likely, he wanted to shock his interviewers. Evidently, the men and women responsible for staffing the Agency did not flinch when even in the middle of the Cold War the young Brennan boasted of casting his vote for a Stalinist sentenced to eight years for "conspiracy to teach and advocate the overthrow of the U.S. government by force and violence."

It appears to have been a preview of Brennan's enduring interest in treasonous behavior, and perhaps a callow affinity for admiring American adversaries and disdaining allies that might have led Obama to see him as a kindred spirit.

Brennan didn't endear himself to colleagues when campaigning for the top CIA spot. "He said we do not steal secrets," says Luke. "People were upset. We're proud of what we do. George Tenet boasted about it, 'we do black ops, we steal foreign secrets.' It is called *espionage*, the core mission of the Agency. The CIA breaks the laws of foreign countries adversarial to the United States. That's the job. At the Agency they say, 'If you want to fight for truth, justice, and the American way, go join the FBI.'"

That's not how Brennan saw the FBI. To him, it was a political instrument. He used it to target a presidential campaign.

He said that in late July 2016 he'd assembled a team of handpicked CIA, FBI, and NSA analysts at CIA headquarters to put together everything they had on Russia and contacts with the Trump team. Brennan said he "was concerned about these contacts because people will go down a treasonous path, sometimes very unknowingly." Brennan's study of Russian methods showed him that they are "very clever at getting people in . . . compromising positions that they then cannot sort of turn back."

On July 31 the FBI opened an investigation on the Trump campaign focusing on four advisors, General Michael Flynn, Paul Manafort, Carter Page, and George Papadopoulos. The investigation was called Crossfire Hurricane. Brennan wanted credit for it.

"I was aware of intelligence and information about contacts between Russian officials and U.S. persons," said the director, "and that serves as the basis for the FBI investigation." He said that he "wanted to make sure that every information and bit of intelligence that we had was shared with the Bureau so that they could take it."

The CIA is prohibited from spying on US citizens, so he used the FBI as a pass-through device. "I made sure that anything that was involving U.S. persons," said Brennan, "including anything involving the individuals involved in the Trump campaign, was shared with the Bureau."

He said he started sharing information with the FBI in the summer. Congressional investigators would have left it at that, but Brennan wanted to talk more. He explained it was "even previous" to the summer. He was feeding information into the FBI long before it opened Crossfire Hurricane. There was, he explained, "ongoing sharing of information with the Bureau, and so it was over the course of the year."

He also passed that information on to senior US officials, including the president. Where did the information come from? He gave conflicting accounts. He said he found out from the press. He claimed the information came from a source inside the Kremlin.

Brennan was very political, says Luke. "He never made a peep about capturing terrorists and the enhanced interrogation program. But when it was convenient, when he wanted the director's job, he became critical of it. He claimed in retrospect that he'd had deep reservations about it at the time. Not even his closest friends and colleagues at CIA recall him voicing them. Here we have another tell—this character's integrity doesn't run too deep."

Brennan was Obama's assistant to the president for homeland security and counterterrorism advisor from 2009 to 2013. He'd wanted the CIA job but withdrew from consideration after he was criticized for supporting the transfer of terror suspects to countries where they might be tortured. When the CIA job came up again in 2012 after David Petraeus was dismissed for sharing classified intelligence with his mistress, Brennan changed his tune. He said he was against the programs he once supported.

"Everyone who had a backbone stuck to what they said," says Luke. "Brennan threw the Agency under the bus. He was in the White House and wanted a bigger job and was willing to be sleazy to get it."

Brennan's proximity to power struck many in the intelligence community as peculiar.

"I would consider him to be part of the Obama inner circle," a former senior intelligence official says. "To be both the director of the CIA and an insider in the Obama Oval Office providing political and policy advice is very unusual. Brennan, while serving as D/CIA, never stopped his political role. I think Brennan is a protagonist in this story."

In the beginning of August, Brennan sent Obama reports about the Trump team's ties to Russia. He said they came from a source inside the Kremlin. The source said that Russian president Vladimir Putin wanted to defeat Clinton and help elect Trump. One former Obama deputy told the press that the president "was deeply concerned and wanted as much information as fast as possible." Obama, said the aide, "wanted the entire intelligence community all over this."

At first, Brennan only told White House chief of staff Denis McDonough, national security advisor Susan Rice, and her deputy, Avril Haines. He kept the Kremlin reports out of the presidential briefing prepared daily by the CIA for fear they'd be disseminated too broadly. During the Clinton administration, he had been responsible for the presidential daily briefing.

Brennan eventually expanded the circle to include Attorney General Loretta Lynch, Vice President Joe Biden, Secretary of State John Kerry, and Defense Secretary Ashton Carter. He told FBI director James Comey about it repeatedly, directly and indirectly.

Brennan also took his findings to Congress. Between August and September, he briefed the Gang of Eight, the chairs and ranking members of the House and Senate Intelligence Committees as well as the leadership from both chambers. He testified that he gave all eight officials the same classified briefing, "the consider[ed] view and assessment and intelligence from the CIA."

Nunes was HPSCI chair at the time. He says Brennan didn't have anything when he came to brief him in his office on Capitol Hill in September. "My staff director and I laughed when he left," says Nunes.

The congressman had warned in April 2016 that the US intelligence community's inability to understand Putin's intentions represented its biggest strategic failure since the September 11, 2001, attacks. "We spent a lot of time looking at Russia," Nunes says of his committee. "We allocated more money for the IC to devote to Russia, and they didn't take it."

Now less than half a year after Nunes's warnings, the director came with dire warnings but without substance or evidence. Brennan testified that he gave every member of the Gang of Eight the same briefing, but Nunes disputes the claim. "He didn't tell me what he told Harry Reid."

Brennan went to the Democrats first. On August 11, he briefed House minority leader Nancy Pelosi, on the 17th ranking member of the House Intelligence Committee Adam Schiff, and Reid, the Senate minority leader, on August 25. Four days later, Reid wrote a letter to Comey, urging the FBI to investigate the ties between the Trump team and Russian officials.

> *There have been a series of disturbing reports suggesting other methods Russia is using to influence the Trump campaign and manipulate it as a vehicle for advancing the interests of Russian President Vladimir Putin. For example, questions have been raised about whether a Trump advisor who has been highly critical of U.S. and European economic sanctions on Russia, and who has conflicts of interest due to investments in Russian energy conglomerate Gazprom, met with high-ranking sanctioned individuals while in Moscow in July of 2016, well after Trump became the presumptive Republican nominee.*

Reid was referring to Carter Page. In March, Trump had named the then forty-five-year-old Naval Academy graduate as one of his foreign policy advisors. The *Washington Post* had given inordinate attention to Page's July 7 speech in Moscow, in which he was critical of Washington's Russia policy. By the end of July, Clinton campaign operatives began feeding the press with stories about Page that were identical to what Brennan had told Reid. The same sensitive information that the director had put on Obama's desk and then briefed to senior officials was at the same time circulating through the media.

Brennan said he raised "the published media reports of Russian attempts to interfere in our upcoming Presidential election" with his counterpart in Moscow. He said that on August 4 he "spoke to Alexsander Bortnikov, the head of Russia's Federal Security Bureau, the FSB, Russia's internal security and intelligence service." Brennan told "Bortnikov that if Russia had such a campaign underway, it would be certain to backfire."

The call logs Durham requested are likely to contain a record of Brennan making an August 4 phone call to the Russian spy chief. The rest of Brennan's story appears to be fiction.

Why would he call a Russian spy chief to complain about news reported in the US press? Did he think the Russians were talking to American journalists about the details of a secret plot? The director claimed that it was a source inside the Kremlin who provided the sensitive information that wound up on Obama's desk. If any of Brennan's account is to be believed, he would have alerted his Russian counterpart to the possibility that the CIA had a mole inside the Kremlin.

It is unlikely Brennan said anything like that to the Russian. It is equally implausible that a different Russian spy chief was openly boasting that Moscow had been cultivating the Republican candidate for president for at least five years. And yet that was the key takeaway from a body of reports circulating throughout Washington in the spring and summer of 2016.

Starting in July, a former British spy named Christopher Steele began providing the FBI with reports about the Trump team's ties to Russia. He said that Moscow had "Trump over a barrel." The information, he said, was sourced to a former head of Russian foreign intelligence.

Steele claimed to have sources deep inside the Russian government, in the foreign ministry, and in the intelligence services. He even had sources, like Brennan's, within Putin's inner circle. His information was similar to what Brennan had given Reid in August. Steele claimed, for instance, that during his July trip to Moscow, Carter Page met with a sanctioned Russian businessman close to Putin.

Steele said that Obama's national security advisor, Susan Rice, saw his reports, as did senior State Department official Victoria Nuland. He didn't say whether Brennan saw it. Brennan said he didn't get any of his intelligence from the former MI6 man. He said that it was only in September that he had first heard of Steele's reporting, and it wasn't until December that he saw the thirty-five-page document consisting of seventeen memos that came to be known as the Steele dossier.

Steele's memos showed that the Russians had compromised the Republican candidate. They showed numerous contacts between the Trump campaign and Russian officials. The message, taken as a whole, was that Trump was treasonous.

The FBI had a relationship with Steele dating back to at least 2010, when he introduced agent Michael Gaeta and senior DOJ official Bruce Ohr to a journalist who briefed them on corruption in world soccer's governing body. In 2013, the FBI made Steele a confidential human source (CHS), and Gaeta became his handler. Over his career as a CHS, the FBI paid Steele $95,000.

Gaeta was working on organized crime out of the US embassy in Rome when Steele called him to London on July 5, 2016. He wanted to show the FBI man his reports on Trump's ties to Russia.

Gaeta had no expertise in counterintelligence matters, so he sent Steele's findings to a colleague at the New York Field Office a week later. The Crossfire Hurricane investigation was opened at FBI headquarters July 31. That day or the day after, Gaeta's New York contact called to tell him Steele's reports had reached the J. Edgar Hoover Building.

In the second or third week of August, Bruce Ohr called Gaeta to check in on Steele's reports. The three of them were working together again. According to Gaeta, the DOJ lawyer told him, "Me and my bosses want to make sure the FBI is handling it and doing something about it."

Ohr, like Harry Reid, was eager to make sure the FBI was moving on the information that Steele and John Brennan were passing along. Toward the end of September, Gaeta was told that the Steele reports corroborated some of the information the FBI's counterintelligence unit already had.

Steele was not credible. He claimed that he had been a senior official in the British foreign intelligence service, as MI6's top Russia hand. His former employers said he only reached mid-level before leaving. They said he had questionable judgment. Senior FBI officials promised their British colleagues to keep derogatory information about their confidential human source under wraps. Failure seemed to follow Steele.

He'd served at the British embassy in Moscow between 1990 and 1993. Between 1993 and 1998, he trained newly minted MI6 officers. His identity as a British spy was leaked in 1999, after which he was not able to return to Russia. He served in Paris and the Middle East and came back to London to run the Russia desk in 2006. That year, high-profile KGB defector Alexander Litvinenko was poisoned in a London hotel under Steele's watch. He left MI6 in 2008, soon after a leak from a British intelligence official claimed that the Russian government was behind Litvinenko's murder.

Steele started his own firm, Orbis, in 2009. In 2010, he was hired by a UK consortium sponsoring England's bid to host the 2018 soccer World Cup. He was tasked to investigate rival bids, in particular Russia's. Steele's reporting, one source told the press, was "incendiary" but not "legally credible." His investigation into Russia's bid was never officially made public.

In 2014, he leaked his findings to the press. According to a report two British journalists gave to Parliament, Steele, identified as the MI6 source, alleged a vast Russian conspiracy to win the 2018 bid. It was managed by Putin himself. The former British spy rationalized why he had no evidence to support his claims.

"What you need to remember about this is the way this was done in Russia is that nothing was written down," Steele told the journalists. "Don't expect me or anyone else to produce a document with Putin's signature saying please X bribe Y with this amount in this way. He's not going to do that. Putin is an ex–intelligence officer. Everything he does has to be deniable."

Putin's point man for the operation, according to Steele, was a Russian oil executive and Putin's former deputy of chief of staff, Igor Sechin. He had bribed another country, Qatar, with energy deals in order to secure the vote for the bid. "If there was collusion," said Steele, "it was done through the energy sector."

Now, in the summer of 2016, Steele was rehashing a version of that same story in his reporting on Trump. The same Russian, Igor Sechin, was trying to bribe Trump advisor Carter Page and with the same lure: energy deals. According to Steele's sources, the Trump campaign was colluding with Russia.

The former senior US intelligence official thinks that the joint Steele-Brennan enterprise was rigged. "I find it hard to believe that Steele, being a past MI6 officer, would've called Moscow thinking those calls would not be covered by Russian intelligence," says the former official. "Even worse than monitoring the Steele calls into Russia, the security services would have seen a perfect opportunity to channel information to Steele to misdirect him. He's not a stupid man, and neither is Brennan. For Brennan to pick up Steele's work and validate it suggests that efforts to build a false narrative about Trump and his campaign being tied to the Russians were premeditated."

The standard version of the story the dossier tells is about a vast conspiracy of collusion between Trump associates and Russian officials. But there's another way to read the dossier.

Turn it upside down and shake out all the Americans, Trump and his circle, as well as Hillary Clinton. Now the main characters are all Russian. Many of them, including the sources Steele claimed for his intelligence reports, are unnamed, like the former senior intelligence officer and the foreign ministry official. Others are named: several businessmen, the Russian foreign minister, the Russian ambassador to the United States, and a former employee at Moscow's US embassy. Most of those named, however, work in the Kremlin. Indeed, that's the main point of Steele's reporting. As he told US officials, the operation was run not by Russian intelligence services, but rather by the Kremlin itself.

The dossier is even more specific. Eight of the Russian figures named are employed, or were previously employed, in the Presidential Administration (PA), the executive office of the president of the Russian Federation, Putin's office.

Here are the eight figures from the PA named in Steele's seventeen reports:

- Anton Vaino: current chief of staff of the PA
- Sergei Ivanov: former PA chief of staff
- Dmitry Peskov: PA spokesman
- Igor Diveykin: deputy head of PA for domestic affairs until October 2016
- Yuri Ushakov: former ambassador to the US, currently the PA's international affairs advisor
- Oleg Govorun: head of a PA directorate dealing with former Soviet republics from 2013 to 2019
- Igor Sechin: deputy head of the PA between 2000 and 2008
- Dmitry Medvedev: former president of Russia; worked for Putin's Presidential Administration between 2003 and 2005

The dossier paints a picture of the office in which they work or worked. It's an office like any other—with rivalries and alliances, firings and hirings, successes, mistakes, even regrets over projects gone wrong. According to the dossier, the office's big initiative, directed by the boss himself, was getting Trump elected. A tool used to accomplish that goal was a portfolio of dirt on Clinton that the office had collected.

In the dossier's account, the Clinton dirt was held by one PA employee, Peskov. Another PA official, Diveykin, discussed the dirt with a Trump campaign advisor. Peskov and yet another PA official, Ivanov, argued about the Clinton dirt. Ivanov thought it was a bad idea to use it.

According to Steele's reporting: "Head of PA IVANOV laments Russian intervention in US presidential election and black PR against CLINTON and the DNC. Vows not to supply intelligence to Kremlin PR operatives again. Advocates now sitting tight and denying everything."

Eventually Ivanov is replaced as chief of staff by Vaino, who had no previous dealings with the Clinton dirt.

The dossier goes on and on about the inner workings of the PA, appointments, and rumors circulated through the office. There are enough details about Russians to fill a Russian novel about a dysfunctional Russian bureaucracy. But why? What does it matter what one PA official thought and that he disagreed with someone else? If Steele's job was simply to show that Trump was in league with a foreign power, why include all the office politics?

Because it suggests an insider's account of the PA. Enumerating minor details about the personalities staffing the office would be seen as evidence that the source was in position to know that Putin himself was managing the pro-Trump operation.

In fact, the CIA really did have a source inside the PA, Oleg Smolenkov. His identity appears to be among the information and intelligence that John Brennan shared with the FBI and placed on Barack Obama's desk.

"Brennan so wanted to show the nefarious nexus between Trump and his campaign and the Russians that he would have done anything to prove it," says the former senior US intelligence official.

Brennan's information was the basis, as the CIA director put it, of the investigation into Trump's ties to Russia. It also seems to have established the dossier's template. Obama officials and Clinton operatives plugged in the names of Trump associates for the purpose of framing the Republican candidate as a Russian agent in order to spy on him. According to Brennan, Putin's efforts were directed at putting Trump in the White House.

THREE

THE SETUP

Steele was working for another client as well as the FBI—Hillary Clinton's presidential campaign. He was hired in May 2016, a pitchman employed to hawk the Trump-Russia narrative to the media by convincing them it was the work of a genuine secret agent: himself. He and his campaign handlers told journalists that his reports were being taken seriously by the FBI.

He met with Jane Mayer of the *New Yorker*, Michael Isikoff from Yahoo News, Matthew Mosk of ABC News, Eric Lichtblau and David Sanger from the *New York Times*, and the *Washington Post*'s Dana Priest and Tom Hamburger. It was apparently lost on the top-name journalists with appointments to meet a real-life James Bond in a Washington, DC, hotel that had it been a real investigation, his talking to the press would have alerted the targets and made his sources vulnerable. But it wasn't a real investigation, and that didn't matter to the reporters. The Trump-Russia story glittered like coins, and it helped their chosen candidate.

Clinton needed a boost. After her cool personality and awkward public demeanor, her largest electoral liability was her emails. The former secretary of state had used a private email server in the hopes of eluding Freedom of Information Act requests that were likely to disclose damning facts. And yet, while protecting herself against the scrutiny of the American voter, she made her government correspondence vulnerable to foreign intelligence services.

In July 2015, the FBI had opened an investigation to see whether she'd mishandled classified information on her unsecure server. The investigation was pro forma. There was no chance she'd be charged since numerous Obama principals had emailed her on her private account. The FBI was not going to indict the entire administration, including the president, for being careless with classified intelligence.

A little less than a year after the investigation began, Comey announced it was over. He usurped the DOJ's prerogative to decide whether or not to indict. Another way to see it, however, is that Comey was just an errand boy who'd saved Attorney General Loretta Lynch the indignity of exculpating a presidential candidate who appears to have broken the law.

What truly concerned the campaign was not an indictment but the prospect that among the thirty thousand emails the candidate had deleted from her server, damning ones would go public. Clinton said the emails she'd destroyed dealt only with personal matters, like condolence notes and yoga routines. But the extraordinary lengths the campaign took to deflect attention away from the deleted correspondence suggests there was something more at stake. Likely they show wrongdoing where her stewardship of US foreign policy intersected with foreign contributions to the Clinton Foundation.

The campaign's fix was simple—get out in front in the event the emails were leaked and shift attention from the subject matter to the delivery mechanism. For instance: The issue is not that the former secretary of state may have made a promise to country A—no, the real problem is that country B stole and leaked her emails, to interfere in the election and benefit her opponent.

In reality, among the many intelligence services that would have had no difficulty accessing the private server of America's top diplomat, it's improbable any would have leaked her communications before the election, or perhaps ever. Unguarded correspondence to and from the woman all believed would be the next US president would be considered priceless. Why squander such a gift, especially when she was likely to win the election no matter what?

The most likely to make her emails public would have been from the small fraction of the press not actively supporting a Clinton victory, or a Trump supporter, or someone who despised her, or perhaps some combination of the three. There was nothing to be done about the message if the emails were released, so her aides resolved to dirty the messenger.

The campaign decided to hang it on Russia. It would be easy to explain. The Russians were active in Europe. Indeed, in January 2016 the UK press reported that a "dossier of 'Russian influence activity' identified operations in France, Hungary and the Netherlands, as well as Austria and the Czech Republic." Moscow had been interfering in US elections since the Soviet era. And, in fact, Putin had accused Clinton of interfering in Russian elections, so the campaign's Russia story could be packaged as his revenge on a woman he greatly feared.

To push the Russia narrative, Perkins Coie, the law firm representing the campaign and the Democratic National Committee, hired two contractors. In late April, they brought on CrowdStrike, a cybersecurity firm that would lend its technical expertise to the premise that Russia was interested in the candidate's emails.

Accordingly, in a June 14, 2016, *Washington Post* story, Crowd-Strike co-founder and Russian-born anti-Putin dissident Dmitri Alperovitch told reporter Ellen Nakashima that the company had "identified two separate hacker groups, both working for the Russian government, that had infiltrated the [DNC's] network." Alperovitch said that he had no "hard evidence" to show how the Russians got in.

Because the servers were never shared with the FBI or apparently anyone else outside CrowdStrike, there was no independent corroboration of the Clinton-funded claims. CrowdStrike president and former FBI agent Shawn Henry later testified under oath there was no evidence Russia "exfiltrated," or electronically removed, information from the DNC's servers. Nonetheless, the *Post* story had laid the foundations for the fake Russia narrative, and just in time for Democratic National Convention at the end of July.

During the convention, WikiLeaks released Clinton-related emails. They were not among the thirty thousand the candidate deleted but instead documented mildly embarrassing intra-DNC debates. In any case, Clinton aides were on the ground ready with an explanation—Russia did it.

Why Russia did it was left to the second contractor that the campaign employed to push the collusion story.

In early April, the Clinton campaign hired Fusion GPS, an opposition research firm founded by two former *Wall Street Journal* reporters, Glenn Simpson and Peter Fritsch, to disseminate the Trump-Russia collusion story to their extensive media network. By the time the convention opened and Clinton campaign manager Robby Mook announced that Russia had hacked the DNC emails to help Trump, it resonated throughout the Fusion GPS echo chamber.

Simpson and Fritsch had been pushing the Trump-Russia story even before they signed on with the Clintons. In the fall, they'd been retained by the *Washington Free Beacon*, a news site funded mostly by Republican donor Paul Singer, then backing Marco Rubio's campaign. In October, Fusion GPS had brought on former CIA contractor Nellie Ohr, DOJ official Bruce Ohr's wife, to explore connections between the Trump circle and Russian organized crime.

Nellie Ohr had studied Russian history and was fluent in the language. She scoured foreign-language as well English-language media for anything tying the Republican candidate to Russia. She and Fusion GPS colleagues compiled numerous Trump-Russia reports by the time the Clinton campaign took over the project in early spring.

A former journalist provided me with several of Fusion GPS' Trump-Russia documents. The most significant was dated May 20, 2016. It describes interactions between the Trump circle, including his children, and businessmen from Russia and other former Soviet states. It also identifies three of the Trump campaign officials whom Steele would name in his collection of memos: Manafort, Michael Flynn, and Carter Page. These pre-Steele documents appear to have shaped the Trump-Russia reporting of numerous prestige press organizations, including the *New York Times*, *Washington Post*, *Politico*, and ABC News.

Simpson explained that after exhausting the open source reporting they'd hired Nellie Ohr to compile, Fusion GPS needed someone to "talk to people inside Russia," and brought on Steele in May. That made little sense. Steele had not been able to travel to Russia since his identity as an intelligence officer was leaked in 1999.

Had Steele really been investigating Trump's ties to the Russian government, it would have been virtually impossible working on his own to ascertain whether his sources were truthful or were instead misdirecting him. But Russian disinformation was never a problem for the former MI6 man—he knew the only disinformation was coming from his employers, American spies, and the Clinton campaign.

Steele's role is illuminated by the dramatic shift in the nature of the Trump-Russia reporting Fusion GPS produced between the May 20 document and his first memo, dated June 20. Pre-Steele, the Fusion GPS material is standard opposition research, using publicly available information to hint at the candidate's alleged connections to apparently shady businessmen from Russia and other Soviet states.

The work attributed to Steele is not opposition research. There is no documentary record supporting the allegations he makes about the Trump circle. Most important, the subject is no longer the Trump campaign's ties to individuals who may be involved in criminal activities. Rather, it is the Trump team's secret relationship with Russian officials and allies of the Russian president.

By alleging Trump's clandestine ties to a foreign power, the dossier was establishing the predicate for the FBI to obtain a Foreign Intelligence Surveillance Act (FISA) warrant on the Trump campaign. A FISA warrant would allow the Bureau to sweep up the campaign's electronic communications—emails, texts, phone calls, and so on—while keeping the spying operation hidden under the guise of a classified counterintelligence investigation.

Normally, there are checks to prevent agents from abusing the secrecy that classified programs and methods afford counterintelligence investigations—like confidential human sources, intrusive surveillance authorities, and the secret Foreign Intelligence Surveillance Court that grants them. In this instance, the FBI's ultimate supervisors, the director and deputy director, were among the culprits abusing US government resources.

Steele's role becomes even more obvious when counting the many times he mistook the details of the "intelligence" that he said he had collected through his sources. Questioned about the dossier by friendly State Department officials, skeptical DOJ investigators, or hostile British lawyers deposing him in a courtroom setting, Steele blundered repeatedly. Simpson had accompanied him on press briefings because his employee didn't know the story that had been manufactured for him to market.

Steele was just an avatar. And the dossier was simply the term of art used to describe a formatted document that contained information John Brennan said he had been giving the FBI prior to the summer of 2016, information he briefed to Harry Reid and sent to the desk of Barack Obama.

The Trump-Russia collusion operation consisted of both a defensive and an offensive component. One purpose was to protect the Democratic candidate against a possible October surprise. Accordingly, Clinton campaign contractors and the CIA director pushed the dossier information about illicit ties between the Trump campaign and Russian officials. If her emails were leaked, the Clinton campaign had already shaped the public narrative—it was Russia that stole the emails and leaked them, in order to help Clinton's treasonous GOP rival.

The other purpose was to discover an October surprise of their own in order to finish off the competition. The dossier was used as evidence for the FBI to obtain a FISA warrant to fish through the Trump campaign's communications in the hope of finding something incriminating. In other words, it was an electronic break-in to benefit Clinton. Thus, the dossier was the centerpiece of the collusion operation.

It was Fusion GPS's job to help identify targets in the Trump orbit to link up with the Putin deputies identified by name in the dossier. Trump's March 21 interview at the *Washington Post*'s offices, in which the candidate named his foreign policy team, provided the Clinton operatives with at least two prospects—Carter Page and George Papadopoulos. The latter was never entered into the dossier—the FBI had other plans for the then twenty-eight-year-old energy consultant from Chicago. But Page was the star of the dossier.

The retired Navy officer was made out to be the central player in the phony collusion story. His past work experience in Moscow and his unorthodox (at least inside the Beltway) views on US-Russia relations made him a relatively convincing patsy. Further, he'd had past exchanges with Russian intelligence officers who'd tried to recruit him. The Crossfire Hurricane team concealed the fact that Page not only deflected their efforts but had even helped the FBI make its case against the Russian spies. The Bureau also tampered with documents showing that Page had assisted other government agencies as well.

Page, like others framed by the collusion operation, was vulnerable. Like most of the Trump team, including the candidate, he was a Washington outsider, with no patronage network inside the capital to protect him in the event someone thought it was useful to ruin his life.

Page became the target of the FISA warrant, the entry point that would give the FBI access to the rest of the campaign, including possibly the candidate himself. According to the dossier, as Brennan had told Reid, Page was the key node of collusion. According to a dossier memo dated July 28, he was one of the intermediaries used by Manafort to manage "a well-developed conspiracy of co-operation between [the Trump team] and the Russian leadership."

The dossier alleged that the source for that claim was an unnamed "ethnic Russian close associate of" Trump. In reality, there was no source. It was just another Fusion GPS smear, this time dirtying Sergei Millian, a naturalized American citizen who couldn't have imagined the criminal scope of the confidence game he'd gotten dragged into or the high-powered players behind it.

The early chapter of Millian's American story is the quintessential immigrant's tale of ambition, hard work, and hustle. Born Siarhei Kukuts in Belarus in 1978, he jumped at the chance to come to the US when he was offered an education grant in 2001. He first made his home in Atlanta and then New York City. He worked as a translator and obtained his real estate license. He also co-founded the Russian-American Chamber of Commerce in the USA to promote business, cultural, and educational exchanges. He wasn't even originally from Russia but figured it would be a good place to make connections, and yet it was this association that would later spike the interest of his tormentors.

In April 2016, a Russian-language news site published a long interview with Millian. The president of the Russian-American Chamber of Commerce in the USA explained how he met Trump in Miami in 2007 and secured an agreement to sell Trump real estate properties in Florida. He said that a Trump presidency would improve relations with Russia.

"In my opinion, if Trump becomes president of the United States, relations with Russia will go upward, or at least not worsen." Millian said that Trump is practical, a businessman. "I know for sure that in Russia he does not have a single business conflict."

Millian tells me that he believes this April story is what caught the attention of Fusion GPS. A spreadsheet apparently compiled by Nellie Ohr listing dozens of names with thumbnail sketches of their associations shows that Millian is right—they had him in their crosshairs. Then they fed him to the media to chum the waters.

Simpson claimed Millian was variously a close Trump associate, a dossier source, an intermediary between Trump and Russia, and a Russian spy. He was none of them.

According to Millian, starting in the summer of 2016, the press began to contact him for interviews. "There were many requests," he explains to me via Twitter direct message, "hundreds." The first was ABC News.

Simpson had reached out to an "old colleague" at ABC News, producer Matthew Mosk, and told him to get Millian on camera.

On July 26, Mosk invited Millian to come to the ABC studios for an interview about Trump. Millian says that a friend advised him it would be good for his business to speak to the media. Mosk published that same day a story about Trump and Russia hacking the DNC. Millian says the story misquoted him. "I never said that I helped arrange 'meetings between Trump and Russian businessmen' during his 2013 trip to Moscow for the Miss Universe pageant."

Mosk's colleague Brian Ross was very interested in the 2013 Miss Universe story, and the Clinton campaign knew it.

In the early spring, longtime Clinton foot soldier Cody Shearer began research for two Trump-Russia reports, less detailed than Steele's memos, even less literate, and considerably more vulgar in its allegations regarding the GOP candidate's sex life. Shearer passed them on to his colleague and Clinton confidant Sidney Blumenthal, who in turn got them to Steele associates.

In one of the reports, Shearer describes a conversation with Ross. "Brian told me that he had been told that Trump had been compromised sexually in Moscow right before the beauty contest he was hosting," wrote Shearer. "He told me that if one could provide a talking head source he would fly to Moscow to tape and air for broadcast."

Ross didn't need to go anywhere, for Simpson delivered a "source" right to his doorstep. Millian shows me a screengrab of a July 28 email from Mosk again inviting him for an interview the next day, this time for TV. Millian says he was surprised when Ross asked repeatedly during filming if he was a Russian spy. Millian shows me another screengrab of an email in which he complained to Mosk about the accusations he was a Russian spy. Mosk said they wouldn't be aired. They were later aired.

Simpson had incriminated Millian by putting him in front of a reporter who accused him of being a Russian spy on television and by inserting him into the dossier. Simpson also told Bruce Ohr that Millian was a Russian intelligence officer. Ohr relayed the message to the FBI, which opened an investigation on Millian.

The Ohrs were central players in the dossier operation. They met Christopher Steele for breakfast in Washington at the end of July, a day before the FBI opened Crossfire Hurricane. Bruce Ohr and Steele had known each other since 2007. In January, they had been in contact about a Russian oligarch with suspected ties to organized crime. Steele worked for the oligarch and asked Ohr to help sort out his visa troubles.

The Ohrs testified they were very surprised to discover that Steele was working for Fusion GPS on the same Trump-Russia project. Steele told them about his part of the operation. He talked about Carter Page and the former Russian spy chief who said they have "Trump over a barrel."

Their July 30 breakfast wasn't just a meeting of old friends; rather it represented a convergence of a broad range of personal ambitions and institutional interests, from Hillary Clinton to the foreign associates she and her husband had cultivated over a quarter of a century, to the top leadership of the FBI and the Oval Office.

FOUR

OCTOBER SURPRISES

The "insurance policy" was Stefan Halper. That's what FBI agent Peter Strzok and his mistress, FBI lawyer Lisa Page, were texting about in mid-August 2016. They weren't discussing post-election contingency plans because they couldn't possibly imagine a Trump victory.

They just wanted to make sure they could spy on the Trump campaign. To do that, they had to make sure they got the FISA warrant on Carter Page (no relation to Lisa Page). So, they sent one of their confidential human sources to record him without him knowing it.

Halper asked Page questions about Clinton's emails and whether the Trump campaign had an October surprise in store for the Democratic candidate. The FBI edited Page's responses and put it in the FISA application—which allowed the agents to sweep up not only his communications but also virtually anything else they wanted from the Trump team.

Nunes had long explained that the "insurance policy" was something specific that the FBI had done to get the FISA warrant, "something as bad or even worse than using the dossier," he'd said. But since most of the context surrounding the Strzok-Page exchange had been redacted, the phrase loomed larger, like it was the coup itself. Instead it was just another manifestation of the moral and political rot—disdain for the law and contempt for other Americans—in which the coup was grounded.

It was Strzok who opened Crossfire Hurricane, an umbrella investigation that focused on four members of the Trump campaign: Carter Page, Michael Flynn, Paul Manafort, and George Papadopoulos. It was predicated, according to Strzok, on "statements Mr. Papadopoulos made about suggestions from the Russians that they (the Russians) could assist the Trump campaign with the anonymous release of information during the campaign that would be damaging to Hillary Clinton."

How did that information warrant opening an investigation of any American, never mind a presidential campaign? The premise was vague: What *statements* exactly had Papadopoulos made? What precisely were the *suggestions* from the Russians? And what *Russians*? Were they government officials? Putin allies? Businessmen? Tourists?

Australia's envoy to the United Kingdom, Alexander Downer, was the source for the Papadopoulos information. At Downer's request, they'd met once briefly at a bar in May. Downer said it was only after Wikileaks released the DNC emails that he understood the importance of what Papadopoulos had allegedly said. After all, Clinton campaign officials claimed that Russia stole and leaked the emails to help Trump. So Downer sought out his American colleague, Elizabeth Dibble, the top foreign service officer at the

US embassy in London, and relayed a conversation he had trouble recalling from two months earlier.

Papadopoulos later said he didn't "remember saying anything to Downer about Russia or Hillary Clinton." Downer's account made no sense. Why would Australia's most senior diplomat in London reach out to a relatively unknown twenty-eight-year-old foreign policy advisor from a presidential campaign that the experts thought was doomed to fail? To help frame the Trump aide.

Downer liked Trump's opponent. As Australia's foreign minister, he had once pledged $25 million to the Clinton Foundation. Before Dibble was stationed in London, she was Hillary Clinton's principal deputy assistant secretary of state for Near Eastern affairs. Her tenure and area of concern intersected with the September 2012 Benghazi attack, when Clinton and other Obama officials misrepresented facts about the terror operation that killed four Americans in the Libyan city. Dibble was also helping frame Papadopoulos.

The opening of Crossfire Hurricane observed no known protocol. Australia and the United States are part of an intelligence-gathering and -sharing arrangement known as Five Eyes, which includes the three other English-speaking powers: Canada, New Zealand, and the UK. Genuine intelligence is supposed to pass through official intelligence channels. In this instance, the FBI opened an investigation based on a rumor that one diplomat exchanged with another.

"They presented it as friendly foreign government information to make it seem legitimate," says Nunes. "And they opened on Papadopoulos. They didn't put him in the dossier because they wanted to make it seem like they had information coming in from everywhere that Trump was colluding with the Russians."

The FBI was under the gun. John Brennan, among others, was pressuring the Bureau to investigate Trump's ties to Russia, so Crossfire

Hurricane was opened on a contrived pretext. On August 10, the FBI started separate investigations of Papadopoulos, Page, and Manafort. The next day, the Crossfire Hurricane team contacted Stefan Halper.

The former aide to three Republican presidents had married into the CIA through the daughter of Ray Cline, one of the Agency's legendary figures. Halper split his time between Washington, DC, and Cambridge University. The Defense Department paid him more than $1 million between 2012 and 2016 to do foreign policy research. His work was subpar, said a Pentagon whistleblower, and he misrepresented his government-funded studies. For one project he claimed to have consulted numerous experts, who, when later asked, said he had not even contacted them.

He invited well-known intelligence professionals to speak at Cambridge, like former Russian spy chief Vyacheslav Trubnikov, whom he also falsely claimed as a source for his research. Trubnikov was also falsely cited as a source for the dossier. Steele identified him as the anonymous Russian intelligence official who said that "the Russians had Trump over a barrel." Trubnikov's was yet another Russian identity used to make the dossier seem authentic.

In 2011, Halper had invited FBI agent Steven Somma to come to Cambridge. Somma had become his handler that year after the FBI cut Halper loose. He'd alienated his previous handlers by pestering them for more money and demonstrating "questionable allegiance" to people he was paid to spy on. Somma gave him another chance.

He approached Halper in August 2016 to know more about what he did for Ronald Reagan's 1980 presidential campaign. Halper reportedly managed a network of retired CIA officers spying on Jimmy Carter's White House.

Reagan's campaign director, William Casey, was concerned Carter might take some sort of dramatic action late in the election cycle to jump ahead of Reagan at the last minute. Casey, later Reagan's CIA director, is credited with coining the term "October surprise." Halper's job on the 1980 campaign was to spot the Carter campaign's plans for an October surprise in time to counter it. The US government funded him with taxpayer money to do the same for the Clinton campaign.

Not everyone wanted to send Halper after the Trump team. Strzok recounted that he met with resistance from colleagues. They'd debated, he said, "how aggressively to pursue investigation, given that aggressive pursuit might put that intelligence source at risk."

Lisa Page thought they didn't need to use Halper to get the FISA warrant. Strzok disagreed. He texted her on August 15: "I'm afraid we can't take that risk. It's like an insurance policy in the unlikely event you die before you're 40."

She said that the "insurance policy" referred to their debate: "Do we burn sources or not burn sources"? Strzok won the argument.

On August 20, Halper sought out Carter Page. They'd met a month earlier when Halper invited him to Cambridge for a conference. He spied on the Trump volunteer during the conference, even though the Crossfire Hurricane investigation hadn't officially been opened. Page had been in Moscow before coming to Cambridge, his last stop on the way home to the US.

In their August meeting, he told Halper that the Moscow trip "was the most incredible experience of my life." He'd been treated respectfully and taken seriously when he shared his ideas about US-Russian relations with a Russian audience. Page told the spy secretly recording him to frame him as a traitor that he didn't understand the negative US media coverage about his speech.

Halper raised the issue of an October surprise. He asked if the Trump campaign could access information that might have been obtained by the Russians from the DNC files. "We would have used [it] in a heartbeat," Halper said of the presidential campaigns he'd worked on. Page alluded to Clinton's more than thirty thousand deleted emails. The "Russians have all that don't they?" Halper asked. "I don't know," Page answered.

The FBI edited Page's comments to make him look suspicious and put them in the FISA application to show probable cause. It was part of what Comey called the "broader mosaic of facts" used to get the warrant. Nunes was right: Dispatching an informant to record an innocent American and change the meaning of his words to make him look like he'd betrayed his country was as bad as using the dossier.

The countdown to the October surprise was underway.

To create the myth that Trump was colluding with Russia to win the election, the Clinton campaign had weaponized three narratives to show how Trump was secretly connected to Russia. The first was about Carter Page, another was about Sergei Millian, and there was a third that dealt with a financial institution owned by Russian nationals, Alfa Bank.

The public face of the operation relied on the media, with Fusion GPS distributing stories to friendly press outfits in the summer and fall. For instance, just as ABC News' Matthew Mosk put Millian on camera to ask if he was a Russian spy, in the same late July time frame *Wall Street Journal* reporter Damian Paletta texted Page to ask whether he'd secretly met with Putin allies during his Moscow trip. Page denied it.

The operation also had a clandestine aspect. Just as Clinton functionaries had framed Page to make him an investigative target, they similarly dirtied Millian. On August 22, Glenn Simpson told Bruce Ohr that Millian was one of the intermediaries between the Trump campaign and the Russians and was believed to be a Russian intelligence officer. Thanks in part to the efforts of Simpson and Ohr, the FBI would later open a counterintelligence investigation on Millian as well.

As zero hour—Election Day—approached, the two aspects of the operation and the three narratives were supposed to merge and go public, presenting a thick account of Trump's treasonous ties to Russia. The problem wasn't just that it was false, but that both the FBI and the Clinton campaign had come to believe their own depraved fairy tale.

The Clinton campaign began cooking up what would become the Alfa Bank narrative sometime in the spring. According to reports written by Clinton operative Cody Shearer, former CIA officer Robert Baer said that "the Russians had established an encrypted communication system with a cutout between the Trump campaign and Putin." Baer told me he'd spoken with Shearer in March or April 2016.

The Clinton campaign eventually settled on Alfa Bank as the "cutout." On July 29, Steele met in Washington, DC, with Michael Sussmann, the Clinton campaign lawyer who brought on CrowdStrike, the cybersecurity firm that alleged without evidence that Russia had hacked the DNC's servers. Now Sussmann was promoting another cyber story that had no factual basis—he told Steele that the computer servers of the Trump Organization and Alfa Bank were in communication.

The story circulated through the press corps all summer. "I fielded dozens of reporters' calls about the allegation on behalf of Alfa Bank, my client," says Jeffrey Birnbaum, a public relations executive.

"What was doubly strange is that no one ever asserted what was communicated" between Alfa Bank and the Trump Organization.

A mid-September dossier report claimed that Alfa's owners were close to Putin, and the link was a Presidential Administration official, also a former Alfa Bank executive. Steele said that Simpson's instruction to produce the report was "definitely linked to the server issue." Taken together, the premise was simple: Because the Trump Organization was in clandestine contact with Alfa Bank, which was close to Putin, the candidate was secretly in touch with the Russian president. Along with Page and Millian, Alfa was the third channel connecting Trump to Putin.

As the month wore on, the press operation became more intense. On September 22, ABC aired a small part of the hour-long interview with Millian that had been filmed in July. The segment was about Trump's alleged business connections to Russia, and Millian's statements were tailored to fit the narrative.

"Business amounted to hundreds of millions," Millian said in the segment. But as the transcript showed, Millian had only been referring to Trump residential properties in Florida that were sold to Russians. The incriminating ABC clip was recycled for a Clinton campaign promotional video posted later the same day to the candidate's website.

The same cycle was repeated the next day for a Michael Isikoff story laundering the Clinton campaign's false allegations about Page. Hours after the story posted, the campaign released a statement about Isikoff's "bombshell report"—and failed to note that the "well-placed Western intelligence source" quoted in the story, Steele, was being paid by the campaign.

The clandestine aspect of the anti-Trump operation was gathering steam, too. Also on September 23, Steele told Bruce Ohr that an Alfa Bank server in the United States was a link between Russia and the Trump campaign. Steele said that Millian's Russian-American Chamber of Commerce in the USA had used the Alfa Bank server earlier in September.

The narratives were beginning to merge, as were the public and clandestine aspects of the operation. In September, Sussmann told the FBI's general counsel, James A. Baker, about the Alfa Bank–Trump server story, as well as journalist Franklin Foer, who eventually published it in *Slate*.

At the beginning of October, Steele was in Rome to meet with FBI officials. They shared details about their investigation of an American presidential campaign. He said he'd never heard of George Papadopoulos. The FBI offered to pay the foreign national, a former spy, significantly for dirt on Americans—did he have more on Page, and could he find anything on other Trump associates, like Michael Flynn? Steele lied to the FBI that the retired three-star general had had an affair with a Russian-born British historian.

Steele also told the FBI that Millian was one of his subsources. He wasn't getting information from him directly but rather through his collector, or primary subsource.

He told a different story about Millian when he met with State Department official Kathleen Kavalec on October 11. He suggested that the American citizen was involved with cyber criminals. Millian, said Steele, was one of three distinct channels connecting Trump to the Kremlin, along with Alfa Bank and Carter Page. He told her he was managing the needs of his client. That was the Clinton campaign. He was keen, he told Kavalec, to see the information he shared with her come to light before November 8.

There was a little less than a month to Election Day, and it was all coming together. Millian was the subject of an FBI investigation. The Trump campaign as a whole was under investigation, and the Bureau was cutting information directly from the dossier and pasting it into the FISA application so they could spy on the Trump circle.

Fusion GPS had several big stories lined up. Franklin Foer was on the Alfa Bank story for *Slate*. David Corn was working with Steele on a big piece about Carter Page for *Mother Jones*. Steele was also speaking with the *Financial Times*'s Catherine Belton for a Sergei Millian article. Most important, the *New York Times*'s Eric Lichtblau and Steven Lee Myers were reporting an article about the FBI's investigation of Trump.

Taken together, the press reports about Alfa Bank, Millian, and Page; the Bureau's investigations; and what the FISA warrant was destined to uncover would combine for a powerful explosive force scheduled to detonate at the end of October—the 31st, to be precise, Halloween, eight days before the election. That was the day the earth was supposed to open and swallow the Trump campaign.

But Crossfire Hurricane came up empty. They obtained the FISA warrant October 21, allowing them to sort through the Trump campaign's contemporaneous communications as well as any past communications that still existed. They'd been hopeful to find some Russia-related dirt, but they would have settled for anything to frame Trump. They found nothing. And now they were exposed.

"Once the FBI drilled a dry hole, they wanted to get out of it as soon as possible," says Devin Nunes. "When the October surprise blew up in their face, they were all in legal jeopardy."

There was yet another twist. In September, the FBI had discovered more Clinton-related emails. During a sex crime investigation of Anthony Weiner for his contact with an underage girl, the Bureau's New York field office found the emails on a laptop belonging to him and his wife, Clinton aide Huma Abedin. FBI headquarters was alerted and slow-rolled it for a month. Likely they hoped they could bury it until after the election. But on October 28 Comey announced he was reopening the Clinton email case.

With that, Comey's FBI career was over. "He's done," says Nunes. "Clinton fires him immediately, the first day she's in."

Nunes surmises that the new job opportunities created by Comey's professional suicide likely contributed to the FBI's change of mind about the *Times*'s Halloween story.

Andrew McCabe must have seen himself as the next FBI director. He was already in good standing with the Clinton camp. Former DNC chair and Clinton fixer Terry McAuliffe had directed more than $675,000 to his wife's failed run for a state senate seat. As the Bureau's number two, McCabe was in position to replace the man the next president was certain to terminate. But he had to make sure that the FBI President Clinton was inheriting would appear to be above reproach.

"Now that they're thinking Comey's gone," says Nunes, "the people who think they're in line to replace Comey wanted to get a story out to clean up their mess and absolve the FBI of any wrongdoing. They'd opened a FISA on Page and got nothing. They wanted to show they'd closed everything out. They're all good guys."

On Halloween everything else fell into place—the *Financial Times*'s story on Millian, Foer's article on Alfa Bank, and

David Corn's piece on Page. But instead of detonating an October surprise, the *Times*'s article deflated it.

"Law enforcement officials," according to the Lichtblau and Myers article, "say that none of the investigations so far have found any conclusive or direct link between Mr. Trump and the Russian government."

The FBI threw cold water on the Alfa Bank story. The Bureau had examined "computer data showing an odd stream of activity to a Trump Organization server and Alfa Bank" but, according to the *Times*, "ultimately concluded that there could be an innocuous explanation like a marketing email or spam, for the computer contacts."

According to the *Times*, the FBI even rejected Brennan's contrived thesis that Putin was interfering to help elect Trump. No, said the Bureau, Russia's actions were "aimed at disrupting the presidential election rather than electing Mr. Trump."

Glenn Simpson was furious with the *Times*, at one time America's most prestigious newspaper. "I think first of all you need to know what an abortion of a story you guys wrote on Halloween," he told Lichtblau. "We told you a lot about how the FBI was investigating the Trump team for its ties to Russia, but your story made it sound as if they found nothing to it. We're quite sure that is wrong."

Even Simpson's wife ripped into the *Times*'s Halloween article. "That bogus story," Mary Jacoby posted on Facebook, "had a profound effect just before the election."

Perhaps that's true. In any case, Donald Trump would be elected the forty-fifth president of the United States the following week—and control of the coup would pass into other hands.

FIVE

FALSE FLAG

Almost everyone in Washington had their knives out for Michael Flynn.

With Donald Trump's victory, the FBI's top leadership was vulnerable—at least to Flynn. As a former director of the Defense Intelligence Agency and a career military intelligence officer, he'd know how and where to find the documentary evidence of the FBI's illegal spying operation.

John Brennan had it out for Flynn, whose plans for reforming intelligence collection threatened the CIA directly. The intelligence bureaucracy as a whole was worried. Flynn had promised a Beltway-wide audit that would force agencies to justify their missions. He'd said he was going to make the entire Senior Intelligence Service hand in their resignations. That amounted to many hundreds, maybe thousands of people across the US intelligence community. He wasn't going to fire them all, but they'd have to detail why their work was vital to national security. Many knew they wouldn't make the cut.

And then there was Barack Obama. The outgoing commander in chief told Trump that his two biggest worries would be North Korean dictator Kim Jong-un and Flynn.

Obama saw the retired three-star general as a signal threat to his legacy, embodied in several Middle East foreign policy initiatives, above all the July 2015 nuclear agreement with Iran, the Joint Comprehensive Plan of Action (JCPOA). Flynn had said long before he signed on with the Trump campaign that it was a catastrophe to realign American interests with those of a terrorist state. And now that the candidate he'd advised was president-elect, Flynn was in position to help undo the deal.

To stop him, the outgoing administration would just run the same playbook they'd used to get the Iran deal through Congress. The White House's communications shop had tasked press allies to smear opponents, lawmakers, and pro-Israel activists as disloyal Americans. If they didn't support normalizing the Islamic Republic of Iran's nuclear weapons program, that's because they were beholden to a foreign power, Israel, and a foreign leader, Prime Minister Benjamin Netanyahu. To discover the plans of those opposed to the deal, the Obama team also spied on their domestic opponents, US lawmakers and Jewish activists.

And so eighteen months after striking the JCPOA, the Obama administration smeared Flynn through the press as an agent of a foreign power, Russia, and spied on him. The collusion story was a handy instrument for many people to advance all manner of personal and political interests. But for Obama, Russiagate was a means by which he would insulate the Iran deal and seal his legacy.

When Obama warned against hiring Flynn he wasn't giving friendly advice to a fellow president about taking on a subordinate who spoke his mind sometimes perhaps too freely. He was threatening the president-elect: if Trump hired Flynn, Obama would make him regret it.

———————————

The retired general had enemies at the very top of the intelligence community. What earned the enmity of thousands of intelligence officials across Washington is what earned him the admiration of those who served under him during combat operations.

"What made Flynn revolutionary is that he got people out in the field," says former DIA analyst Oubai Shahbandar. He served under Flynn in Iraq from 2007 to 2008 and in Afghanistan from 2010 to 2011. "It wasn't just enough to have intelligence; you needed to understand where it was coming from and what it meant. For instance, if you thought that insurgents were going to take over a village, the first people who would know what was going on would be the villagers. So Flynn made sure we knew the environment, the culture, the people."

Flynn described the problem in a 2010 article co-written with Paul Batchelor and current Deputy National Security Advisor Matthew Pottinger, *Fixing Intel: A Blueprint for Making Intelligence Relevant in Afghanistan*. "Moving up through levels of hierarchy," they wrote, "is normally a journey into greater degrees of cluelessness."

Soldiers in the field needed the intelligence collected there, often by other combat units. But there was a clog in the pipeline: the Beltway's intelligence bureaucracy. What that entailed was cutting Washington out of the cycle. Forget the programs and pride of the Beltway-bound intelligence bureaucrats; Americans in uniform in Iraq and Afghanistan needed that information to accomplish their mission.

Influential senior officers like General David Petraeus credited Flynn for helping defeat Al-Qaeda in Iraq in 2007, and in 2012 Flynn was named DIA chief. The next year he secured access for a team of DIA analysts to scour through the documents that had been captured during the 2011 operation to kill Osama bin Laden.

"The bin Laden database was unorganized," says a former senior DIA official. "There had been very little work on it since it was first captured. The CIA had done machine word searches to identify immediate threats, but they didn't study it for future trends or strategic insight."

Flynn arranged for a team from US Central Command (CentCom), based in Tampa, Florida, to come up to Washington.

"We were looking for ties between Al-Qaeda and Iran," says Michael Pregent, a former Army intelligence officer who was working on the bin Laden documents as a contractor. "We're arguing with everyone, NSA, whoever else, telling them what we wanted and they kept saying, there's nothing there, we already went through it. The CIA and others were looking for immediate threats. We said, we're DIA, we're all-source analysts and we want everything to get a full picture."

Just as the CentCom team was preparing for their trip to northern Virginia, they were shut down. "Everything was set," says Pregent. "We had our hotel reservations, a team of translators, and access to all of the drives at the National Media Exploitation Center. Then I get a call in the middle of one of the NCAA basketball tournament games from the guy who was running our team. He said that Brennan and Rice pulled the plug."

Obama's deputies were clearing space for his big foreign policy idea: the Iran nuclear deal. Another aide, Ben Rhodes, had said in 2013 that it was the White House's key second-term initiative, what the Affordable Care Act was to the first term. Evidence that Tehran was coordinating with a terror group that had slaughtered thousands in Manhattan and at the Pentagon would make it harder to convince US lawmakers that it was wise to legitimize Iran's nuclear weapons program.

What was the information about Al-Qaeda's ties to Iran that Flynn wanted his CentCom team to get out? The bin Laden database included "letters about Iran's role, influence and acknowledgment of enabling al Qaeda operatives to pass through Iran as long as al Qaeda did its dirty work against the Americans in Iraq and Afghanistan." One of those letters showed that "that al Qaeda was working on chemical and biological weapons in Iran."

———————————

After decades of anti-Iran campaigning, Republicans were expected to oppose Obama's deal but didn't have the numbers to stop it in the Senate. What concerned the White House therefore was their own party. Senior Democrats on Capitol Hill were uneasy about the deal, as were large numbers of Jewish voters—more than half of whom identify as Democrats.

Jewish organizations offered two major objections to the deal: First, the outlines of Obama's nuclear deal suggested that it might legalize a bomb pointed at the Jewish state. Second, in striking an agreement with Iran, the White House might normalize relations with a regime that embodies anti-Semitism.

In return, Obama confronted Iran deal skeptics in his own party with a hard choice—either support the deal, or you're out. There would be no room in the Democratic Party for principled disagreement over the keystone of Obama's foreign policy legacy. Opponents were portrayed in harsh, uncompromising terms: They had been bought off, or were warmongers, or Israel-firsters.

In a meeting of Senate Democrats in early 2015, Obama had his eye on New Jersey senator Robert Menendez when he talked about pressures "from donors and others" to reject the deal. Menendez was offended. He said he'd "worked for more than 20 years to curb Iran's nuclear ambitions and had always been focused on the long-term implications."

The way that Obama framed it, it was the money laid out against the deal that kept Americans from seeing how excellent it was. "If people are engaged, eventually the political system responds," Obama told comedian-newsman Jon Stewart. "Despite the money, despite the lobbyists, it still responds."

Obama kept talking about money, donors, lobbyists. It sounded like a secret cabal tossing bags of dark foreign cash around Washington, but he was just referring to the American Israel Public Affairs Committee (AIPAC), an American organization run by American Jews promoting America's alliance with its most important Middle East ally. AIPAC leadership trusted the first African American president to do the right thing. They described him to themselves as a great friend of Israel and assured themselves he wouldn't put the Jewish state in danger by legalizing the nuclear program of a regime that regularly called for its destruction.

But Obama didn't trust AIPAC or the ability of the American people to recognize the excellence of the Iran deal. So, he kept much of it from public view.

In 2012, the administration began secret negotiations with Iran. To gain Tehran's confidence, the administration called off a multiagency task force targeting the billion-dollar criminal enterprise run by Iran's Lebanese ally, Hezbollah. The administration told Congress that the nuclear deal would not grant Iran access to the US financial system. A 2018 Senate report showed how the

Obama White House lied to the public and was secretly trying to grant Iran that access. The Obama administration had misled Congress about secret deals it made regarding verification procedures and then secretly shipped $1.7 billion in cash for Iran to distribute to its terror proxies.

The White House's promise that the deal would prevent Iran from ever getting a bomb was validated by its communications infrastructure: The messaging campaign brought together friendly journalists, newly minted arms-control experts, social media stars, and progressive advocacy groups like the regime-friendly National Iranian American Council. As Obama's top national security communications lieutenant Ben Rhodes told the *New York Times*: "They were saying things that validated what we had given them to say."

One strategy employed by Rhodes's assets was to engage critics in esoteric debates over details of the deal—for instance, how many centrifuges would Iranian reactors be allowed to spin? Had Iran's supreme leader declared a fatwa against nuclear weapons? Was this or that nuclear site a military facility?

Among the handful of honest reporters covering the deal, most didn't have enough information, time, or energy to continue fighting a wall of static noise. And that was the point of Obama's media campaign—to drown out, smear, and shut down opponents and even skeptics. Thus, echo chamber allies purposefully obscured the core issue.

The nature of the agreement was made plain in its "sunset clauses." The fact that parts of the deal restricting Iran's activities were due to expire beginning in 2020, until all restrictions were gone and the regime's nuclear program was legal, showed that it was a phony deal. Obama was simply bribing the Iranians with hundreds of billions of dollars in sanctions relief and promises of hundreds of billions more in investment to refrain from building a bomb until he was safely gone from the White House, when the Iranian bomb would become someone else's problem.

The JCPOA was never an arms agreement. In practical terms, it gave Iran time and money to figure out how to build a bomb under an American security guarantee. The Obama team thought that even the Israelis wouldn't dream of touching Iran's nuclear program so long as Washington vouchsafed the deal. They called Netanyahu "chickenshit."

Why did Obama expend so much effort to get the deal? How was it central to his legacy if it was never intended to stop Iran from getting the bomb? Because it was his instrument to secure an even more ambitious objective—to rearrange the strategic architecture of the Middle East.

Obama did not hide his larger goal. He told a biographer, *New Yorker* editor David Remnick, that he was establishing a geopolitical equilibrium "between Sunni, or predominantly Sunni, Gulf states and Iran." According to the *Washington Post*'s David Ignatius, another writer through whom Obama messaged, realignment was a "great strategic opportunity" for a "a new regional framework that accommodates the security needs of Iranians, Saudis, Israelis, Russians and Americans."

The catch to Obama's newly inclusive "balancing" framework was that upgrading relations with Iran would necessarily come at the expense of traditional partners targeted by Iran—like Saudi Arabia and, most important, Israel. Obama never said that part out loud, but the logic wasn't hard to follow: Elevating your enemy to the same level as your ally means that your enemy is no longer your enemy, and your ally is no longer your ally.

Obama demonstrated to Jerusalem the gravity of his intentions every time an administration official leaked reports of Israeli raids on Hezbollah and other Iranian allies in Syria and Lebanon. That put the Israelis on the defensive and also showed the Iranians that Obama could and would bring Israel to heel. Therefore, Tehran should trust him.

"Obama wants this as the centerpiece of his legacy," one US diplomat told the press in Vienna, where Kerry and his team came to terms with the Islamic Republic. "He sees himself as a transformative president in the Reagan mold," said a former Obama advisor, "who leaves his stamp on America and the world for decades to come."

For all of Obama's talk of interests and lobbies, he was himself creating a large international constituency for the deal. Sanctions on Iran had kept foreign companies out of the country for decades, but the promise of new markets for major industries, like energy and automotive, had European and Asian industry chomping at the bit. The American president promised not only to relieve sanctions but also to help drum up business by assuring the world that it was safe to invest in Iran. John Kerry was keen to turn the State Department into Iran's Chamber of Commerce.

Obama's talk of money and donors and lobbies only got louder as negotiators came closer to striking the deal. He was talking *about* the Jews and *to* them. If they didn't back the deal, the sewers would spill over with traditional anti-Semitic conceits about Jewish money and influence, dual loyalties, Jews leveraging their home country on behalf of their coreligionists, and fomenting war. This wasn't a fringe white nationalist figure, but a popular two-term Democrat. Secretary of State John Kerry said it outright: If Congress failed to pass the deal, it would put Israel at risk of being "more isolated and more blamed." There was no alternative to the deal, said Kerry, except war.

Jewish community leaders complained about how the debate over the deal was being framed. "If you are a critic of the deal, you're for war," a senior official at a pro-Israel organization told me at the time. "The implication is that if it looks like the Jewish community is responsible for Congress voting down the deal, it will look like the Jewish community is leading us off to another war in the Middle East."

Nonetheless, Obama kept hammering away at it. In a speech at American University he argued there are only two choices: the Iran deal or war. The one government that does not think this is "such a strong deal" nor "has expressed support" for it is Israel's.

If the smear campaign targeting Iran deal opponents as rich, dual-loyalist, right-wing warmongers was the public face of Obama's push for the deal, there was an even less savory component hidden within the advanced technology of the US intelligence community: The administration was spying on its domestic opponents, American legislators, and pro-Israel activists.

Noah Pollak, a pro-Israel activist who at the time was working against the nuclear agreement with Iran, told me, "The administration did things that seemed incontrovertibly to be responses to information gathered by listening to those conversations."

Pollak said, "At first we thought these were coincidences, and we were being paranoid. Surely none of us are that important. Eventually it simply became our working assumption that we were being spied on via the Israeli officials we were in contact with."

A 2015 *Wall Street Journal* story provided details of the administration's espionage operation. "The National Security Agency's targeting of Israeli leaders and officials also swept up the contents of some of their private conversations with U.S. lawmakers and American-Jewish groups," explained writers Adam Entous and

Danny Yadron. "That raised fears—an 'Oh-s— moment,' one senior U.S. official said—that the executive branch would be accused of spying on Congress."

The names of Americans are minimized in transcripts of intercepted foreign communications to protect their privacy. It is not illegal or even necessarily improper for US officials to deminimize, or "unmask," their identities, provided there are genuine national security reasons to do so.

The story the *Journal* told was evidence that Obama officials knew they were doing something wrong. And so according to Obama aides, it all fell on the shoulders of the National Security Agency, responsible for the bulk of America's signals intelligence. White House officials, according to the *Journal* story, "let the NSA decide what to share and what to withhold . . . 'We didn't say, "Do it,"' a senior U.S. official said. 'We didn't say, "Don't do it."'"

That is, it was not an innocent mistake. Obama aides knew they were abusing surveillance programs ostensibly pointed at Israeli officials in order to know what the Israelis' interlocutors, US lawmakers and pro-Israel activists, were planning to oppose the deal. Obama officials knew that congressional investigators were looking into their surveillance campaign. They leaked the story to friendly reporters to shape it to their advantage.

In June, a month before the deal was struck in Vienna, Michael Flynn was on Capitol Hill testifying on Iran and the flawed deal. He started by describing Iran's destabilizing actions throughout the region, how the regime killed American troops in Iraq and later Afghanistan. He warned about Iran's ties to North Korea, China, as well as Russia. Flynn emphasized that Iran's "stated desire to destroy Israel is very real." Obama's Iran policy is one of "willful ignorance," said Flynn.

As the 2016 election cycle approached, a number of Republican candidates solicited Flynn's advice—including Ben Carson, Carly Fiorina, and Ted Cruz. In a sense, the retired general chose Trump as much as Trump chose him. The Republican candidate's understanding of the bureaucracy was mostly theoretical. To a New York real estate developer accustomed to thin margins, Washington looked wasteful. Dozens of candidates from both parties had hit him up for donations, so he'd seen at close quarters their neediness, their desperation to please. But Flynn had detailed knowledge of how the Beltway bureaucracy worked.

The two hit it off, and Flynn traveled with the candidate regularly. He was vetted for the vice presidency, but Trump decided on Indiana governor Mike Pence, who'd help win both the evangelical and the Midwest vote.

Still, outside of Trump's own family, Flynn was his closest advisor. The foreign policy initiatives he articulated were the president-elect's, and when he spoke to foreign officials, he was speaking for Trump. Flynn not only wanted to undo the Iran deal, he was determined to find the documents detailing the secret deals between Obama and Iran.

With Flynn on the march, the outgoing administration was looking to shield the JCPOA. Obama diplomats consulted with their European counterparts and gave the clerical regime more sanctions relief, even after the Senate agreed 99–0 to renew the Iran Sanctions Act. Kerry called his Iranian counterpart to tell him not to worry.

Notably, Russia weighed in on the Obama team's side. It would be "unforgivable," according to the Russian Foreign Ministry, if the incoming Trump administration forfeited the JCPOA.

Obama agreed to let Russia export more than one hundred tons of uranium, enough to make more than ten bombs, according to some estimates.

"The point was to complicate any effort to tear up the deal," says a senior US official involved in the fight over the JCPOA. "It gave Iran an insurance policy against Trump."

Less than a month after Obama had warned Trump about his top national security aide, the anti-Flynn campaign was well underway.

A December 3 *New York Times* article portrayed Flynn as a dogmatist who brooked no disagreement and insisted that his subordinates corroborate the intelligence assessments he sought. In his worldview, according to the *Times*, "America was in a world war against Islamist militants allied with Russia, Cuba and North Korea." The piece carried the bylines of Matthew Rosenberg, Mark Mazzetti, and Eric Schmidt, with additional reporting by Adam Goldman and Michael Schmidt, all of whom would share in the *Times*'s 2018 Pulitzer Prize for national reporting on the Russiagate conspiracy theory they'd helped generate.

Parts of the *Times* story were recycled in a joint statement signed by progressive advocacy groups allied with the Obama White House in the Iran deal fight, like MoveOn.org and J Street, demanding Trump withdraw his appointment of Flynn. It cited among other concerns his views on Muslims, as expressed in his book, and his position on Iran.

There was action on social media as well, with a one-time intelligence community lawyer destined to become a leading Russiagate conspiracy theorist highlighting sections from Flynn's book. "Shocking," tweeted Susan Hennessey.

The Iran deal communications infrastructure was up and running again. It had only been a year and half since the Obama team had steamrolled congress to win the JCPOA, and now they needed to protect it from the new White House.

It was in this early December 2016 period when the Iran deal operation transformed into Russiagate. The structure was the same; only some of the variables changed. Opponents were no longer tagged as Israel-firsters; they were instead Putin allies or assets. The message, however, was identical: They're disloyal.

The outgoing administration was never concerned about Russian interference in the US political process. Moscow, after all, supported the JCPOA. "Russia" was simply used as a decoy, a false flag, to protect Obama's big foreign policy initiative—and hide the administration's massive spying operation against US citizens.

The clandestine component targeting Flynn began no later than December 2. That day, director of national intelligence James Clapper and UN ambassador Samantha Power unmasked Flynn's name from a classified intercept of communications between foreign officials. It seems that the Obama officials were interested in a Trump Tower meeting Flynn and Jared Kushner held with Russia's US ambassador Sergei Kislyak. The envoy reported back to Moscow, communications that US officials appear to have leaked to *Washington Post* reporters Greg Miller, Ellen Nakashima, and Adam Entous, who'd moved over from the *Wall Street Journal*.

Leaking information from classified intercepts is a felony. Flynn's name was leaked frequently during the transition period and the first several weeks of the new administration. There were at least thirty-nine Obama officials who unmasked Flynn's identity fifty-three times.

Often times, line analysts and investigators will unmask an identity to better understand the national security issue they're detailed to follow. It's done much less frequently by top-level officials who deal with broad policy issues. And it's extremely suspicious when numerous top-level officials are unmasking their political opponents repeatedly.

Power led the list with seven unmaskings of Flynn, a small part of her many hundreds of unmaskings between 2015 and 2016, making her, according to former congressman Trey Gowdy, the "largest unmasker of US persons in our history."

She was one of thirty Obama officials who unmasked Flynn between December 14 and 16. The list includes Brennan, Comey, Treasury secretary Jacob Lew, as well as six other Treasury officials, including Patrick Conlon, the director of the Office of Intelligence and Analysis—Treasury's own intelligence agency.

It appears they were interested in a December 15 meeting Flynn, Kushner, and Steve Bannon had with the crown prince of Abu Dhabi and de facto leader of the United Arab Emirates, Sheikh Mohammed bin Zayed al-Nahyan. Obama's former national security advisor Susan Rice also unmasked Flynn for this meeting. She said that she was irked Emirati leadership had come to the United States without notifying the Obama White House.

Rice's description of her emotional state may well be accurate, though it doesn't explain why she requested the identities of presidential transition officials. But it's not hard to figure out why she and thirty other Obama officials wanted to know about that meeting. Spying on the Trump team's meetings with Arab officials would tell them how the next administration's Middle East policies would affect Obama initiatives, especially the JCPOA. Seven Treasury officials spying on the same meeting suggests that they wanted to know Trump's plans for Iran sanctions.

Kerry had told the Iranians not to worry about sanctions, but what could Obama do to counter Trump if he was planning to reimpose sanctions? Shoot at Flynn.

SIX

THE KILL SHOT

B y December, every institution that had staked its fortunes to a Clinton victory was engaged in a massive cover-up. Barack Obama got the ball rolling.

When he instructed his CIA director on December 6 to undertake an assessment putting together everything the US intelligence community had on Russian election interference, the outgoing president was stamping official US government approval on a conspiracy theory. He knew ahead of time what Brennan was going to find because the CIA director had been telling Obama since August: Putin wanted to help Trump defeat Clinton.

Naturally, after the election Brennan doubled down on the dossier—by cloning it as an intelligence community assessment.

"The ICA was critical for setting up the collusion narrative," says a former senior Obama administration intelligence official. "It gave credibility to everything. The Steele dossier by itself wouldn't have amounted to anything."

It was a neat trick. What Brennan said had started with him and was laundered through Steele was now legitimized by Obama.

"Brennan cooked the process, to keep the experts out," says the former Obama official. "They kept senior Russia analysts at the CIA out of it. They kept out the joint chiefs of staff, the DIA, the State Department's intel shop and others."

Of the country's seventeen intelligence agencies, only the CIA, FBI, and NSA were involved in producing the assessment. "It wasn't even really three agencies," says the source. "NSA said, what you used of ours, you used correctly. [Then NSA director] Mike Rogers folded; he should have called BS."

The core ICA authors were handpicked Brennan acolytes, says the former Obama official. "He kept it small to keep everyone else out. He didn't want anyone looking at process, methodology, and tradecraft," says the source. The flawed methodology and trade-craft obscured reporting that pointed in the opposite direction of the conclusion Brennan sought. It seems they preferred Clinton.

"The Russians assumed she would win," says the former Obama official. "They had experience with her and knew how to manage her. It also obscured reporting that the Russians saw lots of problems in a potential Trump presidency, given his personality and the likelihood that he'd take a harder line approach with them."

Brennan, says the source, "wanted to avoid scrutiny because he was purposefully manipulating intelligence to go one way to support this illusion that Trump had colluded with Russia. That's fraud. He undermined the executive."

John Durham's investigators were reportedly focused on what Brennan did with the ICA.

"The ICA is not a valid document," the former Obama official explains. "We know that in every election something is going on. China is doing a lot right now regarding the 2020 elections. When we got briefed on Russia's actions in 2016, it made no sense. No one disputed Russia meddled in some ways. But there were no specific actions or identifications of intelligence that showed support for their claims that Putin had interfered to help Trump. This was demonstrated when Brennan, Clapper, Comey and Rice testified in classified settings. They had nothing."

Further, says the source, "The ICA discarded evidence that was contrary to its main finding, that Putin supported Trump. It made analytical reaches on fragmentary reporting that was not from reliable sourcing, including the Steele dossier."

Brennan misled Congress, says the former Obama intelligence official. "He said the Steele dossier was not used in the ICA, but it was."

A summary of the dossier was attached to the ICA in a two-page document called Annex A. "The ICA's principal finding is that Putin and the Russian government's influence campaign aspired to help Trump," says the source. "The footnote to support that key judgment about Putin's intentions and strategy refers to Annex A, which is the dossier."

Why, asks the former Obama intelligence official, "was it necessary to complete the ICA before Trump's inauguration?" Because the ICA stood up the dossier, which was coming apart at the seams. The cover-up consisted of a defensive scheme as well as an offensive one to keep the incoming Trump team off balance.

Steele deleted all of his correspondence with Fusion GPS, eliminating evidence of the origins and extent of the operation joining the US intelligence community and the Clinton campaign. Funding for the post-election leg was taken over by the Democracy Integrity Project, run by former Dianne Feinstein staffer and ex-FBI agent

Daniel Jones. He raised more than $2 million for Fusion GPS, and Steele was paid an additional $250,000.

Even though the FBI had officially closed Steele out as a source after he'd violated his source agreement and leaked to the press, the Bureau continued to take his Trump-Russia reporting, via Bruce Ohr. The senior DOJ official also passed on Glenn Simpson's conspiracy theories to the FBI.

Steele told Ohr in December that Millian may have overseen transfers from Russia to the Trump campaign. He told Ohr again that he thought Millian was a Russian spy—because the immigrant had changed his name on arriving in America.

The *Wall Street Journal*'s Mark Maremont reported that Millian was a dossier source. But not "a direct source," wrote the reporter. "Rather, his statements about the Trump-Russia relationship were relayed by at least one third party to the British ex-spy who prepared the dossier."

Framing Millian as an "indirect source" comported well with the FBI's post-election plans. The Crossfire Hurricane team needed to show that the collusion story wasn't just made up out of whole cloth. They wanted to lay out evidence for anyone who came looking that there was good reason to spy on the Trump campaign— reliable sources like Steele and Halper had painted a vast landscape of collusion between Trump and the Russians. But it was only after the FBI began spying on the Trump campaign—and after they could no longer count on a Clinton presidency to scrub their fingerprints from the crime scene—did they discover that the sources might have been wrong.

The FBI claimed that they'd located Steele's primary subsource (PSS) in January. The PSS was interviewed by Halper's handler,

Steven Somma, and DOJ lawyer David Laufman. They claimed to have asked the PSS about the reports Steele had filed with the Bureau. According to the PSS, Steele had misunderstood everything.

The story about Trump in the Moscow hotel, said the PSS, was "rumor and speculation." The PSS had no actual evidence Carter Page was offered a bribe in exchange for undoing sanctions on Russia. "The tenor of Steele's reports was far more 'conclusive' than was justified," said the PSS, who never expected Steele to put the information in reports or present it as "facts." "It was just talk," said the PSS, "word of mouth and hearsay." Some of it, like allegations about Trump's sexual activities, was made in "jest."

The PSS alleged that the information Sergei Millian provided was all during a ten- to fifteen-minute phone conversation. The PSS wasn't sure if it was Millian, but the voice sounded like his from a YouTube video the PSS had seen.

According to the FISA warrants, Steele's information came from the PSS's network of sources, but the PSS told the FBI there was no network. Steele, it turned out, had no real sources at all.

The story about the PSS was concocted to conceal the Crossfire Hurricane team's fraud, and forge evidence showing that the FBI had simply been mistaken. The message they meant to send was that they were incompetent but not criminal.

As another part of the cover-up, the FBI filed reports to themselves that the Russians might have planted disinformation in the dossier to deceive them. According to a January assessment, a memo about Trump's lawyer Michael Cohen was found to be inaccurate. Steele's report, the assessment claimed, might have been influenced by a "Russian disinformation campaign to denigrate US foreign relations."

This, too, was absurd. The ostensible legitimacy of the dossier was premised on Steele's claim to have access to high-level sources inside the Russian government, in fact within Putin's own Presidential Administration. That is, if Steele was to be believed, he was using sources who were likely to try to deceive him—and whom he had little ability to vet.

The dossier's central claim, in the very first memo, was that Trump had been compromised by the Russians—a claim supposedly made by a former Russian intelligence official. For all the FBI's many blunders, surely it would have occurred to top-level officials at headquarters that a claim made by a Russian spy could be weaponized to deceive. One purpose of counterintelligence is to unpack how you know what you know and whether the things you think you know are true. It's quality control. At the very least the FBI would have explored the possibility they'd been targeted by a disinformation campaign before opening an investigation on a presidential campaign. But according to Comey, the dossier was unverified.

So why had it occurred to senior FBI officials only after the election to look for Steele's primary subsource, and only then to question if the Russian government might have planted false information in the former British spy's reporting? Because the FBI knew precisely how the information came to them and who provided it. It was a disinformation campaign, to be sure, but they were not the target. Trump was.

It was only a matter of time before the incoming administration found out. The pressure began to mount when a member of the president-elect's national security team asked Comey if the FBI was investigating Steele's reporting. As a career intelligence officer, Flynn would know where to look for and how to recognize evidence of the Obama administration's surveillance of the Trump team. Getting rid of Flynn is where the interests of the FBI, CIA, and White House intersected.

———————

Flynn, says a retired senior intelligence official, "was the biggest threat to the CIA the agency had seen in years." The 2010 paper he'd produced had put the most glamorous of the intelligence community's seventeen agencies on notice. "'Fixing Intel' was critical of the CIA and worried the Agency a great deal," says the former official. "It was critical of human intelligence not serving the warfighter, and it was critical of not sharing intelligence with allies on the battlefield. The model that 'Fixing Intel' called for was, if not diametrically opposed to the interests of the CIA, at least represented a significantly different approach."

Flynn believed that intelligence best served particular operations. "Flynn apparently had a plan, as a lot of other former DIA directors have had plans, for changing the nature of the US intelligence community by knocking the CIA off its peg," says Angelo Codevilla, a former Navy intelligence officer who served on the staff of the Senate Intelligence Committee.

According to Codevilla, Flynn's initiative entailed "above all, freeing defense intelligence, freeing the Army and Navy and Air Force to run their own operations, especially human intelligence operations and certainly during the so-called war on terror. CIA basically has nothing to offer to soldiers and Marines, in the situations in which they have been put. What on earth are CIA human operators, given who they are and the consequent limitation on their access to people of interest, going to tell our troops about the individuals with whom they deal on the ground in Afghanistan?"

The retired intelligence official explains that "people were worried that the new national security advisor was going to turn over the apple cart. I didn't see it as threat as many of my colleagues saw it as. I had my criticisms of the reforms Flynn called for, but it was a work in progress. But whether you agreed or not, he was coming in to really shake things up."

And that's why, says Codevilla, "Flynn had to be eliminated. Not just because of Trump, but because of himself. He himself was an existential threat to the CIA."

If the Trump team had any ties to Russia, never mind clandestine ones, it's unlikely Flynn would have been in communication with Kislyak so often. Ambassadors are important points of contact between governments but are typically two degrees of separation from the head of state.

To Obama officials, Flynn's communications with Kislyak served as a window onto Trump foreign policy, especially regarding the Middle East, where Obama was determined to leave a lasting impact. Further, the Obama team could tailor communications with the ambassador from Russia to fit the collusion narrative.

On December 23 Flynn spoke with Kislyak about a vote scheduled to take place at the United Nations that day. The outgoing administration had coaxed Egypt to introduce UN Security Council Resolution 2334, holding that Israel was occupying the territories it had taken in the June 1967 war. Israel, according to UNSCR 2334, was in "flagrant violation" of international law. Under the terms of the resolution, even the Western Wall of the Temple Mount, the holiest site in Judaism, was an illegal Israeli settlement.

Trump had convinced Egyptian president Abdel Fattah el-Sisi to withdraw the proposal. But the transition team knew someone else would sponsor the resolution nonetheless. Flynn spoke with a number of foreign officials. He knew that at least five countries had to abstain to block the resolution and didn't think his calls would affect the final vote in one way or another. He compared the exercise to a battle drill, to see how quickly he could get foreign officials on the phone.

The administration knew he called Kislyak, too. Samantha Power unmasked his identity from a transcript of the call. Flynn didn't try to influence the Russian envoy; he just wanted to know where the Russians stood. He knew about Moscow's historical role in the Middle East, where they'd contested American power for more than half a century by supporting anti-Israel and thus anti-US initiatives and backing Israel's Arab enemies, like Syria, in war. Kislyak said that Russia had no choice but to support the resolution.

On the December 23, UNSCR 2334 passed 14–0, with Samantha Power casting a vote to abstain, forsaking America's traditional role of blocking anti-Israel actions at the UN. It was Obama's parting shot at the Jewish state.

Within the week, Obama aides were zeroing in on Flynn. The outgoing White House claimed it was surprised when Putin announced on December 30 that he would refrain from responding after Obama expelled dozens of Russian diplomats and closed two diplomatic facilities. "Great move on delay (by V. Putin)," president-elect Trump tweeted. "I always knew he was very smart!"

The intelligence officials responsible for assembling the president's daily briefing sought information to explain why Putin had chosen not to act precipitously. The FBI said it had an answer. They said they found it in a December 29 conversation between Flynn and Kislyak.

According to McCabe, he was alerted to the information by an analyst and passed it on to Comey, who told Clapper, who in turn briefed Obama. Comey corroborated McCabe's account, but Clapper swore under oath he didn't brief Obama. He may not have been the first one who told the outgoing president. Nearly forty other administration officials were tracking Flynn and unmasking him from intercepts. What would the White House do with the information?

On January 4, Strzok checked to see if the investigation on Flynn was still open. It had begun August 16, more than two weeks after Crossfire Hurricane officially began and less than a week after the FBI started to look at the three other Trump officials. The counterintelligence investigation on Flynn was called Crossfire Razor. He was suspect, according to FBI documents, because he was a Trump advisor, had attended a dinner in Moscow where he sat at the same table as Putin, had done business with companies owned by Russians, and had a top-secret clearance.

It wasn't a real investigation. Rather it was an instrument that legitimized the anti-Flynn operation in which large parts of Obama's government were involved. Had there really been a "covert relationship," as Comey put it, between the former head of the DIA and a foreign power like Russia, it would have been a serious matter.

"He would have had in his head all those special programs that you don't know exist," says Codevilla. "There are about a dozen highly, highly classified military programs, almost exclusively Navy and Air Force programs, that are the DIA's crown jewels. The DIA director knows them far better than any CIA man. And, by the way, very few CIA people are cleared for those things."

The FBI started with nothing on Flynn and found nothing. The paperwork to close the investigation on the now incoming national security advisor was ready January 4. Strzok was happy to find he'd intervened in time. He told an administrator to keep it open—"7th floor involved," he texted, referring to where the offices of the FBI director, deputy director, and other top officials are located.

Obama knew about Flynn's call. Deputy attorney general Sally Yates didn't know how he'd found out. She said that in a January 5 meeting with Comey and the president, she was so surprised by the information she was hearing that she was having a hard time processing it and listening to the conversation at the same time.

Outgoing national security advisor Susan Rice gave a different account of the meeting. She said she was there, too, and so was Vice President Joe Biden. According to an email she wrote to herself memorializing the meeting, Obama told Comey to do everything "by the book."

She wrote:

> From a national security perspective, Comey said he does have some concerns that incoming NSA Flynn is speaking frequently with Russian Ambassador Kislyak. Comey said that could be an issue as it relates to sharing sensitive information. President Obama asked if Comey was saying that the NSC should not pass sensitive information related to Russia to Flynn.

The most sensitive information related to Russia was that the Obama administration was using the collusion narrative as a false flag operation to spy on Trump. Rice's email to herself created evidence that Obama was in the clear and that she and the vice president were witnesses. If anything went wrong with the Flynn matter, it was on Comey. No matter what the FBI director might later say, she and Biden had heard the president insist he proceed "by the book."

On January 6, the outgoing administration ran its offense. Brennan, Clapper, Comey, and Rogers briefed Trump on the ICA, Obama's authorized version of the dossier. Comey stuck around to brief Trump on aspects of Annex A, a summary of the original dossier.

He wanted to see how Trump reacted after he described the memo about prostitutes in Moscow. He didn't tell the president-elect about the dossier's allegations that he'd been compromised by Putin, or that those claims were the source for the ICA's main finding alleging that Putin had interfered in the election to help him win. He didn't say that the Clinton campaign had paid for the dossier or explain that the CIA director had pushed it on the FBI all summer and previous to that, or that the Bureau had used it to spy on his campaign.

After meeting with Trump, Comey got into the car waiting for him and started to write a memo on the secure laptop he was handed as the car started to move. He classified the memo at the "Secret" level. He believed the information "ought to be treated…[like] FISA derived information or information in a [counterintelligence] investigation."

Comey went to the New York field office for a secure videoconference to brief other members of the Crossfire Hurricane team on the intelligence he'd collected on the president-elect. By disseminating news of the briefing to senior officials, Comey gave the press more sources to confirm that Trump had been briefed on the dossier. According to McCabe, CNN was just waiting to hear that the dossier had been briefed before embarking on its role in the anti-Trump operation.

On January 10, CNN first reported news that Trump had been briefed on the dossier. Hours later, BuzzFeed published it and made public for the first time what Washington and New York newsrooms, including BuzzFeed's, had wasted months trying to confirm.

The publication's rationale for making it public was so "that Americans can make up their own minds about allegations about the president-elect that have circulated at the highest levels of the US government." However, BuzzFeed's editorial maneuvers suggest it wasn't really about the public interest at all.

After posting the dossier, BuzzFeed redacted parts of it. One series of redactions was undertaken after individuals and companies who were falsely accused of improprieties took legal action. One redaction, however, was made soon after publication and had nothing to do with legal risk.

The first memo, dated June 20, contains the notorious allegations about Trump arranging for prostitutes to urinate on a Moscow Ritz-Carlton hotel bed that Barack and Michelle Obama once slept in. The story was relayed "by Source D, a close associate of TRUMP who had organized and managed his recent trips to Moscow." According to the dossier, the "Moscow Ritz Carlton episode involving TRUMP reported above was confirmed by Source E, REDACTED."

What BuzzFeed redacted from its earlier version is the description of Source E: "a senior (western) member of staff at the hotel."

Perhaps Steele and Simpson had persuaded BuzzFeed that this source was particularly vulnerable to repercussions and merited special consideration. Or BuzzFeed just agreed to play along.

According to what was later leaked to the press, Sergei Millian was both Source D and E. The double identification was itself enough to make the dossier suspicious. That the source was both a close associate of Trump and Ritz-Carlton staff was evidence it was an incoherent fabrication. Had the American public been able to read what BuzzFeed had redacted, they'd have known on

January 10 that the dossier was a fraud, weaponized to destabilize an incoming administration.

————————————

On January 7, Michael Dempsey, the official in the Office of the Director of National Intelligence who gave the presidential daily briefing, requested to have Flynn's name unmasked from a transcript that appears to include Flynn's December 29 call with Kislyak. The information was now accessible to numerous Obama officials with whom the president's daily briefing was shared, thus increasing the number of possible sources who might leak it to the press.

Adam Entous was offered the leak of the December 29 call. "I didn't know what to make of it," the *New Yorker* writer told a Washington audience. "There were divisions within the newsroom. At that point, I'm at the *Washington Post*. There are divisions about this: Why is it news that Michael Flynn is talking to the Russian ambassador? He should be talking to the Russian ambassador."

Entous's *Washington Post* colleague David Ignatius also got the leak. Clapper told him to "take the kill shot on Flynn."

In his January 12 column, Ignatius wrote about the Obama administration's response to Russia's election interference. He discussed the Steele dossier. Just as the FBI was developing its cover story—incompetence not criminality—Ignatius raised the possibility that "Russian operatives fed the former MI6 officer's controversial dossier deliberately, to sow further chaos."

He also wrote about Flynn's December 29 conversation with Kislyak, and asked, "What did Flynn say, and did it undercut the U.S. sanctions?"

Ignatius's story ignited the Trump-Russia collusion narrative, while masking its nature and purpose. The criminal leak of a classified intercept was evidence that the Obama White House was spying on the transition team's conversations with foreigners, not to protect America against foreign interference but to know the plans of its domestic opponents.

Days after Ignatius published the leak, Vice President Pence said on TV that Flynn had assured him there was no talk of sanctions. Either Pence had misunderstood, or Flynn didn't explain clearly enough. There was nothing in the call about relieving sanctions—Flynn didn't even use the word *sanctions*. Flynn knew the Russians had to respond to Obama's expulsions but he didn't want them to escalate. He sought to calm the situation. Flynn told the Russian ambassador, "Do not allow this administration to box us in." Kislyak acknowledged that's what the Obama team was doing—"transparently," said the foreign diplomat. "Openly."

Pence's televised statement gave Comey and McCabe a pretext to interview Flynn in order to ensnare him in a perjury trap. The Crossfire Hurricane team deliberated options. They asked each other: Do we have to warn him about lying to the FBI at the start of the interview or can we do it at any point? Are we trying to get him to lie so that he's fired, or prosecuted?

The FBI's scruples only went so far as to fear the White House's anger if they were caught. How, they wondered, might that hurt the institution of the FBI? There's no evidence they ever considered the personal damage their actions might cause for a combat veteran who'd served his country in uniform for more than three decades. Nor did they ask themselves how framing the new president's most trusted confidant might affect the country they were sworn to serve and protect.

Comey boasted that he took advantage of a White House that he'd thrown off balance. On January 24, he had McCabe send

Strzok and another agent, Joe Pientka, to interview Flynn at the White House. The new national security advisor mistook their purpose at first. He thought it was business; he thought they were allies in defending America from threats domestic and foreign. Instead, they were sent to entrap him.

Nonetheless, they reported to Comey and McCabe that they didn't think Flynn lied. That didn't matter. Strzok and his mistress Lisa Page rewrote the report of the interview to frame Flynn.

The national security advisor continued to do the job the president had chosen him for—to unravel the previous White House's disastrous foreign policies. After Iran conducted a ballistic missile test and its Yemeni proxies attacked a Saudi naval ship, Flynn announced in the White House briefing room: "As of today, we are officially putting Iran on notice." Former Obama aides berated him: The Trump administration had no choice but to abide by the agreement that legitimized Iran's nuclear weapons program.

The media and its White House sources flipped through the dog-eared pages of the Iran deal playbook and questioned the loyalties of a retired three-star general. Had he sold out his country to Russia?

On February 9, Entous finally got his chance to publish the leaked intercept of Flynn's call with Kislyak that he'd been offered earlier. He and *Washington Post* colleagues Greg Miller and Ellen Nakashima found nine current and former US officials who confirmed that Flynn had discussed sanctions with the Russian ambassador. Few noted that taken together with the Ignatius story this article confirmed the Obama administration had put the Trump team under surveillance—or that the number of officials involved in the leak showed a large criminal conspiracy.

Trump had been warned. Obama was serious. He meant it when he threatened Trump should he bring on Flynn. The new president's hand was forced, and Flynn left the White House February 13.

By then, Russiagate was in overdrive. The most destructive conspiracy theory in US history was well on its way to poisoning minds around the country. It appeared to cast an even deeper spell on the elite urban classes whose peers in the press and government had fueled it in the name of "resisting" Trump. And yet only a small fraction of those who imagined themselves to have the inside story of the Trump team's secret collusion with Russia to defeat Clinton understood the origins of the fantasy world they had been engulfed by.

Russiagate was a purposeful extension of the Obama administration's Iran deal media campaign and of the secret espionage operation targeting those opposed to Obama's efforts to realign American interests with those of a terror state that embodies the most corrosive forms of anti-Semitism.

It's not hard to see why the previous president went after Flynn: The retired general's determination to undo the Iran deal was grounded in his own experience in two Middle Eastern theaters of combat, where he saw how Iran murdered Americans and threatened American interests.

That Obama chose the Islamic Republic as a partner and used tactics against his political rivals that are typically employed by third-world police states partly defines his view of the world and his place in it. That's also why he was the first president in nearly a century who remained in the capital after his term ended.

SEVEN

OUTING SPIES

Before the first weekend in March, the new president was briefed by White House staff that he and other administration officials had been spied on. On Saturday March 4 Trump tweeted: "Terrible! Just found out that Obama had my 'wires tapped' in Trump Tower just before the victory. Nothing found. This is McCarthyism!"

Intelligence chiefs rushed to Obama's defense. "For the part of the national security apparatus that I oversaw as DNI," said James Clapper, "there was no such wiretap activity mounted against the president-elect at the time, or as a candidate, or against his campaign." Clapper was lying around the edges. He also said there was no FISA warrant on Trump Tower.

FBI director James Comey wanted the Justice Department to answer Trump's tweet publicly. According to DOJ officials, Comey was outraged the president had insinuated that the FBI broke the law.

Devin Nunes was precise. "If you take the president literally, it didn't happen," he told Fox News anchor Chris Wallace.

"Was there a physical wiretap of Trump Tower? No. There never was."

The left-wing press embraced Nunes as a conservative maverick, willing to speak truth to power and call out Trump. "Devin Nunes confirms it," wrote the *Washington Post*'s Chris Cillizza. "The evidence of Trump Tower being wiretapped just doesn't seem to exist."

The media's romance with Nunes was short-lived. They'd ignored the rest of what he told Wallace. "The other issue that is still remaining out there is the unmasking of names, the leaking of names. We have a lot of surveillance activities in this country, and I think the concern that the Trump administration has is 'were they actually using surveillance activities to know what they were up to?'" Nunes said. "We know that that happened with General Flynn." Nunes explained that "We don't have the answers to those questions yet...I don't know if the president has those or not."

Trump has known for a fact for three and a half years that he and his circle, including his daughter Ivanka and his son-in-law, Jared Kushner, had been spied on. During the transition period, says a former Trump NSC official, the target list expanded to include incoming administration officials, like the secretary of state, Rex Tillerson, and secretary of defense, retired general James Mattis.

When Trump tweeted about the spying, Nunes already had indications there was spying on the Trump team. Sources had contacted him about the unmaskings in late January. His primary source was from the intelligence community. "They said they started seeing things in November and December," says Nunes. "We didn't really know exactly what it meant yet, but then all these leaks start coming out."

First was the leak of the Flynn-Kislyak call for the January 12 Ignatius story. "A thousand FBI agents should have been kicking down every door in Washington until they found out who was responsible for those leaks," says Nunes. No one did anything about it.

Nunes says in retrospect he should have realized Comey's FBI was on the wrong side of things. "No one ever looked for the leakers. Comey said, we'll turn it over to the inspector general to look into the leaks. It was just another lie of his, another cover-up." And so the leaks continued.

On February 2, the *Washington Post*'s Greg Miller and Philip Rucker published a leaked account of a classified conversation between Trump and Australian prime minister Malcolm Turnbull. The newly elected president was upset to discover another trap his predecessor had set for him.

Less than a week after Trump's election, Obama had told Turnbull the United States would accept more than a thousand refugees that the Australians wouldn't admit. Most of them were from Iran. Obama wanted to embarrass the incoming president. His deal with Turnbull cut against Trump's proposed travel ban preventing foreign nationals from a handful of mostly Muslim nations without US security arrangements from visiting America. Trump let the Australian leader know he was furious.

The night the story posted, Nunes happened to be at dinner with the Australian ambassador to Washington, Joe Hockey. "I read it on his phone," says Nunes. "I said it can't be coming from us. If it's true, this is a leak of a presidential phone call with a foreign leader—it's a major crime. No way this came from us. The ambassador was adamant it wasn't them. I didn't believe him. He was right."

From that night on, says Nunes, "I knew something was wrong."

According to several former Trump NSC officials I spoke with, it was Michael Flynn who had first started to get suspicious about the intentions of the previous administration as early as December, maybe even November. "Flynn was concerned about the questions being asked by the FBI," says one former Trump NSC staffer. "You can deduce from what they're asking that they knew things they shouldn't have known. We knew we were being spied on."

And well before the inauguration, the president-elect already had an idea something was amiss, says a second former NSC official. "People told him, you need to be careful with what you're saying on the phone."

The first thing that struck the incoming team was how DOJ officials handled FISA warrants. "They brought over a book with a list and a short description of what was being filed with the FISA courts," says the second former official. "They expected a blanket approval from us, because that's what they said they'd done with the Obama NSC. They said Obama's NSC had delegated all the FISA approvals to them. But that's not how it's supposed to happen. The national security advisor should be looking at the FISA applications, and the staff should have the opportunity to review what's there."

It appears that this is how Comey and Yates got the White House to renew the Carter Page FISA warrant in January, which allowed the FBI to spy on the Trump White House.

There were concerns with both the DOJ's FISA procedures and the leaks of conversations between foreign officials and transition team members. "We knew all those calls with ambassadors were picked up and some were leaked," says the second former NSC official. "I was trying to figure out what was going on. There were leaks almost every day, and I said this bears looking into. Someone needs to go over and review everything the NSA was doing on particular targets."

He says he was trying to piece together what was happening, with the limited information he had. "If they were spying on the White House through our conversations with foreign officials, how would they do it? To get as much coverage on us as possible, they would have to lower the threshold for intelligence reporting to get as much of it as possible."

He explains that most of what NSA analysts hear in foreign leader phone calls, for instance, has no national security value. "What's important would be something like foreign leader intentions on nuclear power, or what they're doing with Iran," says the second former NSC official. "The NSA analyst listening to gossip between foreign leaders would normally just move to the next conversation. Who cares that the president of Egypt is coming to New York to meet with candidate Trump, or that Jared Kushner has contacts with the UAE and the crown prince of Abu Dhabi is coming to the US in an unofficial capacity? None of that has any national security value."

But if they lowered the threshold for reporting, they'd get more of it. "They would tell the NSA, give us everything you have on official X and Y," says the second official. "They would have said something like, 'We are interested in everything going on with Egyptian president Sisi, or the crown prince of Abu Dhabi.' Then they'd have more reporting on foreign officials speaking to the Trump team or about it." Then Obama officials would leak it to the press.

Around the first week of February, says the second former Trump NSC staffer, they found a binder cataloging unmasking requests. "There were anomalies. I didn't want to jump to conclusions but suggested we find out what it meant. Were these incidental? Was there a pattern that showed what the motivation was?"

The first former NSC official agrees there were anomalies. "Like Samantha Power's multiple unmaskings of Trump campaign people and others with ties to the campaign. And then we get word from sources at the NSA saying that we're still being spied on, while we're in the White House."

The second former NSC official explains how they started to unpack what they'd found. "We looked at the list, who was doing the unmaskings and why they needed to identify them. You could tell by the descriptors which Trump official is which. Why did they need to unmask them? Why is Susan Rice asking for this? This is odd. You don't need unmasking to know what's going on. Also, once we saw the reports, we saw there was no intelligence value."

He saw that he'd been right. He'd tried to game out how the outgoing administration would have used government resources to spy on the Trump team, and here was evidence of that method.

"It wasn't just that there were no implications for national security, nothing about terrorism, for instance," says the second Trump NSC official. "But there was nothing on economics or trade, nothing. So there were two issues: There was reporting of no intelligence value, and there was unmasking. It became clear they were trying to get into the thinking of the incoming administration."

Nunes was told about the evidence but still hadn't seen it by mid-February. He spent weeks trying to sort out logistics, to find where the records he'd been told about were stored, and how to get access to them.

In the meantime, others were piecing together fragments of information coming out of the mainstream press to understand what the various media reports regarding FISA warrants and shar-ing intelligence across the Obama administration meant.

On March 2, radio host Mark Levin broke through. A former DOJ official, Levin devoted his show to explaining how the Obama administration had undermined the Trump campaign and the fledgling presidency. He figured it out by reading the mainstream press from a critical perspective to understand what they were actu-ally describing: It wasn't collusion; the Obama administration was using the national security apparatus to spy on Trump. He called out the previous White House's "police state" surveillance and leak-ing tactics. Levin's broadcast lit a fire.

The briefings from White House officials and Levin's report, say sources, informed Trump's tweet—he knew the Obama admin-istration had spied on him and his circle.

On March 21, Nunes finally obtained access to the documents in a secure facility in the Eisenhower Executive Office Building. "At first I couldn't fathom the scope of it," says Nunes. "These corrupt bastards were unmasking every report with a Trump official in it, every report with anyone remotely related to Trump."

Nunes briefed House Speaker Paul Ryan. "I told him that I was going to speak to the press and the president. I told Speaker Ryan this had nothing to do with Russia. They were just spying."

Two weeks previously the resistance celebrated Nunes for saying Trump hadn't been wiretapped, and now they were about to embark on a still ongoing scorched-earth campaign against him—including phony ethics charges, relentless media attacks, and eventually death threats. Like Trump, he'd gone public with Obama's dirty secret.

"Now we know why they went after me when I revealed the unmaskings," says the congressman. "The FISA issue was primarily about the FBI, but the unmasking was about the Obama White House. That's why they went crazy."

———————————

Some of the spies had managed to get inside Trump's White House.

The National Security Council staff is largely a collection of detailees from different agencies or the military whose one-year stints in the White House can be extended. When a new president comes on in January, he is inheriting his predecessor's NSC staff. The Obama administration's NSC had bloated to around three hundred staffers. When Trump came on in January 2017, he took on hundreds of Obama officials who had expected to be rolled into a Clinton NSC staff.

Not every Obama holdover thought it was their primary assignment to destroy the new president. "They were civil servants, and even if they didn't like Trump, they were good at their jobs," says a former senior Trump NSC staff official. "They helped us get things done."

Others, however, were trying to undercut Trump's policies, in order to preserve Obama's. "We had people who were very supportive of the Obama administration's approach to Iran," says the former NSC official. "They were pro-Iran and pro–Iran deal." Many, says the former official, were moved to places where they could help the new administration or at least cause less trouble.

There were yet others who not only were opposed to the new administration's policies but were targeting the president himself. For instance, only weeks into the new administration, Flynn convened a large staff meeting, after which one NSC staffer was overheard confiding to another, "We can't let him enact this foreign policy." They had "to take him out," said Eric Ciaramella.

The then thirty-three-year-old CIA analyst was at the top of a list circulated by senior Trump officials looking to root out troublemakers and others suspected of trying to undermine the new White House from within. Ciaramella had come over from Langley in 2015 to work with Vice President Joe Biden, who led the Obama administration's Ukraine policy.

"Ciaramella was doing Russia and Ukraine the first few months under Trump," says the former NSC staffer. "He was responsible for Europe. But he was always taking endless notes in staff meetings that had nothing to do with his portfolio. Whenever someone's taking that many notes, it's suspicious. None of it belongs to the individual taking the notes. Those notes are never anybody's personal information. It's classified. It all belongs to the executive branch. Taking notes like that is a sign of someone who is likely to give out information they shouldn't be sharing."

Eventually he was put in a position to give him more access to more information. "When Fiona Hill joined the NSC staff," says the former Trump official, "she didn't want Ciaramella handling Russia or Ukraine because that was her territory. So the new national security advisor made Ciaramella his executive officer."

General H. R. McMaster was in line to become the envoy to anti-ISIS coalition, until Flynn's departure put him in position for the NSA job. He started February 20, a week after Flynn left. "McMaster had known Ciaramella for some time," says the former NSC official. "They ran in some of the same circles."

McMaster's decision to promote an official whom other senior Trump aides had already identified as hostile to the president created more fissures in an already fractious environment. Giving Ciaramella greater access—to more documents, more conversations, more meetings—put Trump policies and the president himself at greater risk. Ciaramella was emboldened.

"Ciaramella," says the former Trump NSC official, "went outside his chain of command to email director of homeland security John Kelly about Trump's phone call with Putin."

Ciaramella emailed Kelly on May 10. That day Trump met in the Oval Office with Russian foreign minister Sergei Lavrov and Ambassador Kislyak. The meeting had been planned on May 2, during a telephone call between Trump and Putin, and was confirmed May 5. A gloss of Ciaramella's classified email notes that on May 5 Trump had also dictated ideas to aide Stephen Miller for the letter firing Comey.

The implication was clear—because the meeting was confirmed the same day Trump had resolved to fire Comey, perhaps Putin had directed Trump to fire the FBI director. On May 9, Comey was fired.

That reasoning was the basis for acting director Andrew McCabe's decision to open a counterintelligence investigation of the president shortly after Comey's exit. McCabe said he wanted to know if Trump got rid of Comey to impede the ongoing investigation into whether Russia interfered with the 2016 election. And if so, was Trump acting on behalf of the Russian government?

In June, Ciaramella was sent back to the CIA, but his efforts to take out Trump were far from over. Perhaps on his return to Langley a senior CIA official should have warned him against political activism. Maybe someone should have reminded him that America's foreign intelligence service exists to advance the national interest by subverting hostile governments rather than its own elected officials in order to tilt the scales in favor of one party.

"It is highly fashionable to promote an anti-Trump atmosphere everywhere, including the CIA," says a former senior intelligence official. "The rules have been bent dramatically to make room for Trump bashing. People who are pro-Trump or neutral about Trump have to keep their mouths shut. Overall, CIA is a very liberal institution, a reflection of the East Coast establishment, a reflection of society."

———————

At the end of May, Ciaramella's former boss testified before the House Intelligence Committee. John Brennan took credit for starting the investigation into the Trump campaign. He said that in the summer of 2016 and previous to that he "was aware of intelligence and information about contacts between Russian officials and US persons." He said, "Every information and bit of intelligence that we had was shared with the Bureau so that they could take it."

At the time of his testimony, plans were underway to get Oleg Smolenkov out of Russia. Intelligence officials told the media that Trump's May 10 meeting with Lavrov and Kislyak worried the CIA. They feared that the president might say something to reveal the US source buried deep inside the Kremlin. In this telling, it was an urgent decision to rescue an American source endangered by an out-of-control commander in chief. Rather, it appears that exfiltrating the Russian bureaucrat was another attempt to make the dossier look real.

On May 15, former FBI director Robert Mueller had been named to lead the special counsel investigation into Russian interference. It was a continuation of the Crossfire Hurricane investigation. Some of the FBI personnel involved in targeting Trump officials before the election joined Mueller's team, like Peter Strzok, his mistress Lisa Page, and lawyer Kevin Clinesmith.

Mueller knew even before he took charge of the special counsel that there was no evidence of collusion. The FBI had been using the Carter Page FISA warrant for more than half a year to collect the Trump team's communications and had found nothing. Further, in interviews with FBI agents, Steele's alleged primary subsource had disavowed the dossier. But outside the intelligence community, few had seen the intelligence showing collusion was a fabrication.

Putting Smolenkov in front of the press would give Russiagate a patina of authenticity. After all, the dossier's architecture was built to appear as if it had come from someone inside the Russian Federation's Presidential Administration, which is where Smolenkov worked.

It seems that Smolenkov was a genuine CIA asset. But he had not provided US spies with anything on Putin's role in helping elect Trump, because that was a story invented by Americans who used Russians as props.

He may have been recruited when he worked as the second secretary at the Russian embassy in Washington, DC, from around 2006 to 2008. The ambassador at the time was Yuri Ushakov, who on his return to Moscow joined the Presidential Administration, where he was Putin's foreign policy advisor. Ushakov is named in the dossier.

The dossier claimed that Ushakov was head of an "independent and informal network" that, along with his successor at the embassy, Sergei Kislyak, "had urged caution and the potential negative impact on Russia from the operation/s" targeting Clinton and favoring Trump. In the dossier's telling, Ushakov lost out to the Presidential Administration faction that advocated for interfering on Trump's behalf.

Ushakov brought Smolenkov into the Presidential Administration, where he was likely in position to provide some useful information to US intelligence. The CIA had reportedly tried to get Smolenkov out in 2016. His preference to remain in Moscow may have been used as phony evidence to credential the FBI's cover-up— maybe Smolenkov didn't want to leave because he was a double agent and had seeded disinformation in the dossier.

In the spring of 2017, US officials reportedly told him that the US press was zeroing in on him. And indeed it was only a little more than a week after Smolenkov fled Moscow that the first report about the CIA's man in the Kremlin appeared.

On June 14, he and his wife and children took their first steps toward the US when they went on vacation in Montenegro. On June 23, the *Washington Post*'s Greg Miller, Ellen Nakashima, and Adam Entous published a story about the unnamed source inside Putin's inner sanctum who told Brennan of the Russian president's plans to interfere in the 2016 elections.

In early August 2016, according to the *Post*'s sources, "an envelope with extraordinary handling restrictions arrived at the White House. Sent by courier from the CIA, it carried 'eyes only' instructions that its contents be shown to just four people: President Barack Obama and three senior aides."

The envelope contained "an intelligence bombshell, a report drawn from sourcing deep inside the Russian government that detailed Russian President Vladimir Putin's direct involvement in a cyber campaign to disrupt and discredit the U.S. presidential race."

Not only that, according to the *Post*'s sources, but "The intelligence captured Putin's specific instructions on the operation's audacious objectives—defeat or at least damage the Democratic nominee, Hillary Clinton, and help elect her opponent, Donald Trump."

A later report from the *New York Times* also spoke of Smolenkov, without naming him, calling him a

> *particularly valuable source, who was considered so sensitive that Mr. Brennan had declined to refer to it in any way in the Presidential Daily Brief during the final months of the Obama administration, as the Russia investigation intensified.*
>
> *Instead, to keep the information from being shared widely, Mr. Brennan sent reports from the source to Mr. Obama and a small group of top national security aides in a separate, white envelope to assure its security.*

It was the same information that Brennan had been pushing on the FBI since before the summer of 2016, the same premise contained in the dossier template filled with Presidential Administration employees, the same key finding in Brennan's ICA. Now, just nine days after Smolenkov and his family had been pulled out of Russia, the *Post*'s sources spoke of a real source inside the Kremlin.

In August 2017, two months after Smolenkov was extracted from Russia, the FBI interviewed the only so-called dossier source they ever spoke with besides the primary subsource. It appears to have been someone from the Presidential Administration, like

Smolenkov. This source was alleged to have given information contained in several dossier reports, in which he is described as a "Kremlin insider," "an official close to Presidential Administration Head, S. IVANOV," "the Kremlin official close to S. [Ivanov]," and "IVANOV's associate." The descriptions fit Smolenkov.

This dossier source told the FBI "that whatever information in the Steele reports that was attributable to him/her had been 'exaggerated' and that he/she did not recognize anything as originating specifically from him/her."

On September 6, the Russian government opened up a criminal case, fearing that Smolenkov had been murdered. The Russians claim that they gave up their search when they discovered he was living abroad, in Stafford, Virginia, only forty miles from Washington, DC. It was peculiar enough he lived so close to the American capital that anyone could have found him, had they been looking. Stafford is less than an hour's drive from the Russian embassy. Even stranger was that in June 2018, Smolenkov registered a house under his own name.

"It makes no sense they'd put this guy out under his own name if he was that sensitive a source," says a former senior intelligence official in the Obama administration. "And if he's so sensitive a source, why are US officials repeatedly talking to the press about an unnamed source who is clearly Smolenkov? It looks like they wanted to put him in front of the media so they could make the dossier look real."

Reporters walked right up to Smolenkov's front door, and men in black SUVs ushered them away.

In Moscow, Presidential Administration spokesman Dmitry Peskov confirmed that Smolenkov had worked in the Presidential Administration. Peskov was also named in the dossier to make it look real. He said that Smolenkov did not have contacts with Putin. He said he couldn't confirm whether Smolenkov was a CIA agent. Only the CIA could confirm that. "I can only confirm there actually was this staffer," said Peskov, "and that he was subsequently fired."

It's possible the Russians were downplaying the gravity of the situation, but the fact that Smolenkov's sponsor, Yuri Ushakov, remained as Putin's policy advisor suggests the Russians knew the story that Brennan, the FBI, and the Clinton campaign had cooked up was a forgery. "Russia's counterintelligence is working just fine," said Peskov.

Did John Brennan use the identity of a genuine CIA asset to push a political operation against a presidential candidate? Since the dossier was rolled into the ICA, the identity of the asset was likely manipulated to target a sitting president as well.

EIGHT

THE SCOPE

With no evidence of collusion, Robert Mueller's special counsel investigation manufactured the appearance of it. The centerpiece of that effort was a July 2017 media campaign about a 2016 meeting at Trump Tower in Manhattan between a Russian lawyer and Trump officials, including the president's eldest son.

The meeting had been arranged by British music publicist Rob Goldstone, on behalf of an Azerbaijani father and son, Aras and Emin Agalarov. In a June 3, 2016, email, Goldstone wrote to Donald Trump Jr. that the Agalarovs had "official documents and information that would incriminate Hillary and her dealings with Russia and would be very useful to your father."

Clearly, someone on the Agalarov side was participating in the multipronged effort to frame the Trump team. Prior to the official start date of Crossfire Hurricane, Trump campaign advisors Roger Stone, Michael Caputo, Carter Page, and George Papadopoulos had all been offered Russia-related dirt on Hillary Clinton. The Trump Tower setup brought the number to seven Trump officials targeted by Clinton operatives and American spies, adding the president's son; his son-in-law, Jared Kushner; and his campaign manager Paul Manafort.

Donald Trump Jr. responded quickly to Goldstone's email. "If it's what you say I love it especially later in the summer."

He wanted to put off the meeting until the end of the summer. The Trump campaign was concerned that the candidate's nomination might be contested at the Republican convention in Cleveland in mid-July. The meeting Goldstone asked for, said Trump Jr., "wasn't something that I would have wanted to deal with right now." When he said "I love it," he explained, "it's a colloquial term of expression," like "if a friend says, 'Hey you want to go grab a beer after work?'—'Sure, I love it.'"

He agreed to the meeting, he says in a phone interview, because of relationship maintenance. "If you're a business guy and someone asks you to do something like that, you do it." He already had a relationship with the Agalarovs. The Trump Organization nearly struck a deal with them a few years earlier for a Trump Tower in Moscow, but it didn't work out. "As a real estate developer," he says, "I'm thinking something else might have worked out down the line."

On June 9, Goldstone escorted Natalia Veselnitskaya, a Russian lawyer, to the Trump Tower in midtown Manhattan for a meeting with Trump Jr., Kushner, and Manafort. She had no dirt on Clinton. She wanted instead to talk about sanctions imposed on senior Russian officials under a 2012 US law.

Veselnitskaya was part of Moscow's effort to repeal those sanctions. She had hired Fusion GPS to assist her. Their role, say sources, was to feed the press with derogatory information about the Magnitsky Act and its driving force, Chicago-born financier William Browder.

Browder's company had become one of Russia's largest investment advisors before he was expelled in 2005, and according to filings, $230 million his company had paid in taxes was misappropriated by the Russian government. Browder hired Russian tax specialist Sergei Magnitsky to investigate. In 2008, Magnitsky was arrested and died in prison in 2009 after he was beaten. To make those behind Magnitsky's death accountable, Browder lobbied Washington lawmakers, who in 2012 passed the Magnitsky Act.

Glenn Simpson met with Veselnitskaya the day before her meeting at Trump Tower, during which she recycled Simpson's talking points about Browder. The Trump officials quickly ended the meeting. Simpson met with her the day after, too.

More than a year later, the *New York Times* broke the news. On July 8 Jo Becker, Matt Apuzzo, and Adam Goldman published "Trump Team Met with Lawyer Linked to Kremlin during Campaign." The next day, the same three reporters filed "Trump's Son Met with Russian Lawyer after Being Promised Damaging Information on Clinton." On July 10, Maggie Haberman added her byline to Becker, Apuzzo, and Goldman's for "Trump Jr. Was Told in Email of Russian Effort to Aid Campaign." Haberman's byline was left off the July 11 story, "Russian Dirt on Clinton? 'I Love It,' Donald Trump Jr. Said."

Finally, the *Times* was done. The same reporting team had written the same story four times in four days. It wasn't reporting; it was a roll-out, a media campaign, as though they were promoting a new cosmetic or rock band. The July 11 and 12 stories on the Trump Tower meeting were cited by the 2018 Pulitzer committee that awarded the *Times* and the *Post* a joint prize for their work promoting the Russia collusion conspiracy theory.

On July 12, the day after the *Times*' last piece on the Trump Tower meeting, the FBI interviewed another figure at the meeting, Anatoli Samochornov, a translator Veselnitskaya had brought along. A contractor for the State Department, Samochornov told the FBI that the June 2016 meeting had only lasted twenty minutes and the main subject was Magnitsky Act sanctions. He said, "There was no discussion of the 2016 United States presidential election or collusion between the Russian government and the Trump campaign."

He said there was no discussion about "dirt" on Clinton and didn't think the Democratic candidate was even mentioned by name. He said that he wasn't fond of Donald Trump Jr., but his account of the meeting was correct. He said that "he would have contacted the FBI if he thought the meeting was nefarious."

The special counsel's office (SCO) never disclosed that a witness had cleared Trump Jr. of any suspicion. Instead, they let the press build the lie until it became one of the pillars of Russiagate. Adam Schiff explained that the meeting represented a "form of collusion." At other times, the California congressman said it was "direct evidence of collusion."

"It's so hard to believe that once lauded institutions are so corrupted," says Trump Jr. of the FBI, Capitol Hill, and his hometown's once great newspaper, the *New York Times*.

Why didn't the press put it together? The fact that Fusion GPS had produced the dossier, the Trump-Russia collusion field guide, and was also employed to advance Russian interests against US law should have been clear evidence that Russiagate was a sinister fable.

But the press already knew what Fusion GPS was going into the 2016 election cycle. Journalists throughout New York and Washington knew that Simpson and Fritsch were paid by corporate and political interests to push narratives. They were aware that Simpson and Fritsch bullied their colleagues, like John Carreyrou, the former *Wall Street Journal* reporter, who won numerous awards for his work on Theranos, the Silicon Valley medical tech firm that was falsifying results. According to an unnamed source in a *Washington Post* article, Fritsch told Carreyrou that his reporting was "too blunt and aggressive, and he encouraged him to soften it."

Fusion GPS was going after members of their own guild, so why didn't the press ever come clean about the dossier? Because Russiagate aligned with their own interests and those of the past and present intelligence officials and Democratic operatives the press depended on for their scoops.

"It was all a PR stunt," Trump Jr. tells me. "There wasn't one specific plan; it was an evolving plan to hurt the president, to put undue pressure and stress on him, to threaten to jail his children, so he'd have to step in to end the nonsense. They wanted to destroy him and his family. As an American I still couldn't fathom in my mind they could be so corrupt and malicious. If they can do it to me, to the president, to Flynn, who won't they destroy to push their political will?"

The FBI arrested George Papadopoulos July 27, 2017, when he was returning to the United States after a trip to the Mediterranean. He was first interviewed by the Bureau six months before, which was half a year after it opened the most important counterintelligence investigation in its history on information Papadopoulos allegedly passed on to an Australian diplomat.

With the SCO tasked to make Russiagate look real, two weeks after Steele's so-called primary subsource had disavowed the dossier, the FBI circled back on the young Trump aide.

The FBI interviewed Papadopoulos in Chicago. They told him they wanted to speak about his friend in New York, Sergei Millian. They really wanted him to talk about someone else.

During the campaign, the FBI had sent at least two confidential human sources after Papadopoulos. One was Stefan Halper, who offered him $3,000 to write a research paper on eastern Mediterranean energy issues. Halper paid for his trip to London and met with him twice on September 15, 2016.

Halper's handler Steven Somma and other agents traveled to London but did not make themselves known to Papadopoulos. However, an undercover agent posing as Halper's research assistant did. She introduced herself to Papadopoulos under a pseudonym, "Azra Turk."

Halper was recording Papadopoulos without him knowing it. He wanted him to confess that the Trump team had an October surprise in the works. He asked him whether he thought the Russians were playing a big role in the election. Papadopoulos said he didn't think so. He asked if the Trump campaign had anything to do with the DNC hack. That would be illegal, said Papadopoulos. Espionage, he told the spy, is treason. The FBI edited Papadopoulos's exculpatory statements out of the FISA applications in order to spy on the Trump team.

It was a month later when the FBI first sent Jeffrey Wiseman, a college friend of Papadopoulos's, to record him. He asked

Papadopoulos if he thought Russia was "playing a big game in this election." Papadopoulos said, "That's all bull." He said no one knows who hacked the DNC. Papadopoulos said that the press reports about the Russians and Trump were conspiracy theories.

In the winter of 2017, the FBI wanted him to talk about Russia. It seems they tried to get him to set up Millian. He said he'd cut ties with his friend, and it would seem odd to him if he tried to reach out to him now. Papadopoulos told them that to the best of his knowledge Millian had no prior knowledge of the Russians possessing Clinton's emails. Unlike Joseph Mifsud.

That was what the FBI wanted from their interviews with Papadopoulos. They had to fix the narrative they'd used to open Crossfire Hurricane half a year earlier. Australian diplomat Alexander Downer had told an American diplomat from the London embassy about statements Papadopoulos made about suggestions from the Russians that they could assist the Trump campaign with the anonymous release of information during the campaign that would be damaging to Hillary Clinton.

But what Russians? For the FBI to start an investigation of Russian election interference based on information Papadopoulos had from the Russians, they needed a Russian. They didn't have one, so they approximated the appearance of one—Joseph Mifsud.

The Maltese-born academic taught diplomats, police officers, and intelligence officers at schools in London and Rome, where he'd lived and worked over the last dozen years. He was a well-known figure on the foreign policy circuit, traveling the world to attend or host international panels and network with famous statesmen, like British prime minister Boris Johnson.

Papadopoulos was introduced to Mifsud in March 2016 in Rome, where the professor was teaching at Link Campus, an academic institution run by a former Italian interior minister who frequently hosted guest lecturers from the FBI and CIA. Papadopoulos was eager to make a name for himself on the Trump campaign and told the professor he wanted to arrange a meeting between the candidate and Putin. Mifsud said he'd introduce him to important Russians who could make it happen—like a think tank researcher and a female student who was falsely said to be Putin's niece.

He traveled to Moscow in April and on his return met with Papadopoulos and gave him startling news. The Russians had Clinton's emails. Papadopoulos asked how he knew. Mifsud chuckled and said, "They told me they have them." Papadopoulos thought it was strange and didn't believe it. There's no evidence he told anyone on the Trump campaign about it. He told the FBI he hadn't thought about it again until they raised the issue in the winter of 2017.

It seems the FBI prompted him. They asked if he received any information from a Russian government official about dirt on Clinton. They asked if anyone ever told him that the Russian government planned to release dirt on Clinton. No, he said. "No?" the agents asked skeptically. They were leading him to complete the circle they'd started with Downer's information in London.

He said he remembered that Mifsud had told him the Russians had Clinton emails. But because he couldn't remember if it was before he joined the Trump campaign or after, the FBI arrested him in July 2017, six months after he was first interviewed, and two months after Mueller was hired.

According to the October 5 statement of offense filed by special counsel lawyers Aaron Zelinsky, Jeannie Rhee, and Andrew Goldstein, Papadopoulos lied in the January 27 FBI interview "about the extent, timing, and nature of his communications" with Mifsud and the two Russians, the think tank scholar and the student.

The special counsel documents are vague about Mifsud, and intentionally so. They do not name Mifsud but identify him only as a professor the defendant "understood to have substantial connections to Russian government officials." The SCO situated Mifsud's ties to Russia in the mind of Papadopoulos. The Mueller prosecutors did not claim that Mifsud is a Russian agent or is affiliated with Russian state interests because there is no evidence that a man with extensive ties to Western intelligence, political, and diplomatic circles is a Russian agent.

Zelinsky, Rhee, and Goldstein misled the court. They filed court documents claiming that Papadopoulos's "material false statements and material omissions" during the January 27 interview "negatively affected the FBI's Russia investigation, and prevented the FBI from effectively identifying and confronting witnesses in a timely fashion." The Mueller lawyers omitted evidence of Papadopoulos's willingness to help the FBI and even locate Mifsud for them.

In his February 1 interview with the FBI, Papadopoulos had told them he was planning a trip to London and "could potentially meet with Mifsud" then. He said Mifsud had recently reached out to him and was going to visit Washington, DC, around February 11. In the February 10 interview, Papadopoulos said that Mifsud had just emailed him to say that he was in Washington, DC, at that very moment.

The FBI did interview Mifsud on February 10 in Washington. According to DOJ documents, he "denied that he had advance knowledge that Russia was in possession of emails damaging to candidate Clinton." The special counsel blamed Papadopoulos for the FBI's failure. His "lies undermined investigators' ability to challenge the Professor or potentially detain or arrest him while he was still in the United States."

That was not true. Papadopoulos had told them that Mifsud had boasted of inside information provided by the Russians themselves. The special counsel complained that Mifsud left Washington the day after the FBI interview and "has not returned to the United States since then." But what did that matter? Journalists knew how to find Mifsud in person or by email, through October 2017. The world's leading law enforcement agency could have asked for help from the governments of Italy and the United Kingdom, between which Mifsud divided his time. It was only after November 1 that Mifsud went into hiding, and he has not been heard from since.

Papadopoulos was Mueller's first big catch, an American who'd had the audacity to exercise his rights and participate in a presidential campaign.

"I believed in America, including its justice system," says Ekim Alptekin.

His faith crashed on the rocks of the American coup he was thrown against, just because he had hired Flynn's company to research the origins of the coup that roiled his own country, Turkey. When the SCO came for Flynn, they pressured the forty-three-year-old Turkish businessman to give him up in order to get the former NSA to turn on the president.

This spring I spoke with Alptekin on the phone over the course of several weeks. Because of his run-in with the Mueller team, he hasn't left Turkey for more than two years for fear of extradition. He's under indictment for making false statements to the FBI and charges related to illicit foreign influence. He can't visit his children in school in the Netherlands. His legal bills are in the millions of dollars, while banks have pulled the plug on his investments, in some cases closing his accounts.

"I tried finding private investors for a large real estate development I own in Istanbul," says Alptekin. "But nobody wants to loan money to someone who remains a target of Mueller's prosecutors and could go to jail for thirty-five years."

On July 15, 2016, a faction of the Turkish military turned on colleagues and countrymen in an effort to topple President Recep Tayyip Erdoğan from power. The presidential palace in Ankara was bombed, as was the parliament. More than three hundred Turks were killed and thousands were wounded after tanks rolled into Turkish cities, including Istanbul, where Alptekin lives. "I saw the city on fire," he says.

The man believed to be responsible for the coup is Fethullah Gülen, an Islamist preacher whose extensive networks inside the Turkish police, judiciary, and educational system had at one time made him a valuable Erdoğan ally. In 1999, Gülen came to the United States for medical care and received a green card in 2008. He now lives in the Poconos Mountains in Pennsylvania.

"The Turkish government had been trying to get Gülen extradited years before the coup," Alptekin says. In order to make the case to US lawmakers, it wasn't enough just to relay information from Ankara. "If it's just coming from Turks, they don't take it seriously."

Further, the wealth Gülen had accumulated through his schools spread across the world bought him power inside of Washington. Gülenist organizations have employed numerous lobbyists, including the now dissolved Podesta Group, once owned by Tony Podesta, younger brother of Hillary Clinton's campaign chairman John Podesta.

In the immediate aftermath of the coup attempt, Alptekin began discussing the Gülen project with Flynn's partner, Bijan Rafekian. "Who could produce a more authoritative report on Gülen than the former DIA director?" says Alptekin. He was convinced Flynn was the man for the job and asked the Turkish government to fund the project. When Ankara dithered, he decided to back it himself and hired the Flynn Intel Group in August 2016.

Alptekin knew that he'd only have Flynn's attention for a few months. "He didn't want to be under any commercial obligation at election time," says Alptekin.

On election day, Flynn published an editorial in *The Hill* that said, "Our ally Turkey is in crisis and needs our support." It was harmful to US interests, Flynn explained, to be sheltering an Islamist radical that was as dangerous to our NATO partner Turkey as Osama bin Laden had been to America. Even worse, wrote Flynn, was that American taxpayers were helping subsidize Gülen's 160 charter schools in the United States.

Trump's victory ended Flynn's involvement with the Gülen investigation. After Flynn left the White House, anti-Trump operatives in the FBI and DOJ continued to target him and, soon, Alptekin.

In May, prior to Mueller's appointment, a former prosecutor named Peter Zeidenberg approached Alptekin through his lawyers and he retained him. Zeidenberg suggested he get in front of any prospective problems and speak with the DOJ about his contract with the Flynn Intel Group.

After Mueller was appointed, Alptekin voluntarily submitted to an interview with SCO prosecutor Brandon Van Grack on May 24. "I thought if I was transparent with the special counsel, they'll understand the stories in the media are false," says Alptekin.

In March, for instance, the *Wall Street Journal* had reported that during a September 2016 meeting he and Flynn had plotted to kidnap Gülen. The story was sourced to former CIA director James Woolsey. Alptekin says Woolsey knew there was no plan to kidnap a US permanent resident.

"If he really thought I was part of a plot to kidnap Gülen," says Alptekin, "why would he pitch me the day after the alleged meeting for a commercial engagement?" Woolsey wanted the job Alptekin had already contracted Flynn for. "If the former CIA director hears about a plot to whisk someone out of America illegally, he waits seven months before reporting it?" says Alptekin. "And then he doesn't tell the FBI but the *Wall Street Journal*?"

Alptekin learned quickly that the Mueller team wasn't trying to find the truth. "I knew how the Gülenists worked," says Alptekin. "They created smoke that was picked up by the US press. And I saw the Justice Department was doing the same thing, using media articles to justify their investigation."

The Mueller team wanted him to help nail Flynn on ginned-up charges for violating lobbying laws. The Flynn Intel Group had registered with Congress under the Lobbying Disclosure Act, applicable when US firms are working on behalf of foreign individuals or companies. Lobbying for foreign countries requires registering under the Foreign Agents Registration Act (FARA).

Investigators are supposed to move from the crime to the perpetrator, but that's not how the special counsel operated. "They started a very broadly scoped investigation into the president's first circle," says Alptekin. "They targeted a person and either found a crime or created one. Then they tried to get their target to lie about others after being faced with the full force of the US government."

Alptekin says that between the SCO and his lawyers, he was being "directed to say the contract was for the Turkish government, and I was a front." He was being pressured on several fronts. In October 2017, the SCO was leaking to the press that Woolsey was speaking to them about the alleged plot to kidnap Gülen. Alptekin's lawyer Peter Zeidenberg called him in Turkey.

"At a certain point," Alptekin remembers, "he started screaming into the phone, 'This is not a movie, there will not be a happy ending, you will play the role that they want you to play. The United States government is asking you to do it.'" Alptekin says he had a witness. "I held up the phone so the witness could hear, and I asked Zeidenberg, 'Are you telling me to lie?' He didn't answer."

Alptekin stuck with the truth and hired a new lawyer. Late in 2018, his new counsel said that Mueller prosecutors invited him to the US for another chance. His lawyer told him: "But they want to be sure you're not going to tell the same story."

They didn't want him to exculpate Flynn; they wanted Alptekin to take him down.

"I'm ashamed to say I briefly considered it, because General Flynn had already inexplicably pled guilty that he lied to the FBI," says Alptekin. "And legal bills were piling up. I couldn't work or travel. But then I thought about what my father told me: You're only a man if you have principles. And it's only a principle if you apply it when it doesn't suit you."

Apltekin says he knew that "General Flynn acted with integrity. Why did he say he'd lied to the FBI? Now we know why—they threatened his son."

───────────

After Michael Flynn left the White House, his lawyers from Covington and Burling wanted to know if he had anything on Trump. Robert Kelner and Stephen Anthony told him it would give them more leverage with the special counsel. Eric Holder, Obama's first attorney general, was a partner at Covington and Burling. Flynn himself was a registered Democrat. He told his lawyers he was unaware of the president doing anything wrong.

In August, nearly half a year since he had left the White House, Flynn was told that the SCO was looking closely at Flynn Intel Group's business, including his son's role at the company. In September, the Mueller team leaked to the press that it was considering charging the younger Flynn for possible FARA violations for FIG's work on behalf of Alptekin.

In November, the SCO turned up the pressure on Flynn to plead guilty. The charges under consideration were FARA related and for making false statements to the FBI in his January 24 White House interview. His lawyers asked for the report of that interview, known as a FD-302, in their November 1 meeting with the SCO. Mueller's team declined to produce it.

On November 3, Flynn's lawyers held a conference call with Brandon Van Grack, lead lawyer on the Flynn case, and other

SCO prosecutors. Flynn's lawyers said their client was innocent. Their request for the 302 was again rejected. The SCO argued that providing it to them would reveal details of their investigation.

The SCO used the press to threaten Flynn. A November 5 NBC News article, "Mueller Has Enough Evidence to Bring Charges in Flynn investigation," by Julia Ainsley, Carol E. Lee, and Ken Dilanian, messaged on behalf of the Mueller team. "If the elder Flynn is willing to cooperate with investigators in order to help his son," the article quotes two sources familiar with the investigation as saying, "it could also change his own fate, potentially limiting any legal consequences." The warning wasn't subtle. The article was illustrated with a photograph of Flynn and his son.

Flynn's first meeting with Van Grack and his SCO colleague Zainab Ahmad was November 16. His lawyers told him afterward that it didn't go well, and he could be looking at fifteen years in prison. They coached Flynn on how to flatter his tormentors. They told him that he was likely to be indicted, and if he didn't plead guilty, his son would likely be indicted, too.

On November 30, Flynn again told his lawyers that he didn't believe he had lied to the FBI in his White House interview. He'd spoken with dozens of foreign officials during a frantic transition period and holiday season. He was on vacation in the Dominican Republic when many of his conversations took place, including the December 29 call with Kislyak. He may have not remembered every detail correctly, he told his lawyers, but he had not consciously or intentionally lied.

He asked his lawyers to find out if the FBI agents who interviewed him believed that he lied. Kelner and Anthony left the room to call the SCO.

Strzok and Pientka had told Comey and McCabe that they thought Flynn had not lied. But Flynn didn't know that. Nor did he know that the original 302 of the White House interview had been rewritten in February by Strzok and his mistress Lisa Page to say whatever those guiding the FBI wanted it to say. And that's why the SCO refused to hand over the 302 to Flynn's lawyers—there was the real one filed shortly after the interview and a forgery. But Flynn didn't know any of that.

When his lawyers returned to the room where he and his wife were sitting and said only that the "agents stand by their statements," Flynn understood it to mean they believed he'd lied. The next day, December 1, he pled guilty to making false statements to the FBI.

———————

With Flynn in hand, the SCO had Trump in its sights. Mueller started asking for an interview with the president. He wanted to talk about how Trump had asked Comey to leave Flynn alone after he'd left the White House. Comey had written a memo to himself about the episode. It was one of the foundations of the obstruction case the SCO was building against Trump. Any move the president tried to make to extricate himself from jeopardy, any attempt to fire anyone, like Mueller, or deputy attorney general Rod Rosenstein, would appear to be cause for an obstruction charge.

If the SCO couldn't bring charges against a sitting president, it could hand them off to Congress for an impeachment charge, but the House would have to be controlled by Democrats to get the votes. The Mueller team was in for the long haul, at least until midterm elections in November 2018.

Rosenstein had bought them all that time with the classified memo he'd filed August 2 outlining the scope of the special counsel investigation. "The following allegations," he wrote, "are within the scope of the Order"—allegations that Page, Manafort, and Papadopoulos "committed a crime or crimes by colluding with Russian government officials with respect to the Russian government's efforts to interfere with the 2016 election for President of the United States."

The special counsel had been appointed to investigate the fiction that the Clinton campaign and John Brennan passed on to the FBI in order to frame Trump and spy on him. The documentary evidence for collusion was only the dossier that Brennan had institutionalized with the January 2017 intelligence community assessment. And now Rosenstein had further credentialed a conspiracy theory.

The scope of degradation and depravity caused by the dossier operation were as yet only dimly visible. The FBI and SCO had turned friends and colleagues against each other to prove the lies they themselves had manufactured. Robert Mueller, credited in all corners as a man of honor, had authorized officers of the US government to target sons to bring their powerful fathers to their knees.

The dossier and the dossier model—a forged document pushed through the US intelligence bureaucracy by political operatives and legitimized by the American media—would be used in subsequent anti-Trump operations. And most astonishingly, just over the horizon was the history lesson Americans had previously understood only indirectly, only by reflecting on the fate of foreign nations broken by their sick belief systems, cruel politics, and the sadistic ease with which warlords and ideologues turned communities, neighbors, friends, and families against each other: Those who can be convinced of the most monstrous lies can be persuaded to believe anything. It appears that this is true even of a free people in a free country.

NINE

UKRAINE THE MODEL

Rudolph Giuliani wanted to go on offense. It had been nearly a year since the special counsel investigation had started and the president's legal team needed someone with criminal investigatory experience. The former mayor of New York came on board in April 2018.

"I wanted to make us a lot tougher against them," Giuliani tells me. "They'd been told the special counsel was going to be resolved in seven months. The president was told it would be resolved before Christmas. I felt I had to reorder the strategy. We needed to get out front publicly because I believed it was not just a legal case. It was a political case."

With a criminal case, Giuliani explains, "if you're going to be indicted, you keep your mouth shut. But there was no jury. There were going to be completely biased characters in the House that were going to impeach him no matter what. It was a case that would be decided by public opinion. If public opinion was against him then the Democrats would surely not only impeach him but also maybe convert some Republicans. So we had to go on television and attack Mueller and his investigation."

We're sitting in the mayor's Upper East Side apartment in the late winter. He's busy and energetic—in addition to defending the president against a conspiracy theory, he's also redesigning his kitchen and starting a new podcast. Friends, colleagues, repairmen, and sound and light technicians rotate through all morning, and the mayor invites them to join him at a long table in the dining room for coffee. In the afternoon, he moves to his office in an adjoining room for a cigar.

He's known Robert Mueller for thirty years. "He worked for me," says Giuliani. "He worked for the US attorney in Boston when I was associate attorney general. I've known him since 1981. I always thought Mueller was a good guy. I never thought of him as a super lawyer, I thought of him as a good guy. That was my initial reaction when he was appointed. Then I saw the people he was appointing. You don't go out of your way to pick ten or twelve activists, people who donated to the Clinton campaign and the Obama campaign. And I said to myself, there's something seriously wrong here."

Mueller's so-called pit bull, says Giuliani, was notorious. "Andrew Weissmann never worked for me, but I knew about him. I knew he was a complete animal. Everywhere he'd been, lawyers complained about him. He's not the kind of guy to put in a delicate investigation. He is the kind of guy you put in if you want to frame somebody."

As the special counsel set about its business, Giuliani saw that his concerns were right. "I thought the way they treated Flynn was disgusting. I saw them raiding Michael Cohen's office. We do that for terrorists, when you're going after bin Laden. You don't do this to lawyers in a white-collar case. And you don't do it in a case that involves the president of the United States. You've got to show a certain amount of statesmanship and objectivity. But the press didn't want to see statesmanship and objectivity. They wanted to see animals."

The mayor and the president have known each other for decades. They are outer-borough New Yorkers (Trump from Queens and Giuliani from Brooklyn) whose ascent to fame began in the 1980s. Trump was finishing construction projects ahead of schedule and under budget as Giuliani brought down the Mafia. When Giuliani appeared onstage with Trump election night, the message was clear—the new president's mandate was to root out corruption in the American capital just as America's mayor had cleaned up the five boroughs.

"I wanted to defend the president because he was being treated so unfairly," says Giuliani. "The Mueller prosecutors weren't just confusing circumstantial evidence. They weren't using ordinary investigative techniques. There wasn't the usual press scrutiny of the tactics of the prosecutor. They're violating the attorney-client privilege as if it doesn't exist. They are leaking like crazy, and then the press is saying the office doesn't leak. So how come I know all about the investigation if the office doesn't leak? It was being handled like a frame-up."

Giuliani knew it was important to assert his strategy immediately. "The first time I met Mueller, I said, 'You realize we're not talking about an indictment.' He said, 'I'll take that under advisement.' And I said, 'No, you won't. The Justice Department has a ruling that says you can't indict a sitting president. You exist under Justice Department rules. If you're saying you're going to set your own rules, then you're violating the terms of your appointment.'

The young guy to his left leans over and whispers in his ear and probably said, 'Hey, the guy's right.' But he didn't acknowledge I was right. He was like a schoolteacher who can't acknowledge he's wrong. And instead, he said, 'We will let you know.'"

The goal was to change how the public—or at least part of the public—saw Mueller and his investigation. The resistance wanted Trump's blood, but a significant number of Americans had just been sold on Mueller's virtues and the integrity of the investigation. Giuliani wanted to demonstrate that it was a show trial; that his client, the commander in chief, had been framed; and that the Mueller team was intent on undoing the 2016 election.

"So when the public heard 'Mueller,' they wouldn't think 'great prosecutor,' 'great FBI agent,' but a guy who hired all Democrats, a guy who entrapped Flynn, a guy who allowed his prosecutors to break in on somebody's house at six in the morning. The idea was to knock him down to size. It was my job to do that to defend my client."

The mayor was several months into the case when he got a call around Thanksgiving time from a former associate who runs an investigatory firm.

"Bart Schwartz was the former head of my criminal division at the US attorney's office," says Giuliani. "He said he had a source who wanted to give me information about Ukrainian government collusion with Democrats to affect the 2016 election. He said the story they made up about Trump and Russia really happened with the Democrats in Ukraine. I'm not thinking at all about the 2020 election. I'm thinking he's going to get me exculpatory information that'll help me defending my client. At this point, I didn't even know Joe Biden was involved."

Biden first met the future president of Ukraine Victor Yanukovych in 2009. As the Obama administration's point man for Ukraine, the vice president was in regular touch with him during his final days as head of state in February 2014.

Three months after Yanukovych fled to Russia, Biden's son Hunter was appointed to the board of a company owned by one of Yanukovych's allies, Mykola Zlochevsky. With his patron out of power, Zlochevsky and his energy company, Burisma, needed protection from rival oligarchs. And that's why he brought on Hunter Biden, the vice president's youngest son, who had no experience in Ukraine or the energy business. His qualifications were limited to the access he guaranteed.

"He wasn't hiring Hunter for a no-show job," says Giuliani. "He was buying protection from the most influential man he could find, Hunter's father, the vice president of the United States."

Biden's relationship to Yanukovych and other Ukrainian figures as well as the Obama administration's role in Ukrainian politics are central to understanding not only the impeachment of Donald Trump but also the earlier Russia collusion conspiracy operation. Ukraine is at the heart of Russiagate, which is why Democratic party operatives, intelligence officials, and the press turned Ukraine-related corruption on Trump in another attempt to destroy him.

Yanukovych was elected president of Ukraine in 2004, but his election was annulled after demonstrators filled the streets for the Orange Revolution. He was too pro-Russia, too pro-Putin, said his opponents. That messaging was intended to win the affection of the Western press. Yanukovych's opponents were simply from a rival political faction.

Labels like "pro-Russia" make little sense in the context of a buffer state situated between Russia and Europe. No Ukrainian head of state can afford to antagonize its nuclear-armed neighbor in Moscow, which had once incorporated Ukraine into the Soviet Union. Further, Ukrainian leaders know that the Germans who lead Europe will not contest Russian arms to keep Kiev in the Western fold. As Trump was to discover, despite the liberal international community's fine words about Ukrainian sovereignty, there is no one willing to spend lives or even money for it.

Yanukovych returned to office in 2006, serving as prime minister through 2007. Fusion GPS co-founder Glenn Simpson was particularly interested in his efforts to win support from Republicans. In 2007, Simpson wrote for the *Wall Street Journal* about Yanukovych's Beltway charm offensive, spearheaded by the firm of Republican strategist Paul Manafort. His work on behalf of Yanukovych caused a minor stir during the 2008 election cycle. As Simpson and Mary Jacoby, his wife, reported for the *Journal* in 2008, Manafort's partner Rick Davis managed the presidential campaign of John McCain, who'd endorsed a Ukrainian political movement in opposition to Yanukovych.

In 2010 Yanukovych was again elected president, and Manafort continued to advise him. He counseled the Ukrainian leader to sign the association agreement offered by the European Union. It was little more than a trade deal that dumped European, especially German, goods into the Ukrainian and, more important, Russian, markets. There were hints the agreement was a first step toward EU accession, but that was fanciful. Ukraine is the poorest country in Europe, and Berlin was not looking to float another economic basket case after bailing out Greece.

Putin saw the association agreement as a threat to Russia's economic stability and therefore his power. Late in 2013 he gave Yanukovych a choice between crippling economic measures and a $15 billion aid package. When Yanukovych withdrew from the EU deal, the streets filled with unemployed toughs, including ultra-nationalists, and students demonstrating for EU membership that would allow them to flee their beloved homeland in search of a future elsewhere. On November 21, 2013, the arrival of protestors at Kiev's Maidan Nezalezhnosti (Independence Square) marked the birth of the Maidan Revolution, or Euromaidan.

The three-month history of Euromaidan shows a nearly miraculous transformation of a relatively primitive civil society as it evolved into a sophisticated operation that toppled a government.

At the outset of Euromaidan, less than half the population had access to the internet, and only 10 to 14 percent had smartphones. But within two months, US Department of Defense analyst Katrina Elledge explained in a 2015 study, protestors were getting their information from Facebook and Twitter, "as a result of its ease of use on mobile devices." Unfortunately, Elledge's study does not explain how mobile devices become more available.

There was IT support and, wrote Elledge, "multiple cyber-related efforts against the Yanukovych government." Euromaidan "hacktivism" included "information theft, defacing websites, and distributed denial of service (DDoS) attacks. Hacktivists made intensive use of social media for PR purposes and to share or clarify information about potential targets." Instructional videos showed "how to make a Molotov cocktail."

Euromaidan was cyber-marketed. PR firms and advocacy networks added "'brand recognition' to Euromaidan," wrote Elledge, by "disseminating press releases in multiple languages via social media." But "Euromaidan PR and the associated Euromaidan Press" also maintained "a core physical presence on the Maidan for easier access to journalists and officials. This pairing of online and off-line activism aided the network's visibility and name recognition."

Much of the organizers' most important work was not in the virtual realm. There was legal aid for demonstrators who were arrested. There was a "People's Hospital" for those suffering injuries. There was even a self-defense force. "Approximately 40 units of an estimated 12,000 volunteers had been self-formed by early February," Elledge wrote, "with an on-call capacity of 25,000. Each unit had varying leadership structures, communication styles, and tactics, but they shared an overarching goal of defending Euromaidan territory."

It was a remarkable feat. An improvised political faction, comprising unemployed ultranationalists and students, of a technologically backward and impoverished nation had mustered enough resources to push a government to the brink. Who paid for the coup? No one knows. But the Obama administration was on the ground.

In the second week of December, US assistant secretary of state Victoria Nuland was in Kiev. She met with Yanukovych and warned that police actions against protesters were "absolutely impermissible." She said that the Obama administration thought it "still possible to save Ukraine's European future."

She met with protestors and was said to have handed out food. An intercept of her conversation with US ambassador to Ukraine Geoffrey Pyatt was posted on YouTube. They discussed which opposition leaders were best suited to go in the government and which should stay out. The Russians were allegedly responsible for leaking the intercept to embarrass Washington. Nuland was criticized for expressing her exasperation with the European Union: "F--- the EU," she told Pyatt.

More important, the leaked conversation showed that the US had seen the coup as an opportunity to shape the Ukrainian government to its liking. Obama's State Department was interfering in the internal political processes of a sovereign government.

Biden was on the phone constantly with Yanukovych: nine phone calls in three months, the last one two days before Russia invaded the eastern sector. On February 21, Yanukovych left Kiev. The White House readout of their final call suggests that Biden had told him the US was withdrawing whatever support it had extended until then:

> *The Vice President further underscored the urgency of immediate dialogue with opposition leaders to address protesters' legitimate grievances and to put forward serious proposals for political reform. The United States is committed to supporting efforts to promote a peaceful resolution to the crisis that reflects the will and aspirations of the Ukrainian people.*

In April, Biden was in Kiev again. He met with a group of Ukrainian politicians, including the man who would be elected president the next month, Petro Poroshenko. Biden took the seat at the head of the table, like a boss. "To be very blunt about it," he said, "and this is a delicate thing to say to a group of leaders in their house of parliament, but you have to fight the cancer of corruption that is endemic in your system right now."

It is not hard to see why Hunter Biden was named to the Burisma board in May. Mykola Zlochevsky needed protection from the domestic rivals now in position to decide his fate and that of his billion-dollar piggy bank. And since it was the Obama administration that had just sent his patron into exile, he perhaps wanted protection from the Americans, too.

In August 2014, Ukraine's prosecutor general, Viktor Shokin, opened an investigation of Burisma, and by the end of the year Zlochevsky fled Ukraine. The man who was paying Hunter Biden more than $80,000 a month was put on Ukraine's most wanted list.

Zlochevsky and his company are corrupt, says a former senior Obama administration intelligence official. "But Ukraine is one of the most corrupt countries in the world. Ukrainian prosecutors were investigating Burisma because it kept the oligarchs who were lined up against the new Ukrainian president on a leash."

The Burisma investigation, however, was bad for the Bidens. Throughout 2015, the vice president was in frequent contact with the Ukrainian president, Poroshenko. In March, they discussed the US sanctions imposed the previous year in response to Russia's occupation of Crimea and parts of the east, where Ukrainian forces were fighting Russian-backed separatists.

Biden called Poroshenko again in June, July, and August. Their conversations ranged from US aid and US sanctions on Russia to Kiev's reform agenda and anticorruption efforts. Given that the Ukrainians were at war with a power often hostile to US interests, it's hardly surprising Ukraine was at the top of Biden's agenda.

And yet the Obama administration refused to arm Kiev in spite of bipartisan support, including John McCain on the right and Adam Schiff on the left. Obama feared that giving Ukraine lethal aid would only provoke Putin to escalate. John Brennan explained that the administration was concerned that sensitive technology would fall into Russian hands. Samantha Power went to Kiev in June to make a speech about fighting Russian disinformation campaigns.

Sometime in the summer, says a former Obama intelligence official, CIA analyst Eric Ciaramella was detailed to the NSC staff where as Ukraine director he answered to the administration official who had the lead on Ukraine, Joe Biden.

"Ciaramella set up all the phone calls and coordinated interactions between the vice president and the Ukrainian president," says the former Obama official. "He did the prep work, and knew what was said in all the calls and meetings between the two, and was responsible for whatever after action or follow-up was decided on."

In September, Obama administration officials seemed to have crossed signals. The ambassador to Ukraine, Geoffrey Pyatt, told the Ukrainians that they were not doing enough to fight corruption. He wanted to know who was slow-rolling the case against Burisma and its owner. Pyatt said that whoever was responsible for subverting the case "should—at a minimum—be summarily terminated."

On September 29, Biden met with the Ukrainian president at a UN meeting in New York. What was the status of the Burisma investigation? And why was the US ambassador pushing the Ukrainians for an investigation that would invariably highlight Hunter Biden's role at the company?

"The Ukrainian president had his own reasons for investigating Burisma," says the former senior Obama administration official. "He's got his own domestic political concerns. He wants to look like he's fighting corruption, and more importantly, the

investigation is an instrument to rein in his rivals, other powerful oligarchs."

The Americans also had their own domestic concerns, says the
former official. "Biden was still thinking about running for president. He didn't leave the race until the middle of October. The
pro-Clinton crowd showed him that the Burisma investigation
could cause him trouble."

The Clinton campaign resolved to make sure Biden didn't have
second thoughts. The *New York Times* had a story about Hunter
Biden and Burisma timed to the vice president's December trip to
Kiev.

On December 7, 2015 Biden and Poroshenko met and held
a joint press conference. The vice president's central motif was
corruption—Ukrainian corruption, of course:

> *All Ukrainians, officials, business leaders, the business*
> *community, everyday citizens—they've got to work together*
> *to root out corruption that has held this country back for*
> *so long . . . The Ukrainian people cannot once again have*
> *their hopes dashed based on the cancer of corruption. . . .*
> *And it's absolutely critical for Ukraine, in order to be stable*
> *and prosperous and part of a secure Europe to definitely,*
> *thoroughly, completely root out the cancer of corruption . . .*
> *And as I told the President at our meeting, as long as you*
> *continue to make progress to fight corruption and build a*
> *future of opportunity for all Ukraine, the United States will*
> *stand with you . . . These new funds—this additional roughly*
> *$190 million—will help fight corruption in law enforcement*
> *and reform the justice sector.*

The *Times* article—"Joe Biden, His Son, and the Case against a Ukrainian Oligarch"—posted that night. "The credibility of the vice president's anticorruption message may have been undermined by the association of his son, Hunter Biden, with one of Ukraine's largest natural gas companies, Burisma Holdings," wrote James Risen.

"Now you look at the Hunter Biden situation, and on the one hand you can credit the father for sending the anticorruption message," a Washington policy expert told the *Times*. "But I think unfortunately it sends the message that a lot of foreign countries want to believe about America, that we are hypocritical about these issues."

Only a day after the *Times* article published, Biden first openly called for the man investigating the company paying his son to be fired. In a December 9 speech in Kiev, the vice president said: "The Office of the General Prosecutor desperately needs reform."

In January, Obama's NSC invited Ukrainian prosecutors to Washington to discuss how to tackle corruption. Ciaramella was at the meeting. The White House reportedly wanted two things. First, they asked the Ukrainians to drop their investigation of the Ukrainian company that employed Hunter Biden. The FBI would handle it. Second, they were interested in reopening an investigation into payments that Paul Manafort's Ukrainian patron made to Americans. They wanted information on Manafort.

It wasn't until March that Manafort was named to the Trump campaign. The former Obama intelligence official speculates that perhaps the White House just sought to dirty a Republican. "There were so many Democrats with questionable ties to Ukraine," says the official. "Not just Biden. One of the biggest donors to the Clinton Foundation was another Ukrainian oligarch, Victor Pinchuk." In 2008, he committed $29 million to the Clinton Global Initiative.

In any case, the January meetings mark one of the origin points of the collusion narrative. The relationship between the man who would serve briefly as Trump's campaign manager and a "pro-Putin" Ukrainian politician was one of the foundations of Russiagate.

Even with Hillary Clinton backing off once Biden was out of the race, the vice president was still on the hook with the Burisma investigation. The president of Ukraine didn't want to give up an instrument with which he fought his domestic foes. On February 2, the Ukrainian prosecutor seized all of the assets belonging to Burisma's owner, Zlochevsky.

The second-highest elected official in the United States called President Poroshenko on February 11; and a week later, on the 18th; and the day after that, on the 19th. Biden urged him "to accelerate Ukraine's efforts to fight corruption." It was clear what Biden meant by *corruption*—he was referring to the prosecutor handling the case involving his son Hunter.

On March 15, Clinton ally Victoria Nuland gave Biden a hand. The assistant secretary of state testified that Ukraine had to get rid of the prosecutor investigating the Burisma case, Victor Shokin, and "appoint and confirm a new, clean Prosecutor General."

Biden called Poroshenko on March 22, and one week later the Ukrainian parliament voted to dismiss Shokin. On March 31, Biden landed in Kiev to announce the $1 billion loan guarantee. Biden later boasted that he'd threatened the Ukrainians in person over the prosecutor. He garbled the timeline and claimed that he compelled them to make their decision within hours—either they satisfy his demand, or they don't get their billion dollars.

His made-up story had the advantage of obscuring the fact that the vice president of the United States had campaigned for more than a year to bury the Ukrainian prosecutor. Out of a country of more than 40 million with a notoriously corrupt political class, the man Biden singled out happened to be investigating the company that was paying his son millions of dollars a year to do nothing. Naturally, Joe Biden was resolved to have him fired.

———————

At the same time, Democrats were turning their problems with Ukraine into Trump's. The dossier operation, like so much of the anti-Trump operation, had a defensive and offensive component— it concealed their corruption and dirtied their opponents.

The Clinton campaign hired Glenn Simpson. The Fusion GPS founder told media allies that Manafort was a Putin asset because of his relationship to pro-Putin Ukrainian politician Victor Yanukovych. Since Yanukovych's ally brought Hunter Biden on to the Burisma board, did that make him a Putin asset? What about his father, the vice president—was he a Putin asset, too? Simpson's keen ability to find where Ukrainian corruption intersected with American sleaze didn't work with Democrats.

Fusion GPS distributed to the press at least two separate dossiers on Manafort and his ties to Ukrainian officials. In a three-day period at the end of April 2016, Michael Isikoff from Yahoo News, Tom Hamburger and Steven Mufson at the *Washington Post*, Peter Stone at the *Guardian*, and *Slate*'s Franklin Foer published articles alleging that Manafort's Yanukovych work showed the Trump team was suspiciously close to Russia.

In March, another channel for Ukraine-sourced Trump dirt had appeared. Ukrainian-American DNC operative Alexandra

Chalupa visited the Ukrainian embassy and discussed Manafort with Ambassador Valeriy Chaly and an aide. Chalupa bragged that the embassy "worked directly with reporters researching Trump, Manafort and Russia to point them in the right directions."

One-time political officer at the Washington embassy Andrii Telizhenko said that his superiors told him to help Chalupa research connections between Trump, Manafort, and Russia. Telizhenko told a reporter that Chalupa said, "If we can get enough information on Paul [Manafort] or Trump's involvement with Russia, she can get a hearing in Congress by September."

Chalupa wanted Kiev to commit fully to the anti-Trump operation. She asked the embassy to convince President Poroshenko to comment on Manafort and his Russian ties during a trip to the US.

She consulted frequently with the DNC. She emailed the DNC communications director that she'd downloaded Manafort dirt to Isikoff, the media operative whose September article on Carter Page was used to obtain the FISA warrant on the Trump campaign. Chalupa said that she'd connected Isikoff to other Ukrainian activists for more dirt on Manafort.

The press kept hitting on the relationship between Trump's campaign manager and Yanukovych to drive the Trump-Russia narrative. Josh Rogin's July 18 article for the *Washington Post* cited it before moving on to new evidence that the Trump team was cozying up to Putin.

Trump staffers, according to the article, "stripped out" the Republican National Convention platform's call for giving Ukraine "lethal defensive weapons." That was not true. A GOP delegate proposed an amendment calling for giving lethal aid to Ukraine. The amendment was toned down by a Trump adviser, changing it to "appropriate assistance." The result was that the amendment was softened but the platform's position on Ukraine was strengthened.

The *Post* article was used by the FBI to obtain the FISA application. So was an August 3 *Politico* article by Michael Crowley that reported how Trump's views on Ukraine had changed since hiring Manafort and Carter Page.

As Fusion GPS distributed the Ukraine-related Trump dirt to the press, the subsequent reporting was integrated into the dossier.

For instance, in a July dossier memo, number 95, written after the DNC emails had been leaked during the Democrats' convention, Steele alleged that in exchange for the DNC hack and WikiLeaks's publication of the emails, the Trump team had agreed to sideline Russia's invasion of Ukraine as a campaign issue. The Clinton campaign was alleging a Ukraine-related quid pro quo.

The dossier also alleged a potential future quid pro quo with Russia over Ukraine. Memo 94, dated July 19, claimed that Rosneft CEO Igor Sechin spoke with Carter Page about "future bilateral energy cooperation" in exchange for lifting "Ukraine-related western sanctions against Russia." A later memo, number 135, upped the ante, claiming that Page would benefit personally in exchange for getting Trump to lift Ukraine-related sanctions. The Trump aide would receive a brokerage fee on a 19 percent stake of Rosneft.

Ukraine was all over the dossier. A memo dated August 22 alleged, "Ex-Ukrainian President YANUKOVYCH confides directly to PUTIN that he authorized kick-back payments to MANAFORT, as alleged in western media." The reference was to a *New York Times* story from the week before claiming that Manafort received illegal cash payments for his Ukraine work, documented in a so-called black ledger.

The black ledger was a forgery. Manafort's Ukrainian payments came through traced wire transfers to banks. The signatures in the black ledger weren't Manafort's. One source for the *Times'* black ledger story was former Ukrainian parliamentarian Serhiy Leshchenko. According to Nellie Ohr, he was a Fusion GPS source, too.

By August, Ukrainian officials came out openly against the GOP candidate. Ukraine's ambassador to Washington placed an op-ed critical of Trump in a US publication. "Recent comments by Republican nominee Donald Trump about the Ukrainian peninsula of Crimea—occupied by Russia since March 2014—have raised serious concerns in Kiev and beyond Ukraine," Valeriy Chaly wrote in *The Hill.*

In Kiev, senior Ukrainian politicians lined up to attack the GOP candidate. A former Ukrainian prime minister warned that Trump had "challenged the very values of the free world." The sitting interior minister said that Trump's comments on Russia and Ukraine provided a "diagnosis of a dangerous marginal." The majority of Ukraine's politicians, said member of parliament and Fusion GPS source Serhiy Leschenko, are "on Hillary Clinton's side."

———————

Mayor Giuliani's source was right. The conspiracy theory about Trump and Russia was true about the Democrats and Ukraine— with an important qualification. The collusion narrative held that Putin had compromised Trump and was running him as an asset. The Ukrainians were not pulling candidate Clinton's strings. It was the other way around.

The Clinton campaign had drawn in the corrupt political class of a small and impoverished buffer state because the Ukrainians had already seen what the Obama administration was capable of, that it toyed with the internal dynamics of foreign governments in the name of transparency, liberty, and sovereignty. The vice president got a prosecutor fired. The State Department formed the Ukrainian government in the aftermath of a coup, which the administration may have assisted. The Ukrainians can't be blamed for being scared.

And so with Christmas a week away and the Obama administration supposed to be closing down shop to make room for the incoming team, Joe Biden didn't have to promise Poroshenko anything when he rang up the Ukrainian president for one last errand. It was about the upcoming vote at the UN on Security Council Resolution 2334. It was the same issue that had Michael Flynn ringing foreign officials around the world and the Trump administration concerned how the anti-Israel initiative would affect Middle East stability.

Ukraine had one of the rotating seats on the Security Council, and Kiev planned to abstain. There were good relations with Israel. There was an influential Jewish community in Ukraine—the prime minister at the time was Jewish—and many Israelis could trace their family histories back to Ukraine. Also, Israel had used its UN vote in favor of Ukraine's territorial integrity after Russia had annexed Crimea in March 2014. But Obama officials demanded Ukraine vote yes.

The Ukrainians had asked for a couple of days, as a courtesy to Jerusalem, before voting in favor of a resolution that Israel was illegally occupying Judaism's holiest sites. But the Obama administration wouldn't hear it. Samantha Power was pressuring the Ukrainian ambassador at the UN and told him they wouldn't accept a delay. And Obama's point man on Ukraine got the Ukrainian president to do what he wanted.

TEN

THE CIARAMELLA DOSSIER

"**W**ell, son of a bitch," said Joe Biden. "He got fired."

The audience laughed. Biden always knew how to make people laugh. He had the common touch. But these weren't common people—it was an audience at the Council on Foreign Relations in Manhattan, and Biden was trying to impress them with a story about himself as a man who got things done. It is easier to get things done using the resources of the US government.

Biden was talking about a trip he made to Kiev to speak with Ukrainian officials. "I was supposed to announce that there was another billion-dollar loan guarantee," Biden said. He said that he had a commitment from the Ukrainian president and prime minister to fire the Ukrainian prosecutor investigating the Ukrainian company that paid his son more than $80,000 a month. Unlike his father, who made many business trips to Kiev, Hunter never visited.

The Ukrainian heads of state and government tried to deflect Biden's demands. "We're not going to give you the billion dollars," Biden told the Ukrainians. "They said, 'You have no authority. You're

140

not the president.'" Biden dared them to call Obama. "I said, call him." The Manhattan audience laughed again. "I looked at them and said, 'I'm leaving in six hours. If the prosecutor is not fired, you're not getting the money.' Well, son of a bitch. He got fired."

Biden had implicated the former president in an extortion scheme, in front of an audience. His statements were on videotape for anyone to view online. Of course no one was going to prosecute Obama or Biden. The making of foreign policy requires the use of various instruments to advance the national interest. Whether leveraging US taxpayer money to get the vice president's son out of trouble served the national interest is another question.

Biden said he never asked Hunter about his business, but he should have warned him that doing business in Kiev was a bad idea, for him and for US national security. Hunter's problems with money, women, and substance abuse would have flagged the attention of foreign intelligence services looking to influence the United States through the troubled son of the vice president. His job on the board of a company under investigation for corruption in a country known for corruption also would have made him and US national security vulnerable. It was the duty of the chief executive to find out what, if anything, had happened.

Donald Trump was impeached, in part, to punish him for asking what Joe and Hunter Biden had been up to in Ukraine. Democrats and the media knew the Bidens were involved in questionable practices. In December 2015, the *New York Times* had reported that Hunter's work for a corrupt Ukrainian company compromised the vice president.

But four years later, the context in which those facts had appeared changed. Hillary Clinton and Biden were no longer vying with each other for the 2016 nomination. Clinton was no longer the establishment pick, and her campaign had no reason to dump dirt on Biden to hurt his candidacy. In 2019, the story was nakedly about Democratic party corruption. So according to the left, facts describing Hunter Biden's work in Ukraine became components of a right-wing conspiracy theory, even though those facts appeared in the *Times*. As Biden came closer to securing the party's 2020 nomination, the cover-up became more urgent.

It was the same with reporting that explained how Ukrainian officials had worked against Trump in 2016. In the lead-up to the 2016 election, an August 28 *Financial Times* story showed how senior officials in Kiev openly backed Clinton. An op-ed from the Ukrainian ambassador to Washington criticized Trump. A January 11, 2017 article in *Politico* explained the role that Ukrainian-American Alexandra Chalupa played in finding Ukrainian-sourced dirt on Trump and distributing it to the US media, the Democratic National Committee, and the Hillary Clinton campaign. Chalupa had bragged that she cooperated with Ukrainian embassy officials in her efforts to smear Trump with dirt about his non-existent ties to Russia.

But the context of those stories changed when the president's personal lawyer Rudolph Giuliani and journalist John Solomon started to unearth accounts of what the Bidens had done in Ukraine and how Ukrainian officials worked against Trump during the 2016 campaign. Starting shortly after he was hired in April 2018, Giuliani went on TV to defend his client. He explained how the collusion narrative that grew into the Mueller investigation was rooted in the Bidens' activities in Ukraine. Beginning in early March 2018, Solomon wrote dozens of stories sourced to Ukrainian officials and Ukrainian government and court documents showing the seedy connections between the Obama administration and the Ukrainian government.

Since Trump was first elected, the goal had been to remove him from office, or at least weaken him. And yet as the 2020 campaign approached, the primary instrument for impeding him, the special counsel investigation, had been disabled by Attorney General William Barr. It was time for another plan. But this one was barely distinguishable from Russiagate, since it was patterned precisely after the Steele dossier operation.

———————

"Our country has been through a lot," Trump told Ukrainian president Volodymyr Zelensky. He was referring to the Russia collusion conspiracy theory. "As you saw yesterday, that whole nonsense ended with a very poor performance by a man named Robert Mueller, an incompetent performance," said Trump.

Mueller had testified on Capitol Hill the day before, July 24, and was incoherent. Fox News's Chris Wallace, no fan of Trump's, called it a "disaster." Mueller refused to answer questions about documents and figures central to the Crossfire Hurricane investigation—Fusion GPS, the Steele dossier, Joseph Mifsud. He stumbled over answers and seemed not to understand questions or fundamental legal principles.

Representative John Ratcliffe asked Mueller if he could cite "an example other than Donald Trump where the Justice Department determined that an investigated person was not exonerated because their innocence was not conclusively determined?"

Mueller said that he couldn't, but, he added, "This is a unique situation."

Mueller had inadvertently made Ratcliffe's point for him. "Nowhere does it say that you were to conclusively determine Donald Trump's innocence or that the special counsel report should determine whether or not to exonerate him," said Ratcliffe. "It's not in any of the documents, it's not in your appointment order, it's not in any of the special counsel regulations, it's not in the OLC opinions, it's not in the Justice manual, and it's not in the principles of federal prosecution."

At the end of the hearing it was clear Mueller had not been in charge of the investigation. He was an avatar for other interests determined to tie down Trump and keep him from implementing his agenda. Now that the investigation was over, Trump wanted to know what was behind the operation that had targeted him starting during the 2016 campaign. It was not only for his sake but also that of the country. So much time and money had been wasted; innocent people had been targeted, bankrupted, charged with crimes they didn't commit, imprisoned. It was time to get to the bottom of it.

Since before election day he'd been accused of colluding with Russia, but when did the Steele dossier operation actually start? Who was involved? Barr and US attorney John Durham had already traveled to Italy to ask questions about Mifsud. Had foreign governments interfered in the election to hurt Trump? After investigating the case for more than a year, Rudy Giuliani was certain of it.

"They say a lot of it started with Ukraine," Trump told the Ukrainian president. "I would like to have the attorney general call you or your people, and I would like you to get to the bottom of it," he said. "Whatever you can do, it's very important that you do it, if that's possible."

Trump had another matter he wanted to raise. "There's a lot of talk about Biden's son, that Biden stopped the prosecution and a lot of people want to find out about that so whatever you can do with the attorney general would be great. Biden went around bragging that he stopped the prosecution, so if you can look into it. It sounds horrible to me."

The president asked if he would speak to Giuliani, too. They discussed the US ambassador to Ukraine, Marie Yovanovich. Zelensky said she'd supported his opponent, Poroshenko, the ex-president Biden said he strong-armed. Yovanovich had started her job in late August 2016, just as Ukrainian officials were openly coming out against Trump. After his election, she was said to be bad-mouthing the president she served. She'd been recalled to Washington in late April.

Other senior US officials whose duties and areas of expertise required it were listening in on the call. Secretary of State Mike Pompeo was listening, and so was Lieutenant Colonel Alexander Vindman, the NSC's Ukraine director. After the morning call, Vindman registered his concerns with two NSC staff lawyers, one of whom was his twin brother, Yevgeny. In the afternoon, Alexander Vindman phoned Eric Ciaramella, who also worked on Ukraine and Russia issues.

The next day Ciaramella wrote a memo about his conversation with Vindman: "The official who listened to the entirety of the phone call was visibly shaken by what had transpired and seemed keen to inform a trusted colleague within the U.S. national security apparatus about the call."

The official described the call as "crazy," "frightening," and "completely lacking in substance related to national security."

The official asserted that the president used the call to persuade Ukrainian authorities to investigate his political rivals, chiefly former vice president Biden and his son Hunter. The official stated that there was already a conversation underway with White House lawyers about how to handle the discussion because, in the official's view, the president had clearly committed a criminal act by urging a foreign power to investigate a US person for the purposes of advancing his own reelection bid in 2020.

"The president," Ciaramella wrote, "did not raise security assistance."

Just two days after the curtain dropped on the Mueller investigation, Ciaramella was rebooting the collusion narrative. According to the story the CIA officer and his colleagues would tell, Trump was again in league with a foreign power to defeat a rival candidate. They rotated Ukraine in for Russia and Biden for Clinton.

The operation's personnel drew from the same sources as the Russia collusion operation—serving officials from powerful government bureaucracies, the CIA, Pentagon, and State Department, as well as elected officials, political operatives, and the press. Therefore, the process was also the same: The actors would work the operation through the intelligence bureaucracy and the media to start an official proceeding, in this case an impeachment process. The play was set to begin.

Ciaramella first expressed his concern to a CIA lawyer. Frustrated that his action wasn't moving quickly enough, he turned to the intelligence community inspector general responsible for oversight of all seventeen of the nation's agencies. On August 12, he filed a whistleblower's report with ICIG Michael Atkinson.

It was a version of the dossier, allegations based on second- and thirdhand sources. Steele said that his information came from anonymous Russians; Ciaramella claimed his came from unnamed Americans.

"In the course of my official duties," wrote Ciaramella, "I have received information from multiple U.S. Government officials that the President of the United States is using the power of his office to solicit interference from a foreign country in the 2020 U.S. elections."

He even replicated a key feature from Steele's memos that helped the FBI obtain the FISA warrant. The dossier alleged that the Trump campaign had agreed to two Ukraine-related quid pro quos. One, in exchange for the hack and release of DNC emails, the Trump team would sideline Ukraine as campaign issue. Two, in exchange for dropping Ukraine-related sanctions on Russia, a Putin ally promised Trump advisors energy deals.

Ciaramella also alleged a Ukraine-related quid pro quo. His August 12 report added a detail missing from the July 26 memo. He claimed in his document he'd learned earlier in July that Trump had "issued instructions to suspend all security assistance to Ukraine." With this, the CIA official had planted the seed that would grow into the basis of the impeachment charges brought against Trump: The president had withheld foreign aid in exchange for something that would benefit him personally—an investigation of his political rival.

Ciaramella and his confederates had simply taken the boastful blunder Biden made in front of the Manhattan audience and hung it on Trump. Now he was the one using US aid to secure a favor from a Ukrainian president. It was an audacious move, but the Ciaramella dossier was also a defensive maneuver. "It was born out of desperation," says one of his former colleagues.

"He wasn't just trying to protect Biden," says the source, a former senior Obama administration intelligence official.

"Remember that Ciaramella is setting up all those phone calls and meetings with the Ukrainian president Poroshenko and then handling all the follow-up. He's like Al Capone's bookkeeper in *The Untouchables*—he knows everything that went on. When he finds out Trump may get the Burisma investigation restarted, he's worried for himself, too."

As Steele had, Ciaramella inserted hearsay and secondhand sources into official intelligence channels. He had help. The form for reporting whistleblower complaints to the ICIG required first-hand information. Ciaramella's complaint, however, was based on secondhand information, from Vindman. In September, the ICIG quietly changed the language in the form to remove the ban on hearsay information. Then he backdated the change in the complaint form to August.

On August 26, Atkinson forwarded the complaint to Joseph Maguire, the acting director of national intelligence. Maguire, though, didn't believe it satisfied the requirements of the whistle-blower statute. It didn't concern an intelligence activity, and it didn't concern a member of the intelligence community; it was about the president.

The Justice Department agreed. "The complaint does not arise in connection with the operation of any U.S. government intelligence activity, and the alleged misconduct does not involve any member of the intelligence community," the Office of Legal Counsel noted in a September 3 memo. "Rather, the complaint arises out of a confidential diplomatic communication between the President and a foreign leader that the intelligence-community complainant received secondhand."

Seemingly closed down, the anti-Trump operatives had a back door into official intelligence channels, the same entrance they'd used for the Steele dossier—the media. A September 5 *Washington Post* editorial reported that Trump was "attempting to force Mr. Zelensky to intervene in the 2020 U.S. presidential election by launching an investigation of the leading Democratic candidate, Joe Biden."

Now that the article had sparked interest in a part of the unfolding operation, Atkinson produced another piece of the puzzle. He notified the Senate and House Intelligence Committees on September 9 that he had a whistleblower complaint. Chairman of the House Permanent Select Committee on Intelligence (HPSCI) Adam Schiff was on relay. That same day, he and two other Democratic committee chairmen announced the opening of an investigation into Trump, Giuliani, and Ukraine. They cited recent press reports, a less than subtle reference to the September 5 *Washington Post* op-ed. It was the same process used during the Russiagate operation: A report based on a fraudulent document is leaked to the press, which publishes it, and intelligence officials cite it as a pretext to justify starting an investigation.

On September 13, Schiff subpoenaed Maguire to get the complaint. That same day, he put out a press release about the subpoena, which forced the whistleblower's complaint into the public for the first time. HPSCI had always treated whistleblower's complaints with discretion—but the point of the Ciaramella dossier operation was to force the complaint into the public.

On September 18, three of the *Washington Post*'s top collusion conspiracy theory reporters, Greg Miller, Ellen Nakashima, and Shane Harris, wrote that the whistleblower's complaint involves "Trump's communications with a foreign leader" and a "promise" that was made. The release of the transcript would show no promise was made.

On September 19, the *Washington Post*'s Aaron Blake showed two of the pieces together. He wrote that the complaint dealt with Ukraine and hinted it had to do with foreign aid. "Lawmakers were concerned," wrote Blake, "that the administration was failing to provide $250 million for the Ukraine Security Assistance Initiative, which is intended to help Ukraine defend itself from Russia."

On September 24, Trump said that he did withhold aid, which had since been released. "But my complaint has always been, and I'd withhold again and I'll continue to withhold until such time as Europe and other nations contribute to Ukraine." Indeed that's what he'd told the *Washington Post* in his March 21, 2016, interview: "I look at the Ukraine situation and I say, so Ukraine is a country that affects us far less than it affects other countries in NATO, and yet we are doing all of the lifting, they're not doing anything. And I say, why is it that Germany is not dealing with NATO on Ukraine?"

Trump's release of the transcript the next day showed that he had indeed made the same point to the Ukrainian president. "We do a lot for Ukraine," he'd told Zelensky. "Much more than the European countries are doing and they should be helping you more than they are. Germany does almost nothing for you. All they do is talk and I think it's something that you should really ask them about. When I was speaking to Angela Merkel she talks Ukraine, but she doesn't do anything. A lot of the European countries are the same way."

By declassifying the transcript, Trump had gained a step on his opponents. The Steele dossier was made of rumors and whispered accounts of things that never happened, but Ciaramella's fiction was based on a real dialogue that anyone could now read for themselves to know the truth. Trump's reluctance to hand out US taxpayer dollars to a foreign government was unlikely to turn supporters against a president who had campaigned on America First. That his adversaries saw it rather as a vulnerability highlighted how far Washington was from the rest of America.

When Vindman later testified that he "became aware of outside influencers promoting a false narrative of Ukraine inconsistent with the consensus views of the interagency," he might as well have been describing a galaxy far, far away. What did the consensus opinion held by the federation of officials from the Departments of State, Defense, and Treasury and the intelligence bureaucracies matter to American voters? They were under the impression that the president they sent to the White House implements the foreign policy they voted for. It says so in the Constitution.

The impeachment hearings brought the deep state to life. Anyone who'd previously wondered if talk of an institutionalized class of Beltway officials, think tank experts, consultants, and contractors was simply another fevered conspiracy theory now saw televised evidence of it. They were smug, entitled, and contemptuous, of the president and those who'd elected him, and of the Constitution to which they only paid lip service.

Nevertheless, on September 24, Speaker of the House Nancy Pelosi announced that House Democrats were starting a formal impeachment inquiry.

Devin Nunes's communications director, Jack Langer, says he saw it coming.

"After the Democrats won the House of Representatives in 2018, and Adam Schiff became chair of the Intelligence Committee, he did a series of interviews in which he talked about goals in the committee," Langer recalls. "He said it was really important to restore comity. The implication was that things were so terrible and dysfunctional under this partisan Nunes chairmanship. So, Schiff was going to restore bipartisanship to the committee."

Langer knew better. He had watched Schiff work with the press to push collusion for two years.

"It was hard to take Schiff's promises seriously. As he was making them he was expanding his staff, because when you become the majority you get a bigger staff. And he's bringing in former prosecutors and specialists in money laundering, which was one of Schiff's big conspiracy theories then—that Trump had laundered Russian money. It struck me that these don't necessarily seem like people who were being hired to do oversight of the intelligence community. Schiff was preparing for an aggressive attack on Trump."

Langer had hoped the Intelligence Committee would return to its normal work. The Russia investigation had taken a toll on Republican staff and he still felt responsible for not being able to protect them, especially Kash Patel, from media attacks.

But even in his new job at the NSC, Patel was a favorite target. He'd never be forgiven for leading the Objective Medusa investigation into FBI crimes and abuses. Vindman and Fiona Hill would testify during impeachment that he'd represented himself as a Ukraine expert and went directly to the president with information on Ukraine.

Patel denied it and brought a defamation case against *Politico* and the *New York Times* for publishing stories based on their false accusations. The suit claimed that the defendants acted in concert with Schiff and his aides to further the anti-Trump Ukraine narrative

"Schiff will do whatever it takes to get Trump," says Langer, "and when he became committee chairman he got all these new authorities to pursue his target. And of course, Schiff loves the limelight."

Schiff kicked things off with a memorable performance. He affected the demeanor of a crime boss and reimagined Trump's call as if it were a passage from a hard-boiled detective novel. "No other country has done as much as we have. But you know what, I don't see much reciprocity here. You know what I mean? I hear what you want. I have a favor I want from you, though. And I'm going to say this only seven times, so you better listen good. I want you to make up dirt on my political opponent, understand? Lots of dirt, on this and on that."

Nunes remembers that in the middle of Schiff's performance Republican members were shocked. "We're all looking at each other," says Nunes. "No one knew what to make of it. Someone leans over and says, 'He's just making it up.'"

Langer says that turning HPSCI into the impeachment committee may have even surprised some Republicans that Schiff was willing to go that far.

"For months, we did virtually nothing aside from impeachment," says Langer. "It just wrecked the committee to have to abandon all the normal responsibilities we have overseeing the intelligence community—to make sure that they're not committing any abuses and to make sure that they're getting all the resources that they need to do the job that they're assigned."

The judiciary committee has authority over impeachment proceedings, but there were two main advantages in giving it to Schiff, says Langer.

"First, it made it easier for them to conduct their initial witness interviews in secret in a classified facility, since that's how HPSCI does business anyway and then selectively leak and spin stuff to the press, which regurgitated whatever ridiculous narrative the Democrats fed to them. The second reason is that the Democrats had no confidence in the chairman of the judiciary committee, Jerry Nadler. He'd led three high-profile hearings—with [former Trump campaign manager] Corey Lewandowski, [Nixon-era White House Counsel] John Dean, and Robert Mueller—that Democrats and their media partners criticized as ineffective. They thought Schiff would do a better job. And Schiff wanted it."

All through October, HPSCI Democrats took depositions from seventeen witnesses whose transcripts they eventually made public. They also convened a secret hearing with Michael Atkinson, who had circumvented normal procedures to get Ciaramella's compromised whistleblower's report to Schiff. The HPSCI chairman marked that hearing as classified and never released the transcript or sent it for a declassification review.

Schiff had first promised that Ciaramella, the whistleblower, would testify, but he changed his mind soon after it was reported that Schiff's staff had met with him before he was passed on to Atkinson, even though the HPSCI chair had publicly denied the committee had any contact with him. It seems Schiff was reluctant to subject Ciaramella to Republicans' questions about his secret contact with Schiff staffers, but there may be another reason Schiff kept his whistleblower under wraps.

"At a certain point he must have found out that he was Biden's guy on Ukraine," says Ciaramella's former colleague in the intelligence community. "If he testifies and the Republicans start asking him questions about Biden and Ukraine, it's over."

The depositions in HPSCI's secure facility in the basement of the Capitol were a rehearsal for the public showcase that began in November.

Before the proceedings began, Nunes gave his Republican colleagues the bad news. "I said, 'We'll lose. We're going to lose every day, and every day will be nasty. We'll lose in the media and every day is going to be a disaster. But don't get worried, stay calm, don't get discouraged, the truth is on our side. We have to be happy warriors.'"

There was an upside to the hearings that Nunes hadn't expected. "The rest of America got to see we were regular people," says Nunes. "The press had made us out to be freaks, but with all the attention to the hearings, people are tuning in and they hear what we're saying. Elise Stefanik, they see a nice and smart young woman. With John Ratcliffe they're watching a very sharp former prosecutor."

Nunes would give the opening statement every day for nearly two weeks. He and Langer saw it as a chance to speak directly to the public. It was also a challenge to write an opening speech for every hearing and in some cases a closing statement as well. They decided to hit on different themes for every speech.

"One of those openings was dedicated to attacking the media," says Langer. "That may seem like a puzzling thing to do. But I think it was important because the media was such a crucial player, both in the Russia collusion hoax and in impeachment. It couldn't have gone forward without their cooperation."

"I'd like to address a few brief words to the American people watching at home," Nunes began the morning of November 19, when Vindman was scheduled to testify. He continued:

If you watched the impeachment hearings last week, you may have noticed a disconnect between what you actually saw and the mainstream media accounts describing it. What you saw were three diplomats, who dislike the pres-

ident's Ukraine policy, discussing secondhand and third-hand conversations about their objections. Meanwhile, they admitted they had not talked to the president about these matters, and they were unable to identify any crime or impeachable offense the president committed.

But what you read in the press were accounts of shocking, damning, and explosive testimony that fully supports the Democrats' accusations.

If these accounts have a familiar ring, it's because this is the same preposterous reporting the media offered for three years on the Russia hoax. On a near-daily basis, the top news outlets in America reported breathlessly on the newest bombshell revelations showing that President Trump and everyone surrounding him are Russian agents . . .

There was no objectivity or fairness in the media's Russia stories—just a fevered rush to tarnish and remove a president who refuses to pretend that the media are something different than what they really are—puppets of the Democratic Party.

With their biased misreporting on the Russia hoax, the media lost the confidence of millions of Americans. And because they refused to acknowledge how badly they botched the story, they've learned no lessons and simply expect Americans will believe them as they try to stoke yet another partisan frenzy.

Because of Nunes's long fight to bring the truth about the FBI's Russia investigation to the public, his colleagues understood that the Ukraine story was just a variation of the same collusion conspiracy theory. With Christmas approaching, House Republicans voted unanimously against impeachment. House Democrats voted to refer two charges of impeachment, abuse of power and obstruction of Congress, to the Senate. Even with a few GOP senators, like Romney, likely to vote with Democrats, the Republican majority was certain to acquit the Republican president. Pelosi's delay in passing the article of impeachment on to the Senate belied her repeated insistence that impeaching the president was an urgent matter. It was a show, meant to block out Trump's agenda.

Nunes had won the battle of public opinion, but the showdown came at a cost—Schiff knew that Nunes had beat him. He wanted revenge. In an appendix to his three-hundred-plus-page report on impeachment, Schiff published metadata of Nunes's phone records: the length of some of the calls he made and how many calls. The information came from subpoenas Schiff had filed for the phone records of Rudy Giuliani and a source of his, Lev Parnas. In his report, Schiff splashed records of Nunes's calls alongside those of Kash Patel, another Republican HPSCI staffer, and even the journalist John Solomon.

"It's a little ironic," says Nunes, "that this whole thing started for me when I found evidence that the Obama administration had unmasked Trump officials and then I was unmasked."

Nunes was also, again, under fire from the press. CNN's Vicky Ward reported that he'd secretly been in Vienna the previous year to meet with Victor Shokin, the very same Ukrainian prosecutor Biden had fired. The story was sourced to Parnas. He was under indictment for charges unrelated to the Ukraine affair. He apparently thought that smearing Nunes would prompt Schiff to rescue him from legal trouble.

According to Parnas's lawyer, his client had information that "Nunes had told Shokin of the urgent need to launch investigations into Burisma, Joe and Hunter Biden, and any purported Ukrainian interference in the 2016 election."

Nunes had been on a congressional trip to Libya and Malta at the time of the alleged meeting, and Shokin denied ever meeting him. By then Nunes had already devised a strategy for press lies. He filed defamation suits. On December 3, he brought a $435 million suit against CNN for the Parnas story. It was the only way to get back his good name. The bigger game, he explained, was to make the media responsible again. "A functioning democracy needs a real press corps," says Nunes.

Among his other suits, he'd brought a case against Fusion GPS for its "systematic effort to intimidate, harass, threaten, influence, interfere with, impede, and ultimately to derail" his investigation into the FBI's crimes and abuses regarding the Page FISA warrant and other matters.

Fusion admitted that it had targeted Nunes. Glenn Simpson and Peter Fritsch's book, *Crime in Progress*, was published around Thanksgiving. "Fusion had no illusions about being able to topple Nunes, but the notion of digging into his record made many at the firm salivate," wrote Fusion GPS's co-founders. "He was a threat to Mueller's ability to do his job," they wrote.

The goal was to stop Nunes's investigation of the FBI and DOJ investigators who'd plotted against the president. "When Fritsch asked Fusion staff for volunteers to look into Nunes," the Fusion GPS co-founders wrote, "every hand shot up."

In their book, Simpson and Fritsch describe how they invented anti-Nunes narratives that were published by McClatchy, a now-bankrupt newspaper chain known for its unrestrained attacks on Nunes and for running some of the most outlandish Russia collusion conspiracy theories.

Just as the operation keyed to the Ciaramella dossier was passed on the Senate, the DOJ issued its report about the investigation based on the Steele dossier.

In March 2018, the Justice Department's inspector general Michael Horowitz had announced that it would examine the circumstances of the Page FISA warrant. Nunes had been managing expectations for a year and a half before the IG report dropped on December 9.

"I'd been saying that the big thing was going to be the Durham investigation," says Nunes. "We just wanted the IG report to provide evidence. No assessments, or interpretations, just what people said, what's in their emails. We wanted data."

The report was a catalogue of FBI malfeasance, documenting seventeen major errors and omissions in the original warrant and three renewals to spy on the Trump campaign. But when the report was released, the media instead focused on the IG's conclusion that the opening of the Crossfire Hurricane investigation was properly predicated.

In later Congressional testimony, Horowitz explained that the finding on predication was limited. Despite media misreporting, he did not exclude political bias as a cause of the problems in the FISA warrant. Indeed, he said that he could not explain or understand "why this all happened." When asked why James Comey said the report vindicated him, Horowitz responded that "the activities we found here don't vindicate anyone who touched this."

Durham rejected the predication finding altogether. The day the report was issued, he released a statement:

I have the utmost respect for the mission of the Office of Inspector General and the comprehensive work that went into the report prepared by Mr. Horowitz and his staff. However, our investigation is not limited to developing information from within component parts of the Justice Department. Our investigation has included developing information from other persons and entities, both in the U.S. and outside of the U.S. Based on the evidence collected to date, and while our investigation is ongoing, last month we advised the Inspector General that we do not agree with some of the report's conclusions as to predication and how the FBI case was opened.

Barr agreed with Durham. The investigation should not have been opened with the evidence the Crossfire Hurricane team had.

The Inspector General's report now makes clear that the FBI launched an intrusive investigation of a U.S. presidential campaign on the thinnest of suspicions that, in my view, were insufficient to justify the steps taken. It is also clear that, from its inception, the evidence produced by the investigation was consistently exculpatory. Nevertheless, the investigation and surveillance was pushed forward for the duration of the campaign and deep into President Trump's administration. In the rush to obtain and maintain FISA surveillance of Trump campaign associates, FBI officials misled the FISA court, omitted critical exculpatory facts from their filings, and suppressed or ignored information negating the reliability of their principal source.

The abuses detailed by Horowitz were so extensive that the media couldn't sustain its focus on predication. They confronted some of the architects of Crossfire Hurricane. Comey admitted that he was wrong when he'd said there were no problems with the FISA. McCabe said he was "shocked and horrified" by Horowitz's findings. Still, both Comey and McCabe blamed the problems on lower level officials.

The abuses Horowitz described were surely shocking but they obscured the larger point. Even a cursory reading of the reports shows that with few exceptions, the scores of past and present FBI and DOJ officials interviewed had invented cover stories and fabricated or forgot details. Because Horowitz did not have the power to issue subpoenas or convene a grand jury, his investigators were frequently unable or unequipped to challenge the improbable answers the Crossfire Hurricane team provided.

Most notably, there is no evidence Horowitz sought to interview Steele's so-called primary subsource. That was the centerpiece of the FBI's cover-up, designed to show they had been fooled and opened the Crossfire Hurricane investigation in good faith. The Bureau was incompetent, not criminal.

Nonetheless, the IG report did produce evidence of criminality. FBI lawyer Kevin Clinesmith had altered evidence to frame Carter Page. Clinesmith had been sent an email by a CIA liaison explaining that Page had been a source for the Agency. In an email to an FBI colleague applying for a renewal of the warrant on Page, Clinesmith had changed the meaning of the liaison's email by inserting the words "not a source" into it.

"We didn't know about that," says Nunes. "Everything else we pretty much knew. Doctoring an email is beyond where I'd expect anyone to go. They've given a whole new definition to 'dirty cops.' By the time you get to the highest levels of government, they're supposed to have enough training and supervision to get to the top. Integrity has to be the focal point of their work. That and avoiding politics. But all of them were horribly political. They were all talking politics all the time."

Clinesmith had lamented to his colleagues after the Trump election. "I am numb," he wrote. "I am so stressed about what I could have done differently." He vowed to forge on. "We have to fight this again," he wrote. "Viva le resistance [sic]."

"FBI agents talking about politics like that is one thing if you're at a cocktail party," says Nunes. "It's another when you're running an investigation on the people you hate. It would be funny if it wasn't so sick."

Langer saw the IG report as vindication of Objective Medusa's investigation, especially the February 2018 Nunes memo.

"We made one core argument in the whole memo," says Langer, "which was that the FBI used unverified Steele dossier allegations in the FISA warrant on Carter Page. That's indisputable after the Horowitz report. And yet the mainstream media was very reluctant to use the IG report as a basis to go revisit the debate over the memo, even though that was one of the biggest media stories of the year. The press shelled the Nunes memo because Schiff told them to. They said, 'it's full of lies and exaggerations and spin and cherry picking. It's compromising national security. It's a nothing burger.'" None of them used the IG report to revisit the memo debate.

Schiff at the time had also written a memo to contest Nunes's findings. In it he denied there were any abuses involved in the Carter Page FISA. Schiff was asked about the IG report. "He coughed up a ridiculous excuse," says Langer. "He said, 'well, we had no idea back then that these kinds of things were happening.' But the Nunes memo revealed it was happening. Schiff had access to the same documents we did. So he knew."

While the Senate was voting to acquit the president, there was already more trouble on the way. It was coming from abroad. Trump allies warned him about the coronavirus. On the night of January 30, Senators Ted Cruz and Tom Cotton were counseling him to shut down travel from China.

"Administration figures were worried about the economic consequences of locking out China," says a senior US official. "But Cotton and Cruz were insistent. They said as soon as impeachment was over, Trump will be blamed for the pandemic. They told the president his enemies would use the same tactics they'd used with the Iran deal, the dossier, and impeachment."

He closed the border on January 31 but the pandemic had already hit.

ELEVEN

THE PARTY

The novel coronavirus that swept out of the Chinese city of Wuhan in midwinter to infect millions around the globe underscored the case Trump had been making about the People's Republic of China (PRC) long before he came to office. "China is not our friend," Trump famously tweeted in 2013. "They are not our ally. They want to overtake us, and if we don't get smart and tough soon, they will."

Trump's position on China was why the swamp had been fighting him from the beginning. The influence that Beijing exerts in Washington, in addition to the money it dispenses, had over three decades shaped the priorities of policymakers on both sides of the partisan divide. In promising to challenge China, Trump the outsider had thrown down his gauntlet and nearly everyone inside the Beltway rose to the challenge.

The superpower conflict between the United States and Soviet Union helped push China onto center stage nearly fifty years ago. And over the past three decades, Beijing has come to dominate the international system, thanks not only to the world's largest pool of cheap, unregulated labor and a burgeoning consumer marketplace, but also to the craven delusions and greed of American political and business elites.

The collusion conspiracy theory that filled the news cycle and congressional agenda for three years in order to derail Trump's presidency also diverted attention from America's real major foreign threat. It wasn't Moscow. The Russiagate head fake benefited a large number of elected US officials and businessmen who had gorged themselves at China's trough for nearly thirty years. To rationalize impoverishing American workers and compromising US national security, they said they were making the world safer and freer with their efforts to tame the Chinese Community Party (CCP) and usher China into the community of nations.

Since only America stood in the way of China's status as a global leader, Washington was home to an enormous ecosystem sustaining a broad coalition of international media, tech oligarchs, politicians, and corporate interests. They got US policymakers to agree to deplete American resources to the advantage of a Chinese juggernaut that promised great rewards to those who lit the way for the inevitable, unstoppable rise of China.

Trump was elected not just because voters, especially in onetime industrial states, thought he was the only candidate willing to protect them from the devastation wrought on the US economy and social fabric by the CCP and their American partners. He promised that America would get it all back. He struck a chord when he talked about economic nationalism and bringing manufacturing jobs back home as part of his America First program. He said America would win.

Trump's warnings about Beijing went back decades. "Chinese government leaders, though they concede little, desperately want us to invest in their country," Trump wrote in his 2000 book, *The America We Deserve.*

> *Though we have the upper hand, we're way too eager to please the Chinese. We see them as a potential market and we tend to curry favor with them even at the expense of our own national interests. Our China policy under Presidents Clinton and Bush has been aimed at changing the Chinese regime by incentives both economic and political. The intention has been good, but it's clear to me that the Chinese have been getting far too easy a ride.*

He'd been saying for years that America needs to take manufacturing jobs back from China. "We need to bring manufacturing jobs back home where they belong," he tweeted in February 2012. In January 2013, he tweeted, "Trade with China has killed over 29% of US manufacturing jobs in the US http://wapo.st/13dNkpL China is robbing us blind!" In April two years later he asked on Twitter: "How do you take care of our people if you don't make anything? We don't make anything. We are rapidly losing our manufacturing to China etc."

He said he'd be tough with the Chinese on trade.

"China dumps everything that they have over here," he said during the 2016 debates. "We can't get into China. I have the best people, manufacturers, they can't get in. When they get in, they have to pay a tremendous tax."

He toyed with the idea of a 45 percent tax on Chinese goods. "The forty-five percent is a threat that if they don't behave, if they don't follow the rules and regulations so that we can have it equal on both sides, we will tax you," candidate Trump said. "It doesn't have to be 45, it could be less. But it has to be something because our country and our trade and our deals and most importantly our jobs are going to hell."

As the newly elected Trump promised to curb Chinese ambitions, PRC president Xi Jinping told a Davos audience in 2017 that "No one will emerge as a winner in a trade war." The globalist echelon class did not need to be inspired by anti-Trump messaging to stay on side.

The president imposed tariffs that brought the Chinese to the negotiating table. In mid-January, as PRC officials were in Washington signing phase one of the deal, Beijing was lying about the nature of the coronavirus. The Chinese said there was no evidence of human-to-human transmission. There was. Perhaps as many as 5 million Wuhan residents left the city after the virus erupted and before the January 23 quarantine.

Because China lied, public health authorities were unable to take early measures that might have prevented the respiratory disease from spreading to the four corners of the world. Further, by closing down domestic flights from Hubei Province, of which Wuhan is the capital, and continuing to let international flights leave the country, the communists defended themselves while channeling death into the rest of the world.

The consequences of the plague alone, never mind the possible intentions of CCP leadership, show that Americans were right to wonder whether COVID-19 was in fact a bioweapon. China's first account of the coronavirus as a viral mutation that jumped species in a Wuhan wet market was soon disproved.

Whatever the origins of the virus, the Chinese leveraged it as a weapon of social and economic warfare. Could the ruins of a shooting war be much worse than those of a virus that left hundreds of thousands of Americans dead and a large part of the population unemployed, turning the businesses, life savings, and dreams of millions to ashes?

The United States, senior US officials say, would likely lose in any major confrontation, financial or military, with China. Even the medicines we would need to treat our wounded are in Beijing's hands.

Few in Washington want to call it war—and for good reason. The massive amount of wealth that America's political and business elites transferred to the CCP over the past thirty years put the United States under China's thumb. The Chinese have a stake in everything from finance to education, and they are assisted by American partners whose economic interests are now tied to China.

Consider, for example, China's infiltration of the US education system. Between 2012 and 2018, Hanban, a propaganda arm of the Chinese government, contributed $113,428,509 to US schools—more than seven times the amount US schools actually reported.

American tech firms like Google, Qualcomm, and Intel are among the companies that asked the Commerce Department to lift the ban on selling chips to Huawei, a Chinese telecom. "For technologies that do not relate to national security," an official at the Semiconductor Industry Association told the press, "it seems they shouldn't fall within the scope of the order."

The idea that helping Chinese companies was inherently virtuous became so prevalent in Washington that nearly no one noticed when one-time Democratic vice presidential candidate Joe Lieberman signed on to lobby for ZTE, another Chinese telecom firm with reported ties to the Chinese military and intelligence services. He joined his former Senate colleague Norm Coleman, a Republican.

The former legislators knew that China was targeting American industry. The same month that Lieberman signed on with ZTE, the Justice Department asked Canadian authorities to detain the chief financial officer of Huawei. Meng Wanzhou, the daughter of the company's founder, was named as a defendant in a case charging Huawei with racketeering and conspiracy to steal trade secrets. A month later, grand juries in New York and Washington state indicted Huawei for stealing intellectual property from T-Mobile.

And yet American officials continued to sell their talents and contacts to Beijing. In April 2019, the same month that US intelligence reported that Huawei was funded by Chinese state security, the Obama administration's former director for cybersecurity, Samir Jain, joined Huawei. "This is not good, or acceptable," Trump tweeted in response to the news.

How will America fight with much of its ruling class on the other side?

"This question will consume US policy—foreign, domestic, and economic—for the next decade," says Wisconsin congressman Mike Gallagher. "How do we responsibly decouple strategic sectors of our economy from China, while working with our allies to keep the free world united in the face of this totalitarian adversary?"

Gallagher was part of a group of Republican lawmakers drafting anti-CCP laws in the midst of the pandemic, which included, among others, Representative Dan Crenshaw and Senators Tom Cotton, Ted Cruz, and Josh Hawley. Any Democrats who considered joining their GOP colleagues in calling out the CCP withdrew after Democratic officials reportedly warned that even stating facts by identifying where COVID-19 originated "would fuel anti-Asian racism in the US."

In March, Gallagher and Cotton introduced a bill calling to end US dependence on China for pharmaceutical manufacturing and incentivize American entrepreneurs to make pharmaceuticals at home.

"It's time," Cotton tells me. "Most Americans are amazed to learn we are dependent on our main enemy for things like penicillin. We shouldn't send all this critical stuff to China—a country that plainly has hopes to become our chief geopolitical rival."

Both Cotton and Gallagher note that the PRC became even more dangerous to American interests since Xi took power in 2012. "His anticorruption campaign amounted to a crackdown on his political adversaries," says Cotton. "He has more power than any Chinese leader since Mao."

Cotton has taken the lead against China on Capitol Hill. "Some of us have been sounding the alarm on China for years. Too many of our business, media, academic elite, though, have ideological blinders and vested financial interests."

Even worse, says Cotton, they colluded with the Chinese Communist Party. "American professionals—like bankers, consultants, and lawyers—taught the CCP how to take jobs from America, which will lead to less expensive goods. In other words by outsourcing jobs, we promoted cheap Chinese labor—sometimes literally slave labor—at the expense of US labor. Now because of the Wuhan coronavirus, more people understand that market efficiency is not the only or the highest good for the United States."

He explains how the China optimists and accommodationists who have dominated the American foreign policy debate since the end of the Cold War got it wrong. "It was clear about fifteen years ago that capitalism would not change China," says Cotton. "In fact, China was changing capitalism. Giving them permanent most-favored-nation status for trade in 2000 did not slow down their transgressions. It may have accelerated it. The experiment failed."

————————

With Trump imposing huge tariffs on Chinese goods, America's most famous living diplomat expressed concern about the future of the US-China relationship. Trump's actions, Henry Kissinger said, had landed the two sides in "the foothills of a cold war."

Kissinger, who has spoken with the president about China, was also worried for his legacy. His overtures to China paved the way for the 1972 meeting between the president he then served and Chairman Mao Zedong. Richard M. Nixon's opening to Beijing is typically seen as a geostrategic masterstroke to divide China from its rival communist power, the even more threatening Soviet Union. In retrospect, it also marked the beginning of a nearly half-century-long delusion about the nature of the CCP.

And yet Kissinger's vision of China as America's bride-in-waiting derived from much older ideas about the country. More than a hundred years before Nixon's trip, China's defeat at the hands of France and Great Britain opened the country to foreign trade as well as foreign visitors, most notably Protestant missionaries. Thousands of American families joined their British counterparts in the Far East. They believed it was fertile ground for spreading the Gospel.

These missionary pioneers would come to shape American foreign policy and attitudes toward China for generations to come, as their offspring filled positions of influence in the government, academia, and media. Henry Luce, for instance, the founder and editor in chief of *Time* magazine, the twentieth century's most influential publication, was raised in China by missionary parents.

Long after the 1949 Communist Revolution, Luce continued to wage a rearguard action, complaining that President
Harry Truman's State Department and the liberal establishment
had "lost" China to the "Reds." It's true that some US officials
preferred the communists to the ostensibly pro-Western nation-
alists, but no one "lost" China. Luce's argument derived from the
same self-aggrandizing idea that motivated his parents and their
missionary colleagues—China was theirs for the taking. Mao's
revolution should have made clear that Chinese politics and society, like those of every country, are moved primarily by its own
internal forces.

Yet the conviction that China was ripe to be remade in America's image continued to form the thinking of the American policy
establishment. The optimism was not wholly misplaced.

America's use of economic development to drive political liberalization had shown repeated successes in the post–World War II
period. "It's the strategy we used most consistently since the end
of WWII," says Matthew Turpin, who served as China director for
Trump's National Security Council staff in 2018–2019 and held a
similar position at the Pentagon under the Obama administration
from 2013 to 2017.

"We used it with postwar Italy and Germany and Japan in the
1940s," says Turpin. "In the '70s we used it with Spain, and in the
'80s we used it with South Korea and Taiwan. And we used that
approach after the fall of the Berlin Wall with the countries of
Eastern Europe. The strategy has a logic to it. So, we thought the
same with China. Building China's economy and accustoming its
leadership to the peace that is a natural consequence of prosperity
would lead to political liberalization."

The problem is that Chinese leadership saw through America's strategy. You didn't need to be steeped in Marxist doctrine to understand that the capitalists saw China as an untapped resource just waiting to be exploited. China was a self-baiting trap, and all Mao and his successors had to do was wait for the Americans to wander in.

If anyone should have understood the darker currents running through humanity, it was America's forty-first president, George H. W. Bush. A WWII Navy pilot who lost men in the Pacific, Bush had served as US ambassador to China and also as director of the CIA before becoming vice president. In those roles, he came to know China well, while overseeing Cold War proxy fights and operations that cost many thousands of lives and decided the fate of hundreds of millions more.

But Bush was determined to see China as a partner rather than a rival. Perhaps he thought it was his historical role to usher in a post–Cold War era of peace. "I see a world of open borders, open trade and, most importantly, open minds," he told the UN in 1990. According to Bush, the new order is "a world that celebrates the common heritage that belongs to all the world's people, taking pride not just in hometown or homeland but in humanity itself."

Others who were present at the birth of globalism saw it as a nightmare poised to swallow the American dream. Missouri Democratic congressman Richard Gephardt championed a message of economic nationalism similar to Trump's. The 1988 Democratic presidential candidate said that American workers were hurting from foreign competition that was rigged against them by their own political and business class. Gephardt described the US ruling class in much the same way Trump would come to define the "Swamp."

The establishment, said Gephardt, was "a loose term for academics, editorial writers, and some who have a vested economic interest in not changing some of these problems, who believe you have to accommodate decline."

In his efforts to defend the American worker from bad deals with Japan and South Korea, Gephardt, like Trump, was accused of every thoughtcrime conceivable in the new open-borders America—protectionism, xenophobia, and of course racism. When China became the central trade issue a decade later, he must have figured he was safer tacking to the language of human rights—that is, the human rights of foreign nationals.

"Human rights must be at the very core of our foreign and international economic policies," Gephardt said in 1997. He was arguing to revoke China's most-favored-nation trade status. "It is time for a new policy of firm engagement that finally advances our national interests and ideals."

He noted that the trade deficit with China had ballooned to nearly $40 billion, clear evidence that Clinton's policy had failed American workers. "We can't compete with slave labor," said Gephardt. He was referring to China's use of prisoners in the manufacturing sector. He called China's political system "free-market Stalinism."

Gephardt's description was apt but his argument incorporated a decisive flaw. Tying the US-China relationship to China's human rights record, rather than to America's national self-interest, downplayed the likely impact that aligning with a hostile totalitarian regime might have on Americans.

What would happen, for instance, if American industry handed off much of its manufacturing base to Stalinists? Obviously, it would impoverish American workers. And what if a natural catastrophe befell America, and US officials found themselves at the mercy of a hostile power that decided to extort or punish Washington by withholding vital goods like medical equipment or pharmaceuticals? The ensuing panic alone might cripple the country for weeks, months, maybe longer.

The debate over what was best for China came at the expense of obscuring the issue that should have been foremost on the minds of US lawmakers: what was best for working Americans and US national security.

It seems Kissinger, the master strategist, never asked these basic strategic questions. There was too much money at stake. "Kissinger was completely 'played' by the party," one experienced DC China hand tells me. "His consulting enterprise, Kissinger Associates, built its 'business' around enabling the Chinese Communist Party and convincing Western business leaders that they needed to leave their 'business judgment' at the border and simply accept the party's conditions as the price of entry into the China market."

Political analysts marvel at the PRC's monumental achievement—in a short period of time, they'd lifted hundreds of millions of people out of poverty. Equally remarkable is that so few in Washington were bothered that the improved condition of China's peasantry was the direct result of the intentional impoverishment of the American working class. When Trump made China a central piece of his 2016 campaign, Obama mocked him for what he called hollow promises to take back America's manufacturing sector. "Well, what, how exactly are you going to negotiate that?" asked Obama. "What magic wand do you have?"

For Obama and Biden, there was nothing to be done for American workers except retrain them to compete in a tight job market that had no room for them. Why worry about China? Because it wasn't their problem, they framed it as an opportunity. America wasn't *competing* with China. Rather, we were integrating our economy with theirs in order to draw Beijing into the liberal international system. And why shouldn't America's ruling class profit personally from a magnanimous arrangement that profited the world?

Biden gave his son Hunter a seat on Air Force Two while he was on an official trip to Beijing in 2013. Once there, the younger Biden introduced his Chinese business partner to America's number two official. He acquired a director's seat and became a shareholder in BHR Partners, a multibillion-dollar private equity firm that was 80 percent controlled by Chinese parties. According to the *Financial Times*, the state-run Bank of China International Holdings was one of the biggest stakeholders in the firm.

In October 2017, Hunter Biden paid roughly $425,000 for a 10 percent stake in BHR Partners, but BHR didn't come close to its $1.5 billion funding target. A fund it started in May 2018 raised a little more than $11.2 million that was used to finance the restructuring of a cheesemaker. He resigned from the board in October 2019 to avoid bringing undue scrutiny to his father's presidential campaign. His lawyer said his client had earned no money at the time from his investment.

Thanks to his father, Hunter Biden hit pay dirt in Ukraine, but his effort to make money with China was representative of how the vast majority of Americans experienced the Beijing boom. The vice president's son wound up on the losing end of an arrangement that US officials like his father had promoted.

The CCP understood from the outset that Washington's plan was to use business to drive China into the liberal international system. The Americans were open about their intentions. By

enriching the party's elite and legitimizing their power over peas-
ants they transformed into consumers, the Americans would make
it too costly for the CCP not to participate in its own destruction.

Mao called the American strategy "Peaceful Evolution." The
PRC's countermove was simple: We will use business to enrich
America's ruling class and thus dissuade them from protesting too
much about how we conduct our politics—or how we are taking
jobs away from their constituents.

———————

The career of Senator Dianne Feinstein best embodies the marriage
of US China policy and doing business with the PRC. It's hardly
surprising she opposed Trump's aggressive China tariffs. Her
promotion of trade with China to advance the interests of her
constituents turned into apologetics on behalf of the CCP, as it
aided her political ascent and made her rich. In October, *USA
Today* listed Feinstein as the sixth-richest member of Congress,
with a net worth of $58.5 million—a sum that vastly understates
her actual wealth. Richard Blum, her husband, is worth at least
another $1 billion.

When Feinstein was first elected to the Senate in 1992, Blum's
interests in China amounted to less than $500,000. She was named
to the Senate Foreign Relations Committee in 1995, and by 1997,
according to the *Los Angeles Times*, "Blum's interest had grown to
between $500,001 and $1 million."

In 1994, Blum's company, Blum Capital, had entered a joint
venture to found Newbridge Capital, specializing in emerg-
ing markets, including China. In 1996, Newbridge acquired a
24 percent stake in a Chinese state-owned enterprise producing
iron used in making cars for $23 million. The deal was initiated

by an investment company run by a former official from the state-owned investment company CITIC who was also a former vice minister of petroleum. Newbridge also invested $14 million for a 24 percent stake in a food and beverage company run by another former CITIC executive.

Blum said in 1997 that less than 2 percent of the approximately $1.5 billion that his firm managed was committed to China. He held a $300 million stake in Northwest Airlines when it operated the only nonstop service from the US to Chinese cities. In 2002, Newbridge was negotiating to acquire 20 percent of Shenzhen Development Bank. After some rough seas, it paid $145 million for an 18 percent share two years later. It was the first time a Chinese bank came under control of a foreign entity.

Feinstein said that Blum's business in China had no effect on her foreign policy or trade positions regarding the country. "We have built a firewall," she said of her relationship with her husband. "That firewall has stood us in good stead."

Yet the record shows that the marriage between Blum's business and Feinstein's political career is a very close one.

Feinstein first visited Shanghai in 1978, shortly after the United States and China opened diplomatic ties. San Francisco's newly elected first woman mayor struck up a friendship with her counterpart, Jiang Zemin, who was mayor of Shanghai at the time. Under their guidance, Shanghai, China's leading industrial city, and San Francisco, home to one of America's largest Chinese immigrant communities, struck up a sister-city relationship. The two siblings did well by each other.

"China made friends first," Feinstein told the press, "and then they did business with their friends." Feinstein considers Jiang a "good friend." She spoke of how she and Jiang danced together. Then they started to make money. In the mid-1980s, a firm in which Blum invested struck a $17 million deal with a state-owned business for a retail and residential complex outside Shanghai.

In 1989, Jiang became general secretary of the Chinese Communist Party. Three years later Feinstein was first elected to the Senate. Serving two of the largest Chinese diasporas in the United States—the San Francisco/Oakland/San Jose area (629,243) and the greater Los Angeles area (566,968)—Feinstein respected the wishes of many, but hardly all, of the Golden State's Chinese Americans who wanted warm ties with their ancestral homeland. More important, her long-standing ties to senior Chinese Communist Party officials advanced the financial interests of her constituents. It is because of California's trade relationship with China that the state is the world's fifth-largest economy.

The relationship benefited Feinstein personally. In 1993, Jiang became president of China and invited Feinstein and Blum to Beijing to meet with party leadership. According to a 1994 *Los Angeles Times* story, Blum was planning to bundle $2–3 million of his own with another $150 million from other investors to invest in state-owned enterprises, including telecommunications equipment.

Feinstein said at the time that Blum's economic interest in China was "news to me." The couple denied that his business in China profited from her then fifteen-year friendship with the president of China. "[Blum] is in San Francisco running his business, I am in Washington being a United States senator, and they are two separate things," Feinstein told reporters. "I don't know how I can prove it to people like you. Maybe I get divorced. Maybe that is what you want."

There's a logic to Feinstein's self-pity—she was being singled out for doing what everyone else was also doing or wanted to do. Taking a piece of the action was good for America, the winners told themselves. Business with China kept the peace. It was a central tenet of the post–Cold War order—with mutual financial interests at stake, no one makes war against their trade partners.

As the US Senate deliberated whether to withdraw most-favored-nation trade status from China in 1994 because of human rights abuses, Feinstein—then a freshman senator—established herself as a strong advocate of closer ties. Expressing disapproval of Beijing, she argued, would be "counterproductive." Punitive measures would only "inflame Beijing's insecurities" and halt reform.

In a 1996 editorial, she wrote: "Tying most-favored-nation to improvement in human rights is ineffective at best and counterproductive at worst. Revoking the trade status would be seen by China as the United States promulgating a complete break in Sino-American relations, putting in grave danger U.S. strategic interests in Asia."

Feinstein explained that Americans needed to be patient:

Just 30 years ago, China was engaged in the massive upheaval of the Cultural Revolution and Great Leap Forward, during which 20 million Chinese were either killed or imprisoned. Human rights were at their lowest point. Since then, the positive changes in China have been dramatic. Chinese society continues to open up with looser ideological controls, freer access to outside sources of information and increased media reporting. More people in China vote for their leadership on the local level than do Americans.

That last line is illustrative. Nearly the entire American establishment had convinced itself that treating the PRC like a normal country was a sign of virtue. But it takes a rare kind of contempt to push propaganda on American voters and tell them they're less civic-minded than the subjects of the Chinese Communist Party.

Feinstein made a habit of comparing the PRC to the United States to the detriment of her own country. She called for a commission of comparative human rights looking at China and America and studying, for instance, "the success and failures [of] both Tiananmen Square and Kent State." Members of the Ohio National Guard killed four students at Kent State in a 1970 anti-Vietnam war protest, an act that was widely condemned at all levels of American society. In 1989, the CCP's People's Liberation Army deliberately killed hundreds, if not thousands, of students in the middle of Beijing in order to maintain its grip on power.

Feinstein talked to her friend Jiang about Tiananmen soon after the massacre. "China had no local police," Feinstein said that Jiang had told her. She was messaging on behalf of the CCP. "It was just the PLA. And no local police that had crowd control. So, hence the tanks . . . But that's the past. One learns from the past. You don't repeat it. I think China has learned a lesson."

She was named to the Senate Intelligence Committee in 2001 and became chair in 2009, giving her access to America's most closely guarded secrets. According to reports that surfaced in 2018, Feinstein had employed a staffer who had been recruited by Chinese intelligence. Feinstein fired him around 2013, after he'd worked for her for twenty years—starting around the time her friend Jiang became president. Feinstein brushed off concerns that US national security had been compromised. "He never had access to classified or sensitive information or legislative matters." Charges were never filed against the staffer.

That was not the only time the Chinese government targeted Feinstein. In 1997, she was warned by the FBI that the Chinese might try to push money into her campaign. She said she had "no reason to believe" that the CCP had actually contributed to her campaign. "None whatsoever."

She had a point. Why would Beijing waste money on her campaign when it was already in business with her husband?

She said that her husband never sought to exploit her access to increase his opportunities in China. On a January 1996 trip to China, Blum and Feinstein went to dinner with Jiang. They dined in the room where Mao died.

"We were told that we were the first foreigners to see his bedroom and the swimming pool," said Feinstein. She said her "husband has never discussed business with Jiang Zemin, never would, never has." Of course, the fact that he was having dinner with the Chinese leader hosting them for an exclusive visit of a Communist Party historical site would have been more than enough for lower-ranking Chinese officials to know exactly where Blum stood with their bosses.

After the 1997 FBI briefing, Feinstein expressed her frustration to the press about accusations that she was being manipulated by the Chinese. "If there is credible evidence," she said, "'tell me what it is. Enable me to protect myself. That's the job of the FBI." According to her, none of the FBI agents "told me where or when or how or what to look for."

In 2000, Feinstein achieved her longtime policy goal when Congress conferred permanent most-favored-nation status on

China. The Senate voted in favor with eighty-three yeas, including Joe Biden. The Republican governor of Texas and presumptive GOP candidate for president praised the bill: "Passage of this legislation will mean a stronger American economy, as well as more opportunity for liberty and freedom in China," said future president George W. Bush. And so, the deal was done.

America's political and business elites told themselves that the new breed of Chinese communists were interested in money, just like capitalists. That fiction required American officials to ignore what they should have observed during the almost fifty-year-long Cold War struggle against Soviet communism. Moscow apparatchiks and their Iron Curtain courtiers very much enjoyed the luxuries that money afforded them, like Western-made shoes and tailored suits, access to fresh vegetables and Swiss bank accounts. The politburo confiscated private wealth not on behalf of the proletariat but to enrich themselves.

America's ruling class were paid to ignore what was obvious about their new Chinese partners, but no one is seduced against their will. What distinguished communists was not their disdain for money or their trenchant critiques of consumer capitalism. Rather, it was their paranoid imperative to crush whatever they perceived as a challenge to their indomitable pursuit of power.

By the time Xi Jinping began to consolidate his hold in 2012, it had become clear that Beijing wasn't interested in joining the liberal international system.

Australian official John Garnaut, a respected former journalist who spent years reporting from China, explained the CCP's paranoid worldview in an important speech he delivered in 2019. "The Western conspiracy to infiltrate, subvert and overthrow the

People's Party is not contingent on what any particular Western country thinks or does," said Garnaut. "It is an equation, a mathematical identity: The CCP exists and therefore it is under attack."

In April 2013, the CCP's Central Committee issued the "Communique on the Current State of the Ideological Sphere." Document No. 9, as it came to be called, explained the confrontation with the Washington-led liberal international system in stark terms. Party cadres were required to wage an "intense struggle" against "false trends," including constitutional democracy, human rights, and freedom of speech, which the Communists defined as instruments used to weaken the party.

Xi and his top deputies made Mao's observation their own. They knew what the Americans were plotting with their strategy of "peaceful evolution." What's most valuable about Document No. 9 is the picture it paints of the CCP, a self-image drawn in the sharp hues of confrontation, as well as the message it sent to Washington: China is not America's friend.

TWELVE

OBAMA'S COUP

On March 13, Trump declared a national emergency. The emergency orders, he said in a Rose Garden speech, conferred broad new authority to give doctors, hospitals, and healthcare providers maximum flexibility to respond to the virus and care for patients. The president asked hospitals around the country to activate their emergency preparedness plans.

Some communities were better prepared than others. "Every city is different," says Dr. Steven Hatfill, a virologist at George Washington University. "What works in Detroit may not work in Orlando. A response has to be tailor-made. You have to plan responses at the community level. A pandemic is nothing more than just a series of small-level epidemics in local communities."

Hatfill had been targeted by then FBI director Robert Mueller in the wake of the 2001 anthrax attacks as a suspect. DOJ and FBI officials fed his name to the press. In 2008, the government settled a suit that Hatfill filed for $4.6 million. Robert Mueller never apologized for turning Hatfill's life upside down. Mueller never admitted he was wrong.

Hatfill speaks deliberately, slowly, as if to modulate his speech patterns to create the calm with which it is necessary to think and make good decisions in a time of uncertainty. It was important to ward off panic.

People could feel it was still an early phase in the course of the pandemic. Things might change in the days ahead. They might change quickly. Hatfill is proud of how his Washington, DC, neighbors are managing. "I walk out in the morning and see bus drivers are going about their work, keeping the city moving," Hatfill says. "You need to have a certain swagger, the confidence that you can meet the challenges ahead."

The distinction between essential and nonessential workers appeared as if organically. Those who need to leave their homes to work—bus and taxi drivers, nurses, doctors, policemen, grocers, chefs, waiters, truckers, deliverymen, and so on—are essential to the maintenance of society. Lawyers, journalists, political activists, and others whose well-being is dependent on the services performed by the former do not need to leave their homes.

Pandemics are a function of civilization. As we started to build our first towns and then cities, we made it easier for viruses to spread from place to place. "Before the colonial era, most African villages were separated," says Hatfill, who did medical research in Africa. "And if one village caught something, it was hard to transmit it to the next one."

That changed as villages grew into cities. Building civilization altered ecosystems, and transportation made movement between places easier. Viruses, like the humans who transmitted them to one another, moved more quickly. To defeat a pandemic it's useful to return as much as possible to a premodern condition. Equally important as restricting movement is to invest authority in local communities so that they are able to protect themselves. That takes planning, says Hatfill.

"You have to care to realize there's a threat, and then you have to institutionalize the plan. Tell the next guy who replaces you. Planning helps the community to manage their medical surge requirements and leaves the leadership free to do other things like making sure that there's an income so people can shop and get groceries and things like that. Where you see disasters is where you don't see preplanning as a local community and you become medically overwhelmed. Then the population becomes very fragmented. And then you have panic."

Trump was eager to reopen the country by Easter. But on March 29 he extended the guidelines and businesses stayed closed. Now it was another month of stasis.

Americans were concerned but not panicked—not yet—even as unemployment numbers surged weekly and one of the strongest economies in US history shrank daily. It was bad for Trump. His reelection bid was tied to jobs and the economy, but there was another issue, too.

In fighting the California water wars, Nunes had discovered that the struggle wasn't really over the environment, as the activists claimed. Rather, it was about political power. Water was the key resource that Central Valley farmers and the owners of businesses that depended on agriculture needed to sustain their operations. Deny them water and they lose their ability to make a living. Without money, they can't afford the political operations, campaigns, and lobbying to defend their industry, families, communities, schools, and businesses. The water wars weren't about the natural ecosystem of the delta. The left was targeting a political ecosystem. They were trying to destroy their opponents' economic base.

At first there was no one directing the war against Trump's base: small businessmen, small landowners, mom-and-pop stores, neighborhood restaurants. The giants, like Amazon, thrived, but that was the work of the coronavirus, not Trump's opponents. That would change when the violence started and the small businesses that survived the pandemic were looted and destroyed.

In the meantime, though, Americans had not panicked. Many became angry with newly imposed restrictions that limited their movement. Some of the guidelines seemed random. Why were beaches off-limits? Why couldn't parents take their kids to the playground? The evidence showed that the coronavirus was more likely to spread in congested spaces, like New York City apartment buildings.

And then the guidelines seemed punitive. As early as late March, photographs of New Yorkers sunbathing in the city's parks filled the pages of the local press. In late April, New York mayor Bill de Blasio tweeted threats after an outdoor funeral for an orthodox Jewish rabbi had drawn a large crowd. "My message to the Jewish community, and all communities, is this simple: The time for warnings has passed. I have instructed the NYPD to proceed immediately to summons or even arrest those who gather in large groups. This is about stopping this disease and saving lives. Period."

In time it became clear that while the guidelines may have been drafted to save lives by keeping the medical system from collapse, they were being used by political officials to choose winners and losers. Some parts of the country were being punished and others rewarded.

When demonstrators went to Lansing, Michigan, in mid-May to demand the governor reopen the state, they were cast as villains, ruthlessly ignoring the guidelines drawn to protect the lives of the most vulnerable. And yet when a demonstration on behalf of Black Trans Lives Matter drew a closely packed crowd of thousands in Brooklyn weeks later, they were portrayed as joyful celebrants of the new awakening.

The transformation happened quickly.

"Pandemics accelerate time," says historian Victor Davis Hanson. "There's panic, loss of life, disruptions, fear. They tend to be more determinative than other events."

Hanson explains how plagues transformed societies.

"The standard understanding of the Black Plague of 1347 to 1351 is that it destroyed hierarchies. Fifty million people died across class lines, customs and traditions, and therefore the contagion introduced a level of fluidity that helped to end the medieval age and brought in the Renaissance, the modern period. So, it allowed people to come out of the woodwork who otherwise didn't have the requisite social standing or birth, but they were necessary because of population decline. There's a certain type of person or class who comes to the fore, during periods like the Black Plague and other sorts of upheaval."

Hierarchies are turned over; values change. "We're reminded of what's existential," says Hanson. "We're wealthy, we're sophisticated. And then all of sudden we're in our Manhattan apartment and the thermostat is broken and the cupboards are empty and we want that guy to drive that truck from Bakersfield loaded with food to get here. This coastal elite culture is very fragile. It has no margin of error. This is a reminder that ultimately all that matters are food, fuel, and transport."

If pandemics overturn the established order, how are the winners and losers of the new order decided?

"If people continue to be kept in their homes and they're not working," says Hanson, "then the forces of precivilization are going to get an edge. I'm not scared about the virus. I'm scared about the politics."

The pandemic had primed America for bloodshed. The paradox was that when the burning and looting started, COVID-19 was not an issue. The guidelines, lockdowns, and enforced prohibitions against public gatherings all fell away on May 26 when demonstrators gathered in the streets of Minneapolis to protest the apparent murder of a forty-eight-year-old African American man the day before. In an open letter, 1,200 public health officials rationalized the sudden and surreal about-face that licensed mass gatherings:

> *We do not condemn these gatherings as risky for COVID-19 transmission. We support them as vital to the national public health and to the threatened health specifically of Black people in the United States. We can show that support by facilitating safest protesting practices without detracting from demonstrators' ability to gather and demand change. This should not be confused with a permissive stance on all gatherings, particularly protests against stay-home orders.*

The apparent randomness was purposeful. It was meant to be disorienting and destabilizing, like the violence that followed.

George Floyd's death at the hands of four indifferent Minneapolis police officers was captured on video and circulated immediately. It was precisely because no one in America believed that he deserved to die with a knee on the back of his neck that the protests that swept throughout the country burned with orgiastic intensity.

Demonstrations erupted in thousands of towns and cities across America. Then riots. Police officers were attacked. They were dragged through the streets of Chicago and beaten by mobs in New York. One law enforcement officer was killed in California, and a retired police captain was shot to death in the St Louis pawnshop he was guarding. Civilians caught in the cross-fire were killed, too. Stores and homes were razed and looted. The financial, psychological, and social cost to major cities across the country—from Seattle and Los Angeles, to Chicago and Atlanta, to New York and Washington, DC—was extensive and in some cases perhaps irreparable.

Taken together with the more than 100,000 killed by the coronavirus and the subsequent loss of more than 20 million jobs, the violence and destruction of the nationwide protests tore a gaping hole in the fabric that binds America as one. The violence of the protest movement looked like it was leading to larger conflict. Who could see it as anything other than a dangerous, maybe irreversible, turning point in American history?

"As tragic as these past few weeks have been," said Barack Obama, "as difficult and scary and uncertain as they've been, they've also been an incredible opportunity for people to be awakened to some of these underlying trends. And they offer an opportunity for us, to all work together to tackle them to take them on to change America and make it live up to its highest ideals."

Obama had reason to be optimistic. It was his coup. It had been his coup from the beginning.

———

Why did none of the Washington, DC, journalists who had regular access to Obama during his presidency ask why he was still in Washington? The Obamas had claimed that they wanted their youngest daughter, Sasha, to finish up at her DC private school, but she graduated from high school in 2019. In the fall she matriculated at the University of Michigan. Why did none of the reporters who had messaged on behalf of Obama administration officials for eight years ever ask why his top aide, Valerie Jarrett, had an office in his mansion in the Kalorama neighborhood, a ten-minute downhill bike ride to the White House? They didn't ask because Democratic party insiders understood the fifty-eight-year-old former president was still the de facto leader of the party. Voters didn't know.

Obama reemerged on the public political stage when it was time to alert the public that they need not worry about the condition of the nominal candidate. Joe Biden is just an avatar.

Obama knew better than anyone that his old friend was not at the top of his game. "You don't have to do this, Joe," Obama told his former Vice President in 2019 when he decided to run for president again. "You really don't." It couldn't have been much of a surprise to Obama when he saw Biden misspeaking or forgetting his lines and showing signs of something more serious than the verbal miscues that characterized the former senator's career.

Democratic Party supporters were understandably worried. Obama needed to get out the message. And yet the coronavirus made in-person visits to his Kalorama mansion more difficult, and normal political signaling through cutouts and whisper campaigns less effective. The pandemic also presented a rare political opportunity. It had stripped Trump of his campaign's two major selling points—jobs and the economy. Further, it suspended the huge rallies from which he drew much of his political energy.

And so Obama dispensed with the polite fiction that he spent his time screening documentary films for his $50 million Netflix deal and decided to go public.

Since he'd left office, his social media was typically full of anodyne good cheer, holiday greetings, book recommendations, and other corporate-seeming niceties. Then, on April 10, Obama tweeted three times to promote articles about making vote-by-mail standard practice nationwide.

> No one should be forced to choose between their right to vote and their right to stay healthy like the debacle in Wisconsin this week.

> Everyone should have the right to vote safely, and we have the power to make that happen. This shouldn't be a partisan issue.

> Let's not use the tragedy of a pandemic to compromise our democracy. Check the facts of vote by mail.

According to one of the articles he tweeted, some Republicans approve of the idea, even if Trump is against it. So why hadn't the Founding Fathers thought of voting by mail back when Ben Franklin was postmaster general? Because what is obvious today was also obvious 240 years ago, and to everyone who has ever studied the issue since: Voting by mail is an invitation to voter fraud.

Yes, Democrats saw the lockdown as an opportunity to push their agenda. Hillary Clinton, for instance, clumsily restated Rahm Emanuel's slogan during an appearance in a Biden video town hall: "Don't let a crisis go to waste!" But the reason Obama tweeted about vote by mail—not once, but three times—wasn't simply to push a particular policy. It was an opportunity to pull back the curtain and reassure the party: *Relax, I'm here.*

Once he'd gotten voters' attention, he proceeded to lay down the party's articles of faith.

Identity politics:

We can't deny that racial and socioeconomic factors are playing a role in who is being hit the hardest by the virus. It's a reminder for our policymakers to keep our most vulnerable communities at the forefront when making decisions.

Immigration:

Dreamers have contributed so much to our country, and they are risking their lives fighting on the frontlines of this pandemic. They deserve permanent immigration status and a pathway to citizenship—as they are Americans in every way but on paper.

There was a redundant advertisement for his avatar:

I'm proud to endorse my friend @JoeBiden for President of the United States. Let's go.

In a tweet promoting an article about Putin's "war against American science," Obama tipped his hat to the DNC-funded conspiracy theory that tied down Trump's presidency for three years:

Democracy depends on an informed citizenry and social cohesion. Here's a look at how misinformation can spread

through social media, and why it can hurt our ability to
respond to crises.

And climate change. By shutting down the country to fight the
coronavirus, the precedent had been set to do the same because of a
national climate "emergency" that would allow the party to rewrite
regulations and laws to enrich friends and bankrupt opponents:

> We've all had to adapt to cope with a pandemic. Climate
> change will force far harsher changes on our kids. All of
> us should follow the young people who've led the efforts to
> protect our planet for generations, and demand more of our
> leaders at every level.

Obama wouldn't have needed to intervene so openly had
Kamala Harris won the nomination. Washington insiders on
both sides agreed that since she had Obama's backing, she was the
obvious front-runner. After she proved inert and unlikable on the
stump, Obama waited for the other candidates to sort themselves
out, like an NCAA tourney bracket, until it was down to Biden
and Bernie Sanders.

For Obama and the politburo he guides, the problem with
Bernie wasn't that his agenda was too progressive. The fact that the
Sanders foreign policy team was so easily grafted on to the Biden
campaign is evidence there is a unified Democratic Party policy,
formulated in the shadow White House in Kalorama. The problem
with Sanders was that the Vermont socialist stubbornly insisted on
being his own political brand.

Obama would choose the vice president, through whom, if
elected, he and his aides, would guide the country. This would give

the forty-fourth president another four to eight years to complete the transformative work he did not have time to finish in his first two terms in office.

———————

This was the purpose of the coup: to block the agenda that Trump was elected to implement until Obama could retake control through a member of the party he'd shaped in his own image.

Trump cut directly against his predecessor and not just his policies, like the Iran deal and the Affordable Care Act. There was also Trump's posture. He promoted America First, but it was more specific than that. He liked Americans. That was how a celebrity New York millionaire with a Queens accent charmed audiences around the country.

Obama saw America as a valuable cog in a larger global machine. Americans didn't understand that yet, or why he was determined, as he said, to fundamentally transform their country. But that was the future. It was useless, for instance, to try to bring manufacturing jobs back from China. Even if it could be done—and he thought it was not possible—why bother? That moment in history was over. If Americans wanted to cling to their old way of life, that was their choice. The world was passing them by, and there was nothing he could do about it.

Obama seemed not to like them much anyway. He was disdainful of their tastes and affections. When Democratic party officials shut churches and gun stores early during the pandemic, they were echoing Obama's lament, complaining of the embittered masses, clinging to their guns and religion.

The 2016 Democratic candidate tried to impersonate his cool contempt when she called non-Clinton supporters "deplorables."

It lost her no votes when she confessed what everyone knew was in her heart. And yet she laughed awkwardly to hear herself sound like him. She would protect his legacy, too.

Obama would have been aware of the anti-Trump operation even before the Crossfire Hurricane investigation officially opened July 31, 2016. The Clinton campaign was using his spies, after all. John Brennan was an Oval Office insider. The CIA director said he gave the FBI information about contacts between Trump associates and Russian officials even before the summer of 2016. Why would he withhold that from the president he served?

In early August, Brennan was briefing him on his part in the operation and the real CIA asset he was using to frame Trump. He sent Obama "a report drawn from sourcing deep inside the Russian government that detailed Russian President Vladimir Putin's direct involvement in a cyber campaign to disrupt and discredit the U.S. presidential race."

Throughout the preelection period, Obama was kept abreast of developments. On August 8, Peter Strzok texted Lisa Page: "Internal joint cyber cd intel piece for D, scenesetter for McDonough brief." They were preparing Comey to brief Obama's chief of staff, Denis McDonough. On September 2, Page texted Strzok about readying talking points for Comey: "potus wants to know everything we're doing."

Two days after Trump won, Obama warned him not to hire Flynn and spent his remaining weeks in the White House making good on his threat. The outgoing president took control of the operation the Clinton campaign had funded. On December 6, he directed Brennan to produce an official document (the intelligence community assessment) that would legitimize it.

On January 4, he told Comey to "look at things" regarding the Flynn investigation. "Have the right people on it," said Obama. Strzok found that the Crossfire Razor investigation was still open. Deputy attorney general Sally Yates was surprised to find during her meeting at the White House with Obama and Comey that the president already knew about the situation with Flynn and the calls between him and the Russian ambassador.

Of course Obama knew about it. Starting on election day, thirty-nine officials from his administration began unmasking Flynn's identity from classified intercepts at least fifty-three times. And that was only one Trump official. As Nunes had explained, they'd unmasked people who were only remotely associated with Trump. There was a book full of unmaskings done by Obama officials. He had nurtured a culture of espionage throughout his administration. Even his ambassador to Italy was spying on the Trump team.

On January 5, Brennan briefed Obama on the ICA. He'd directed him to finish before he left office so there was no chance the incoming administration could prevent the smear campaign from going public. Now it was official and permanent—Trump owed his presidency to Putin.

Obama covered his tracks. Susan Rice's January 20 email to herself memorialized the same meeting weeks before that Yates attended. Except, in contrast to her account, Rice claimed that she and Biden were present, too. Rice had made herself and the vice president witnesses to Obama's integrity. Whatever Comey might wind up saying about Obama's instructions to him about Flynn or anything else related to the Russia investigation, she heard the president tell the FBI director to go "by the book."

Obama had purposefully interfered with the peaceful transition of power. His former DNI confirmed it. "If it weren't for President Obama," said James Clapper, "we might not have done the intelligence community assessment that we did that set off a whole sequence of events which are still unfolding today, notably, special counsel Mueller's investigation."

The sequence helps explain why no Democrats ever called out Russiagate for the absurd lie that it was. It wouldn't have been hard for a Democratic senator or representative, a former Cabinet member, or a retired ambassador to say, *I don't like Trump or his policies either, but let's put aside this fake and ultimately dangerous conspiracy theory. It's bad for the country, and it's not good for the party to become known as the party of make-believe.*

None of them did because they knew Obama was part of Russiagate. They knew Obama spied on adversaries as well as Democrats. They didn't want to cross him. He showed them how it would go in the first few months of his administration.

In April 2009, a reporter was leaked the substance of a classified intercept that swept up a conversation between California congresswoman Jane Harman and an alleged agent of Israel. It captured her promising to intercede on behalf of two employees of the American Israel Public Affairs Committee. What was odd about the story was that the conversation was picked up years before, during the Bush administration. And yet it was leaked under the Obama White House.

The Obama administration spied on journalists, like James Rosen and Sharryl Attkisson. John Brennan spied on Congress to find out what the Senate Intelligence Committee came up with in its report on the CIA and torture. The White House spied on

Congress, again, and pro-Israel activists during the fight over the Iran deal. And they spied on Michael Flynn to protect the deal.

In May, documents hinting at Obama's role in framing him were declassified. He'd already shown his hand the month before with the series of tweets on voting by mail. He wasn't going to let go of Flynn.

After the Justice Department withdrew its case, Obama leaked a phone conversation in which the former president said that the attorney general's decision made him worry for the rule of law. The leak went to Michael Isikoff, author of several major collusion stories. In the recording, Obama said that Trump's first national security advisor was guilty of perjury. That was incorrect. How did Obama not know that Flynn wasn't charged with perjury but rather with making false statements to the FBI? It was a fine point, but Obama was a lawyer.

A week later, the judge in the Flynn case executed an extraordinary maneuver. He solicited an amicus brief from a former judge showing how Flynn might be charged with perjury.

Obama had not only taken credit for the coup; he was directing parts of it.

———————————

Obama's party had identified Trump to themselves as a racist, fascist, and White nationalist for four years. But how could he be held responsible for the death of an African American man in Minneapolis in broad daylight? Minnesota has a Democratic governor and two Democratic senators; Minneapolis has a progressive mayor; and the precinct that sent four officers after George Floyd was in Representative Ilhan Omar's district. For the party of resistance, the protests were a tactical bridging maneuver away from the coronavirus lockdowns, which were starting to run their course.

Like COVID-19, the protests highlighted that America has two classes. But this time those who stayed at home were the essential workers, except for the police who had to go to the streets. They were filled with students, activists, media, and the unemployed. It looked like Ukraine, except in a country of more than 300 million. Two lawyers were arrested in Brooklyn for distributing Molotov cocktails and throwing them at a police van. The police kept finding stashes of bricks and chunks of cement hidden where protestors would presumably know how to find them. It looked organized, like a network under central control somewhere.

There were, as the press reported, peaceful protestors, at least at first. But no one who went to the streets after several nights of rioting was looking to protest peacefully. They were volunteering themselves as human shields, instigating violence, or causing it.

Going to the street is dangerous. Numbers matter, because they are the mechanism by which a party shows its strength and intimidates rivals. If you're in the minority faction, you have to back down, unless you own most of the weapons. And yet during the George Floyd protests, those who did have most of the weapons—police officers—backed down anyway.

The mayor of Minneapolis and Seattle officials ordered police to abandon precincts under siege. In Charleston, South Carolina, bar and restaurant owners called the police repeatedly as their properties were being looted. Later, standing among the ruins of their businesses, they didn't blame the police but the authorities who held the police back. Even the governor of New York, Andrew Cuomo, said it was New York City mayor de Blasio's fault that the New York Police Department failed to protect New Yorkers.

Street politics are a consequence of the absence or the break-down of democratic procedural norms. The Founding Fathers did not need the example of the French Revolution birthed in blood the same year the US Constitution came into force in order to under-stand the dangers of people going to the streets to fight for their political ideas. The violence that frequently results when politi-cal power is counted in large numbers massed in public squares is a constant throughout human history. That's what the framers sought to save us from.

But memorials and monuments of them were under attack, too. In Portland, Oregon, a statue of George Washington was pulled down and the city announced it would not be restored. The rioters defaced symbols of US history and tradition. They spray-painted "1619," referring to the *New York Times* project to revise Ameri-can history and identify the founding of the country with slavery. Famous historians of the period said that the "1619" project was laced with falsehoods, but it had already been adopted by class-rooms across the country. In branding the mayhem with "1619," the attack on US cities bore the imprimatur of an ideological proj-ect created, branded, and marketed by America's most powerful media, cultural, and academic institutions.

If the issue really was systemic racism, as the scores of protes-tors and their advocates in the press claimed, then the problem was the system itself. Logically, the system would have to be collapsed. But the people to whom the system belonged had no intention of breaking it. It belonged to the Democratic Party, which is why they had been able to weaponize it against Trump and his supporters. The press, the intelligence services, all that belonged to the Demo-cratic party, even Black Lives Matter was theirs.

Obama had cultivated BLM support during his presidency. Five police officers were killed in Dallas during a July 2016 BLM protest against police violence. They had been killed by a black sniper who told the police he was targeting white officers.

The president spoke at their funeral. "We have all seen this bigotry in our lives at some point," said Obama. "None of us is entirely innocent. No institution is entirely immune. And that includes our police departments. We know this." The day after the funeral, Obama hosted BLM officials at the White House.

The organization that helped raze and loot American cities in the spring of 2020 was a frontline militia as well as a fund-raising mechanism. The "Donate" tab on the BLM website links to ActBlue, a Democratic Party financial instrument that pushed more than $1.5 billion in small donations into the 2018 midterms.

———————

Democratic Party money was also backing an information warfare campaign targeting Trump and his base. In May the press reported that retired general Stanley McChrystal was advising Defeat Disinfo, a political action committee using technology developed to counter ISIS propaganda. Pentagon-funded research had been retooled to sabotage the president's re-election campaign.

McChrystal had been critical of Trump in the past. After defense secretary Mattis's 2018 resignation, he praised the retired Marine general and slammed Trump's plan to withdraw forces from Syria and Afghanistan.

"If you pull American influence out, you're likely to have greater instability, and of course it'll be much more difficult for the United States to try to push events in any direction," said McChrystal.

"There is an argument that says we just pull up our stuff, go home, let the region run itself. That has not done well for the last fifty or sixty years."

He'd led elite special forces units before being named as commander of US troops in Afghanistan in 2009. He later acknowledged that he didn't have a plan for Afghanistan. "I wish I did," he said he told Secretary of State Mike Pompeo.

"If we pull out and people like al-Qaeda go back, it's unacceptable for any political administration in the US. It would just be disastrous, and it would be a pain for us," said McChrystal. "If we put more troops in there and we fight forever, that's not a good outcome, either. I'm not sure what the right answer. My best suggestion is to keep a limited number of forces there and just kind of muddle along and see what we can do."

He was relieved of duty in 2010 after the publication of a magazine article in which his staff criticized Vice President Biden. In 2011, McChrystal teamed up with First Lady Michelle Obama in an initiative assisting military families.

His new project was sponsored by Democratic Party operatives and former Obama officials. A former DNC finance director was helping raise money. Defeat Disinfo, according to press reports, was an extension of Main Street One, a New York–based intelligence firm funded in part by Higher Ground Labs, an incubator for Democratic Party initiatives. It was run by a former Obama fund-raiser and a strategist who worked on both Obama presidential campaigns. Several former Obama officials were on the board.

McChrystal said his aim was to ensure "the accuracy of information leading up to the election." The artificial intelligence and network analysis designed to counter ISIS was recast to disrupt the

Trump campaign. Defeat Disinfo relied on a network of more than 3.4 million influencers across the country, some of whom, according to press reports, were paid to take sides against the president.

For nearly a week, protestors gathered in Lafayette Park in front of the White House and clashed with police. It was a US version of Euromaidan. The night of May 31, they set fire to St. John's Episcopal Church across the street from 1600 Pennsylvania Avenue, known as the Church of the Presidents, where US commanders in chief have prayed for more than two hundred years.

It had been a tough week; the country had been through a lot. Trump wanted to show resolve. In the late afternoon of June 1, he broke off from a press conference and led part of his Cabinet through the park, where protestors had gathered. Park Police scattered the crowds that the previous night had sown chaos in the surrounding neighborhood.

As the Trump team walked out, to their left was the Hay-Adams hotel, one of the city's most beautiful and historic landmarks, home once to John Hay, Lincoln's personal secretary and two-time secretary of state, and the historian Henry Adams, a descendant of Presidents John Adams and John Quincy Adams. The hotel's scaffolding had been set on fire by protestors the night before but was soon extinguished.

There was still evidence of the fire that had burned in the basement of St. John's Sunday night. Trump climbed the front steps. With him were, among others, Attorney General Barr, defense secretary Mark Esper, and chairman of the Joint Chiefs of Staff General Mark Milley, chief of staff Mark Meadows, and national security advisor Robert O'Brien. Trump held up a Bible and spoke a few words.

"We have a great country. That's my thought. We have the best country in the world," said Trump. "We will make it even greater. And it won't take long. It's not going to take long. You see what's going on, it's coming back, it's coming back strong. It'll be greater than ever before."

Two days later, Trump's former defense secretary James Mattis fired a shot across his bow. He released a statement that appeared to zero in on the president. "The Nazi slogan for destroying us . . . was 'Divide and Conquer.' Our American answer is 'In Union there is Strength," wrote Mattis. Like the Antifa anarchists laying waste to US cities, the former Trump Cabinet member was calling the president a Nazi.

He described the church walk as a "bizarre photo op for the elected commander-in-chief" and called out "military leadership standing alongside." That was the purpose of Mattis's statement. He appeared to be chastising Trump, but he was in fact warning Trump's two top defense officials, Esper and Milley.

"We must reject any thinking of our cities as a 'battlespace,'" wrote Mattis, referencing a phrase that Esper had used in the preceding days when the administration was discussing the possibility of sending active-duty forces to US cities ravaged by the violence.

"At home, we should use our military only when requested to do so, on very rare occasions, by state governors," wrote Mattis. He was referring to the 1992 Los Angeles riots during which Governor Pete Wilson called in ten thousand Marines to quell the violence. Mattis understood the present problem well enough—either by intention or through incompetence, state and local authorities throughout the country had prevented police forces from protecting American lives and property. If they wouldn't do it, what choice did the president have but to intervene? Mattis sided with chaos.

Esper was the first to fall out. The day that Mattis's threat was published, he delivered a statement in the Pentagon press room. Esper said that he now disagreed with Trump, and there was no reason yet to send in active-duty troops.

Milley folded the week after. He apologized for joining the president in a show of resolve with a walk across the park. "My presence in that moment and in that environment created a perception of the military involved in domestic politics. As a commissioned uniformed officer, it was a mistake that I have learned from, and I sincerely hope we all can learn from it."

Mattis had written that Trump was dividing America. In fact, it was he who had purposefully sown disunity. By warning civilian and military Pentagon officials to distance themselves openly from the president they served, Mattis had helped destabilize the US government.

Obama had seized the advantage. "We're in a political season, but our country is also at an inflection point," his top aide, Valerie Jarrett, said in June. "President Obama is not going to shy away from that dialogue simply because he's not in office anymore."

In fact, the Party of Obama had been waging a proxy war against Trump and his supporters for more than three years. Their first instrument was the Russiagate conspiracy theory, which hatched a fraudulent impeachment process staged by the same political operatives, intelligence officials, and media personalities who pushed "collusion" into the public sphere. They even weaponized real crises to undermine the US government, like the coronavirus and the ensuing three-month-long lockdown that was portrayed as a matter of life and death, only to be randomly lifted to combat racism, after leaving nearly 20 million Americans jobless. The successive failures of their campaign to destroy Trump and undo the 2016 election only made them angrier and more willing to take desperate measures.

The point of the protests and the coup of which they were a central component was plain: If you want peace and stability, restore the Party of Obama and let him complete his work, the transformation of America. Choose Trump and you choose war.

JUSTICE AND MICHAEL FLYNN

In late winter, Kash Patel was detailed to the Office of the Director of National Intelligence to serve as deputy to Richard Grenell. Trump's ambassador to Germany had been one of the administration's most effective officials. When the president named him the acting DNI, he became the first openly gay Cabinet secretary in US history. He and Patel, the first Indian American to serve as deputy, were tasked to clean out the stables.

"The DNI had veered from its original mission," says Patel. "It ballooned in size. Its task is to oversee the intelligence community and bring resources together. The president wanted it streamlined. We reduced the agency by eliminating billets that duplicated the efforts of other agencies. No one was fired. We just sent people back to their home agencies, which signaled a greater need for them."

DNI's number one function, says Patel, "is to provide the president with the presidential daily briefing, digesting all the intelligence across the intelligence community, prioritizing the collection we believe he wants to see, and taking his guidance on what else he wants to see."

Trump, says Patel, wants transparency. "He's the most transparent president we've ever had."

The documents that the forty-year-old former DOJ terrorism prosecutor and Grenell declassified over the period of a few short months lends evidence to his assertion. They show that Trump was spied on during his campaign, the transition period, and then during his presidency. Had there been any genuinely incriminating evidence found in the Trump team's communications, an intelligence community intent on undoing the 2016 election results would have made it public. Instead, anti-Trump conspirators fabricated the collusion conspiracy theory.

Patel had been Nunes's lead investigator into HPSCI's investigation of FISA abuses and related matters. He'd told Nunes that there were so many elements to it that they'd have to cut off the head, like Medusa. Patel named their investigation Objective Medusa.

He said that the work that he and Nunes, Jack Langer, Damon Nelson, and the others had done was righteous. He said that in the end they had cut off the head. He told me last year that they just couldn't show it yet. The documents declassified by him and Grenell showed at last the full evidence of Objective Medusa's success.

"Declassifying the transcripts of all of our HPSCI interviews of Obama officials showed there had never been any evidence of collusion" says Patel.

Susan Rice, Samantha Power, Andrew McCabe, and other Obama aides who had filled the media cycle for three years with rumors of secret deals between Trump and the Russians had been lying all along. The interview with CrowdStrike founder Shawn Henry showed there was no evidence to support one of the pillars of the Russiagate narrative—that the Russians had hacked the DNC's emails.

"We declassified the footnotes to the inspector general's report," says Patel. "That shows the FBI knew that Steele and his sources were full of it. And yet they still kept renewing the FISA warrants to spy."

Declassification of Rod Rosenstein's memo demarcating the scope of the Mueller investigation showed that it too was based on the dossier. "They knew that Steele's reporting was garbage," says Patel, "but they used it to stand up the special counsel."

Patel and Grenell also declassified the documents showing how the Obama administration had spied on Michael Flynn and framed him.

A list of thirty-nine Obama administration officials showed how they'd unmasked Flynn's identity fifty-three times from transcripts of classified intercepts.

The transcripts of Flynn's December 23 and 29 conversations with Sergei Kislyak showed that he had never discussed sanctions with the Russian ambassador.

The memo for the opening of Crossfire Razor August 16, 2016, showed that the FBI had no basis for investigating a retired three-star general and former DIA chief.

The January 4 memo closing the Flynn investigation showed the FBI had found no derogatory information on him.

January 4 text messages between Peter Strzok, Lisa Page, and others were evidence that FBI leadership had nonetheless kept the investigation open as a pretext to interview Flynn for the purpose of framing him.

An FBI interview with Sally Yates showed that in a January meeting with Comey and Obama, the president was aware of the FBI's actions against Flynn. A passage from an email Susan Rice wrote to herself about the same meeting contradicted Yates's account. It claimed that there were witnesses, she and the vice president, who had heard the president tell the FBI director to "go by the book."

Peter Strzok's handwritten notes indicate that Obama had not. Rather, Obama told Comey, "Make sure you look at things and have the right people on it." Biden suggested they use an obscure law, the Logan Act, to target Flynn. Comey protested that the Flynn-Kislyak calls "appear legit." Nonetheless, even after Obama and Biden had left the White House, the operation targeting Flynn and the president continued.

Handwritten notes of a senior FBI agent and emails between members of the Crossfire Hurricane team showed that they were deliberating tactics for the January 24 interview with Flynn. What could they conceal from him? What could they elicit from him? Did they want to ensnare him in a perjury trap? For what purpose? To have him fired or prosecuted.

February 10 text messages between Strzok and Page showed that they secretly edited the record of Flynn's January 24 interview seemingly to incriminate him. Strzok and the other agent who'd interviewed him did not believe he had lied.

The documents declassified by Grenell and Patel persuaded Attorney General Barr to grant the motion filed by Flynn's lawyer Sidney Powell and withdraw the DOJ's case against Trump's first national security advisor.

Judge Emmet Sullivan decided, however, that he was not yet ready to let Flynn's case go. He solicited a former judge to write a brief explaining how Flynn might be prosecuted for lying to the court.

Patel knew when Objective Medusa began in the spring of 2017 that it would be a long road to get to justice. A grind, Nunes calls it. Three yards and a cloud of dust.

"We started the investigation to make sure that people were held accountable," says Patel. "Just because you have a high government position doesn't mean you're immune from being held accountable. What we're waiting for now is the final act of accountability."

And yet the man ultimately responsible is unlikely ever to be held accountable. The deep state wasn't the protagonist in the anti-Trump operation, it was an instrument that Barack Obama used in his ongoing effort to transform America.

———————————

"The ocean was our backyard," says one of Michael Flynn's older sisters, Barbara. The Flynns were raised in Newport, Rhode Island, not in the wealthiest part of the famous New England resort town. "Nine kids in a 1,200-foot square house with one bathroom," she says.

Barbara Flynn remembers the summers. "There were lifeguard competitions with college swimmers, and here's this wiry high school kid who beats them all. And then after he won, he coached and cheered on the rest of us. If ever you followed someone into war, it'd be Mike. You know he would survive, he would win, and he'd do the right thing. We called him Iron Mike."

Their father had also been in the Army, serving in World War II and Korea. Their mother was a lawyer with a strong sense of duty, patriotism, and family.

"It's important to have strength from your family," says Barbara. She remembers when her brother called when he left the

White House the second week of February 2017. "Mike calls us the night before, he calls every brother and sister and says, 'I'm going to be resigning, and you're going to hear the news.' He says, 'We'll get through this.' And that's when all of us started to call each other."

The Flynns, she says, talk all the time. "Everyone of us is talking to each other ten to fifteen times a day, maybe more." They decided they needed to do something for their brother Mike. Barbara remembers it was in a conversation with her youngest brother, Joe, that they hit on the idea of a legal defense fund.

"There's no way an average person can take on the weight and might of a corrupt Department of Justice with its unlimited resources," says Barbara. "The legal defense fund became not just a rallying point; it gave us a massive lift. It gave our family a way to keep pushing. It gave us a way to fight back."

"At first Mike was against it because he didn't want it to look like he was pandering," says Joe. "Also, he figured it would be over soon."

He had been advised by his lawyers at Covington and Burling to plead guilty to making false statements to the FBI. They told him it was the best option. It would keep the hunters from his son.

"I invited Sidney Powell to the December 2018 hearing where Mike was going to plead," says Joe. Neither Flynn nor his wife, Lori, had met Powell before. "I'd met her a few months before that in Dallas when I was raising money for the legal defense fund," Joe says. "We spoke over coffee for a few hours. I said, 'I need you to come to this trial.' She came to the trial and sat with us."

Judge Sullivan accused Michael Flynn of treason and then called a recess. Joe says that it was Lori who brought attention to the gravity of the situation. "She said, 'He's giving us a pause, and we're going to take a pause, because otherwise they're going to send my husband to jail today,'" says Joe Flynn. "Lori is the real hero. And also the biggest victim, watching her husband who she's known since they were both fourteen being accused of things everyone knows is not true."

Joe remembers that the Flynns held a family meeting that night. "We're asking, 'Michael, did you commit these crimes?' He says, 'No, I didn't commit these crimes. I agreed to this because we thought this was the best course of action, because I was told if I go against a jury in Washington, I'm going to go to jail for ten years.'"

The Flynns resolved to fight, and Powell took over the case. "She's fearless," says Joe. "She's relentless. And Mike and Lori's whole demeanor changed after she came on. They decided, 'We're going to fight this. We're not going to go like sheep to the slaughter.'"

Barbara says her brother was named after Saint Michael. "For Catholics, the Archangel Michael is the angel who fights, leading warriors against evil. Mike and our mother had a very special relationship. We were all close to her, but there was a spiritual bond between them. And I remember when Mike became a colonel. We would start bragging that Mike's a colonel now. And then he became a one-star general and we're bragging more. And my mother stops me. She said, 'Oh, no, Barbara, this is serious stuff. Mike has a role to play. He is about to enter into the most serious time in our country's history.'"

I sought out General Flynn. And he wrote:

As a Soldier, I fought on many foreign battlefields around the world in support of US policy objectives but never in my wildest dreams did I ever believe I would be fighting for my life and liberties on the domestic battlefield for justice and truth. Through this struggle, I now better appreciate that reaping the blessings of freedom, we must endure the fatigues of sacrifice. A coup d'état is a real thing. It is not something that should ever happen in the United States of America—not in our country—but it did. The events of these past four years have tested the will-power of our nation. It is not a government we fight for, instead it is an idea built on a foundation of God-given freedoms and individual liberties that we must be prepared to defend—that is the essence of our constitutional republic. We must not fear what lies ahead. To all Americans, what we choose to do in this life should never be stopped by fear. Instead, we need to embrace the uncertainty and accept the risk that comes with sacrifice and then work to overcome the sheer magnitude of life's challenges, especially during this crucible of our nation's history. Our nation is worth fighting for—God bless and protect America.

ACKNOWLEDGMENTS

Thanks to the publications and staff where some of this material first appeared in different form: Alana Newhouse, David Samuels, Matthew Fishbane, Liel Leibovitz, and Jacob Siegel at *Tablet*; David DesRosiers, Tom Kuntz, Peder Zane, and Liz Sheld at *Real Clear Investigations*; John Solomon and Daniel Wattenberg at *Just the News*. Sohrab Ahmari and Stephen Lynch at the *New York Post*.

Thanks to my agent, Keith Urbahn, and his colleagues at Javelin. Thanks to my editor, Kate Hartson, and Sean McGowan and the staff at Center Street.

Thanks to Angelo Codevilla, Will Fetters, Mayor Rudolph Giuliani, Victor Davis Hanson, Barbara and Michael Ledeen, Svetlana Lokhova, Amanda Milius, Sidney Powell, Gary Rosen, Peter Theroux, UH, and the Office of Strategic Studies for your insight and support.

Thanks, as ever, to the Nunes family: Mrs. Elizabeth Nunes, and Evelyn, Julia, and Margaret. Thanks to Congressman Nunes's staff. Thanks to Jack Langer and Kash Patel and all the Objective Medusa team for your continuing inspiration. Thank you, Devin Nunes. And to my beloved wife, Catherine, thank you.

NOTES

CHAPTER ONE: CLOUD OF DUST

Page 1: **We've all been through a lot together:** President Trump statement on Senate Acquittal, C-Span, February 6, 2020.

6: **unemployment rate:** US Department of Labor, "Unemployment Rate 3.6 Percent in April 2019, Lowest since December 1969," *Economics Daily*, May 8, 2019.

CHAPTER TWO: THE DIRECTOR

15: **Attorney General William Barr:** Katie Benner and Julian Barnes, "Durham Is Scrutinizing Ex-CIA Director's Role in Russian Interference Findings," *New York Times*, December 19, 2019.

17: **Helsinki summit:** Jeremy Diamond, "Trump Sides with Putin over US Intelligence," CNN, July 16, 2018.

19: **Communist Party USA's presidential candidate:** Tal Kopan, "Polygraph Panic: CIA Director Fretted His Vote for Communist," CNN, September 15, 2016.

19: **interest in treasonous behavior:** "Transcript: One-on-One with Former CIA Director John Brennan," MSNBC, August 17, 2018.

19: **concerned about these contacts:** US House of Representatives, Permanent Select Committee on Intelligence, "John Brennan Testimony: Russian Active Measures During the 2016 Election Campaign," May 23, 2017.

21: **Brennan sent Obama reports:** Greg Miller, Ellen Nakashima, and Adam Entous, "Obama's Secret Struggle to Punish Russia for Putin's Election Assault," *Washington Post*, June 23, 2017.

23: **Reid, the Senate minority leader, on August 25:** Eric Lichtblau, "CIA Had Evidence of Russian Effort to Help Trump Earlier than Believed," *New York Times*, April 6, 2017.

23: **Reid wrote a letter:** "Harry Reid's Letter to James Comey," *New York Times*, August 29, 2016.

23: **Reid was referring to Carter Page:** "A Transcript of Donald Trump's Meeting with the *Washington Post* Editorial Board," *Washington Post*, March 21, 2016.

23: **July 7 speech in Moscow:** Andrew Roth, "Trump's Russia Adviser Criticizes U.S. for 'Hypocritical Focus on Democratization,'" *Washington Post*, July 7, 2016.

25: **"Trump over a barrel":** US House of Representatives, Committee on the Judiciary, joint with the Committee on Government Reform and Oversight, "Interview of Bruce Ohr," August 28, 2018, p. 27.

25: **Susan Rice, saw his reports:** *Peter Aven, Mikhail Friedman, and German Khan v. Orbis Business Intelligence Limited*, Deposition of Christopher Steele, March 17–18, 2020.

25: **FBI had a relationship:** US House of Representatives, Permanent Select Committee on Intelligence, "Interview of F.B.I. Special Agent MTR," December 20, 2017.

25: **Michael Gaeta and senior DOJ official Bruce Ohr:** Lee Smith, *The Plot against the President: The True Story of How Congressman Devin Nunes Uncovered the Biggest Political Scandal in US History* (Center Street, 2019), 81–82.

25: **FBI made Steele a confidential human source:** DOJ Office of the Inspector General, "Review of Four FISA Applications and Other Aspects of the FBI's Crossfire Hurricane Investigation," December 9, 2019, 86.

25: **FBI paid Steele $95,000:** DOJ Office of the Inspector General, "Review of Four FISA Applications," 88.

26: **That day or the day after:** "Interview of F.B.I. Special Agent MTR," US House of Representatives, Permanent Select Committee on Intelligence, December 20, 2017.

26: **Bruce Ohr called Gaeta to check in:** DOJ Office of the Inspector General, "Review of Four FISA Applications," 99.

26: **MI6's top Russia hand:** DOJ Office of the Inspector General, "Review of Four FISA Applications," 257.

26: **newly minted MI6 officers:** *Peter Aven, Mikhail Friedman, and German Khan v. Orbis Business Intelligence Limited*," Deposition of Christopher Steele, March 17–18, 2020.

27: **leak from a British intelligence official:** Mark Urban, "Litvinenko Killing 'Had State Involvement,'" BBC, July 7, 2008.

27: **"What you need to remember…":** Heidi Blake and Jonathan Calvert, "Written Evidence on the 2022 World Cup Bidding Process," *Sunday Times*, November 2014; Heidi Blake and Jonathan Calvert, "Written Evidence Submitted by the *Sunday Times* Insight Investigations Team," November 2014, http://data.parliament.uk/writtenevidence/committeeevidence.svc/evidencedocument/culture-media-and-sport-committee/the-2022-world-cup-bidding-process/written/15880.html

CHAPTER THREE: THE SETUP

31: **He was hired in May 2016:** Glenn Simpson and Peter Fritsch, *Crime in Progress: Inside the Steele Dossier and the Fusion GPS Investigation of Donald Trump* (Random House, 2019), 61.

31: **Met with Jane Mayer:** Simpson and Fritsch, *Crime in Progress*, 110–111.

32: **investigation was pro forma:** Laura Jarrett, "Key Dates in the FBI Probe of Hillary Clinton's Emails," CNN, June 14, 2018.

33: **"dossier of 'Russian influence activity'":** Peter Foster and Matthew Holehouse, "US Intelligence Agencies to Investigate Russia's Infiltration of European Political Parties," *Telegraph*, January 16, 2016. Prior to interfering in America's 2016 election, Steele had been hired for a project he referred to as "Project Charlemagne," an investigation of Russian election interference in Western Europe. The *Telegraph* article appears to describe that earlier Steele project.

34: **CrowdStrike president:** Ellen Nakashima, "Russian Government Hackers Penetrated DNC, Stole Opposition Research on Trump," *Washington Post*, June 14, 2016.

34: **Shawn Henry later testified:** "Interview of Shawn Henry," US House of Representatives, Permanent Select Committee on Intelligence, December 5, 2017.

34: **Clinton campaign hired Fusion GPS:** Adam Entous, Devlin Barrett, and Rosalind S. Helderman, "Clinton Campaign, DNC Paid for Research That Led to Russia Dossier," *Washington Post*, October 24, 2017.

34: **Robbie Mook announced:** Jeremy Herb, "Mook Suggests Russians Leaked DNC Emails to Help Trump," *Politico*, July 24, 2016.

35: **former CIA contractor Nellie Ohr:** Simpson and Fritsch, *Crime in Progress*, 27.

35: **Dated May 20:** Lee Smith, *The Plot against the President: The True Story of How Congressman Devin Nunes Uncovered the Biggest Political Scandal in US History* (Center Street, 2019), 45.

35: **"talk to people inside Russia":** Simpson and Fritsch, *Crime in Progress*, 62.

37: **Questioned about the dossier:** US Department of State, "Notes from Meeting with Chris Steele and Tatyana Duran of Orbis Security," October 11, 2016; DOJ Office of the Inspector General, "Review of Four FISA Applications and Other Aspects of the FBI's Crossfire Hurricane Investigation," December 9, 2019; *Peter Aven, Mikhail Friedman, and German Khan v. Orbis Business Intelligence Limited*, Deposition of Christopher Steele, March 17–18, 2020.

39: **Russian-language news site:** Ria Novosti, "Sergey Millian: Donald Trump Will Improve Relations with Russia," April 13, 2016.

39: **A spreadsheet:** "New DOJ Docs Show Nellie Ohr Sent DOJ/FBI Anti-Trump Russia Dossier Materials through Her Husband Bruce Ohr," Judicial Watch, August 14, 2019.

40: **Simpson had reached out:** Simpson and Fritsch, *Crime in Progress*, p. 97.

40: **Mosk published that same day:** Brian Ross, Matthew Mosk, Rhonda Schwartz, and Megan Christie, "DNC Hack Prompts Questions about Trump's Ties to Russia," ABC News, July 26, 2016.

40: **Shearer passed them on:** Jonathan Winer, "Devin Nunes Is Investigating Me. Here's the Truth," *Washington Post*, February 8, 2018.

41: **The Ohrs were central players:** "*JW v. DOJ Ohr*," Judicial Watch, July 23 2019.

41: **The Ohrs testified:** US House of Representatives, Committee on the Judiciary, joint with the Committee on Government Reform and Oversight, "Interview of Bruce Ohr," August 28, 2018. US House of Representatives, Committee on the Judiciary, joint with the Committee on Government Reform and Oversight, "Interview of Nellie Ohr," October 19, 2018.

CHAPTER FOUR: OCTOBER SURPRISES

43: **It was Strzok who opened:** "Key Obamagate Doc Uncovered," Judicial Watch, May 22, 2020.

43: **Elizabeth Dibble:** Kimberley Strassel, "The Curious Case of Mr. Downer," *Wall Street Journal*, May 31, 2018.

44: **Papadopoulos later said:** George Papadopoulos, *Deep State Target: How I Got Caught in the Crosshairs of the Plot to Bring Down President Trump* (Diversion Books, 2019).

44: **Downer liked Trump's opponent:** John Solomon and Alison Spann, "Australian Diplomat Whose Tip Prompted FBI's Russia-Probe Has Tie to Clintons," *The Hill*, March 5, 2018.

45: **Defense Department paid him:** Lee Smith, *The Plot against the President: The True Story of How Congressman Devin Nunes Uncovered the Biggest Political Scandal in US History* (Center Street, 2019), 26.

45: **Trubnikov was also falsely cited:** Smith, *The Plot against the President*, 285.

45: **FBI agent Steven Somma:** University of Cambridge Faculty of History, "Intelligence Seminar: Michelmas Term 2011."

45: **FBI cut Halper loose:** DOJ Office of the Inspector General, "Review of Four FISA Applications and Other Aspects of the FBI's Crossfire Hurricane Investigation," December 9, 2019, 313.

45: **William Casey:** Leslie H. Gelb, "Reagan Aides Describe Operation to Gather Inside Data on Carter," *New York Times*, July 7, 1983.

46: **Strzok recounted:** US House of Representatives, Committee on the Judiciary, joint with the Committee on Government Reform and Oversight, "Interview of Peter Strzok," June 27, 2018, 45.

46: **Strzok disagreed:** US Senate Committee on Homeland Security and Government Affairs, "Chairman Johnson Releases Interim Report Including Strzok-Page FBI Text Messages," February 7, 2018.

46: **"Do we burn sources":** US House of Representatives, Committee on the Judiciary, joint with the Committee on Government Reform and Oversight, "Interview of Lisa Page," July 13, 2018, 44.

46: **Halper sought out Carter Page:** DOJ Office of the Inspector General, "Review of Four FISA Applications," 317.

47: **"broader mosaic of facts":** Ian Schwartz, "Baier to Comey: If Dossier Was "Salacious," Why Did You Use It to Get FISA Warrant?" RealClear Politics, April 26, 2016.

48: **counterintelligence investigation on Millian:** DOJ Office of the Inspector General, "Review of Four FISA Applications," ix.

48: **Michael Sussmann, the Clinton campaign lawyer:** *Peter Aven, Mikhail Friedman, and German Khan v. Orbis Business Intelligence Limited*, Deposition of Christopher Steele, March 17–18, 2020.

49: **claimed that Alfa's owners:** *Peter Aven, Mikhail Friedman, and German Khan v. Orbis Business Intelligence Limited*, Deposition of Christopher Steele.

49: **Simpson's instruction:** Chuck Ross, "Dossier Author Christopher Steele Had Previously Undisclosed Meetings with Lawyers for DNC, Clinton Campaign," *Daily Caller*, April 27, 2020.

49: **on September 23, Steele told Bruce Ohr:** DOJ Office of the Inspector General, "Review of Four FISA Applications," 119.

50: **Sussmann told the FBI's general counsel:** House Permanent Select Committee on Intelligence, "Report on Russian Active Measures," March 22, 2018, 57 n. 43.

50: **Steele was in Rome:** DOJ Office of the Inspector General, "Review of Four FISA Applications," 108.

50: **Kathleen Kavalec:** US Department of State, "State Department Handwritten Notes of Meeting with Christopher Steele," May 5, 2019. US Department of State, "Notes from Meeting with Chris Steele and Tatyana Duran of Orbis Security," October 11, 2016.

51: **Franklin Foer:** Franklin Foer, "Was a Trump Server Communicating with Russia?" *Slate*, October 31, 2016.

51: **David Corn:** David Corn, "A Veteran Spy Has Given the FBI Information Alleging a Russian Operation to Cultivate Donald Trump," *Mother Jones*, October 31, 2016.

51: **Catherine Belton:** "The Shadowy Russian Émigré Touting Trump," *Financial Times*, October 31, 2016.

51: **New York Times's:** Eric Lichtblau and Steven Lee Myers, "Investigating Donald Trump, FBI Sees No Clear Link to Russia," *New York Times*, October 21, 2016.

51: **But on October 28 Comey announced:** "Letter to Congress from FBI Director on Clinton Email Case," *New York Times*, October 28, 2016.

53: **Simpson was furious:** Glenn Simpson and Peter Fritsch, *Crime in Progress: Inside the Steele Dossier and the Fusion GPS Investigation of Donald Trump* (Random House, 2019), 140.

CHAPTER FIVE: FALSE FLAG

55: **And then there was Barack Obama:** Gerald F. Seib, Jay Solomon, and Carol E. Lee, "Barack Obama Warns Donald Trump on North Korea Threat," *Wall Street Journal*, November 22, 2016; Michael D. Shear, "Obama Warned Trump about Hiring Flynn, Officials Say," *New York Times*, May 8, 2017.

57: **Ben Rhodes:** Washington Free Beacon, "Obama Adviser Likened Iran Nuclear Deal to ObamaCare," *Fox News*, November 2, 2014.

57: **"The bin Laden database…":** "The Bin Laden Papers," *Wall Street Journal*, September 14, 2015.

58: **One of those letters showed:** Thomas Joscelyn, "Top Intel Official: Al Qaeda Worked on WMD in Iran," *Weekly Standard*, July 12, 2016.

59: **Robert Menendez:** Michael Shear, "Obama and Senator Robert Menendez Spar on How to Handle Iran," *New York Times*, January 15, 2015.

59: **comedian-newsman Jon Stewart:** Lee Smith, "Obama Blows His Jewish Dogwhistle with John Stewart," *Tablet*, July 22, 2015.

59: **secret negotiations with Iran:** Jay Solomon, "Secret Dealings with Iran Led to Nuclear Talks," *Wall Street Journal*, June 28, 2015.

59: **To gain Tehran's confidence:** Josh Meyer, "The Secret Backstory of How Obama Let Hezbollah Off the Hook," *Politico*, 2017.

59: **2018 Senate report:** US Senate, Permanent Subcommittee on Investigations, "Report: Obama Administration Secretly Authorized Iranian Access to US Financial System," June 6, 2018.

60: **Rhodes told the *New York Times*:** David Samuels, "The Aspiring Novelist Who Became Obama's Foreign-Policy Guru," *New York Times Magazine*, May 5, 2016.

61: **geopolitical equilibrium:** David Remnick, "On and Off the Road with Barack Obama," *New Yorker*, January 20, 2014.

61: **David Ignatius:** David Ignatius, "Obama's Diplomatic Opportunity," *Washington Post*, October 4, 2013.

62: **US diplomat told:** Toby Harnden, "Obama All Out for Iran Deal This Week," *Times*, July 5, 2015.

62: **Secretary of State John Kerry said it outright:** Lorenzo Ferrigno, "Kerry: If Congress Rejects Iran Deal, Israel Will Be Blamed," *CNN*, July 24, 2015.

63: **senior official at a pro-Israel organization:** Lee Smith, "Obama to Jewish Leaders: Lay Off the Iran Deal, and I Will Lay Off You," *Tablet*, August 6, 2015.

63: **Noah Pollak:** Lee Smith, *The Plot against the President: The True Story of How Congressman Devin Nunes Uncovered the Biggest Political Scandal in US History* (Center Street, 2019), 149–150.

64: **Flynn was on Capitol Hill:** US House of Representatives, Joint Foreign Affairs and HASC Subcommittees, "Michael T. Flynn Testimony on Iran," June 10, 2015.

64: **"willful ignorance":** Fionna Agumouh, "Former DIA Director: Obama's Middle East Policy Is One of 'Willful Ignorance,'" *Business Insider*, June 10, 2015.

65: **secret deals between Obama and Iran:** Tim Mak, "Trump Team Wants You to See the Iran Nuke Documents Obama's Kept from View," *Daily Beast*, December 5, 2016; Eli Lake and Josh Rogin, "Congress Alarmed by Iran Pact's Secret Understandings," *Bloomberg*, July 24, 2015.

65: **more sanctions relief:** Carol E. Lee and Jay Solomon, "Obama Seeks to Fortify Iran Nuclear Deal," *Wall Street Journal*, November 20, 2016.

65: **Senate agreed 99–0:** Laura Rozen, "Obama Administration, Allies Try to Buy Time for Iran Nuclear Deal," *Al-Monitor*, December 21, 2016.

65: **Russia weighed in on the Obama team's side:** Alexander Winning and Peter Hobson, "Russia Says Loss of Iran Nuclear Deal Would Be Unforgivable: Interfax," Reuters, December 15, 2016.

66: **Obama agreed to let Russia:** Laurence Norman, "Obama Administration Seeks to Secure Iran Deal," *Wall Street Journal*, January 10, 2017.

66: **recycled in a joint statement:** "53 Orgs to Trump: General Flynn Is Unfit to Be National Security Advisor," J Street, December 5, 2016.

67: **clandestine component targeting Flynn:** US Office of the Director of National Intelligence, "Follow-Up Unmasking Requests re Former National Security Advisor," May 8, 2020.

68: **"largest unmasker of US persons in our history":** US House of Representatives, Permanent Select Committee on Intelligence, "Interview of Samantha Power," October 13, 2017, 25.

68: **one of thirty Obama officials:** US Office of the Director of National Intelligence, "Follow-up Unmasking Requests."

68: **Flynn, Kushner, and Steve Bannon:** Ellen Nakashima, Adam Entous, and Greg Miller, "Russian Ambassador Told Moscow That Kushner Wanted Secret Communications with Kremlin," *Washington Post*, May 26, 2017.

68: **Susan Rice also unmasked Flynn:** Manu Raju, "Exclusive: Rice Told House Investigators Why She Unmasked Senior Trump Officials," CNN, September 18, 2017.

CHAPTER SIX: THE KILL SHOT

69: **intelligence community assessment:** US Office of the Director of National Intelligence, "Background to 'Assessing Russian Activities and Intentions in Recent US Elections': The Analytic Process and Cyber Incident Attribution," January 6, 2017.

70: **John Durham's investigators:** John Solomon, "Why the Obama Intelligence Assessment on Russia Collusion Is under Investigation," *Just the News*, June 15, 2020.

71: **Annex A:** Sean Davis, "Declassified Intelligence Community Annex on the Steele Dossier Proves the FBI Misled Trump and Obama," *Federalist*, June 11, 2020.

71: **Steele deleted:** *Peter Aven, Mikhail Friedman and German Khan v. Orbis Business Intelligence Limited*, Deposition of Christopher Steele, March 17–18, 2020.

72: **He raised more than $3 million:** Chuck Ross, "Dark Money Org Gave $2 Million to Group Working with Fusion GPS, Steele," *Daily Caller*, March 10, 2019.

72: **Steele told Ohr in December:** "Judicial Watch Gets Bruce Ohr FBI 302s," Judicial Watch, August 29, 2019.

72: **Steele's primary subsource:** DOJ Office of the Inspector General, "Review of Four FISA Applications and Other Aspects of the FBI's Crossfire Hurricane Investigation," December 9, 2019, 186.

73: **another part of the cover-up:** Talia Kaplan, "Former Acting DNI Grenell on Declassifying Russia Probe Docs, 'Transparency Is Never Political,'" Fox News, June 14, 2020.

76: **December 23 Flynn spoke with Kislyak:** "Read the Transcripts of Michael Flynn's Calls with Russian Diplomat," PBS News Hour, May 29, 2020.

77: **UNSCR 2334 passed 14–0:** United Nations Meetings, Coverage and Press Releases, "Israel's Settlements Have No Legal Validity, Constitute Flagrant Violation of International Law, Security Council Reaffirms," December 23, 2016.

77: **surprised when Putin:** Missy Ryan, Ellen Nakashima, and Karen DeYoung, "Obama Administration Announces Measures to Punish Russia for 2016 Election Interference," *Washington Post*, December 29, 2016.

77: **According to McCabe:** Andrew G. McCabe, *The Threat: How the FBI Protects America in The Age of Terror and the Age of Trump* (St. Martin's, 2019), 199.

78: **Comey corroborated McCabe's account:** US District Court for the District of Columbia, "Government's Motion to Dismiss the Criminal Information against the Defendant Michael T. Flynn," exhibit 5, May 7, 2020.

78: **Clapper swore under oath:** US House of Representatives, Permanent Select Committee on Intelligence, "Interview of James Clapper," July 17, 2017, 35.

78: **Strzok checked:** US District Court for the District of Columbia, "Government's Motion to Dismiss the Criminal Information against the Defendant Michael T. Flynn," exhibit 7, May 7, 2020.

78: **Crossfire Razor:** US District Court for the District of Columbia, "Government's Motion to Dismiss the Criminal Information against the Defendant Michael T. Flynn," exhibit 2, May 7, 2020.

78: **He told an administrator:** US District Court for the District of Columbia, "Government's Motion to Dismiss the Criminal Information against the Defendant Michael T. Flynn," exhibit 7, May 7, 2020.

79: **Obama knew about Flynn's call:** US District Court for the District of Columbia, "Government's Motion to Dismiss the Criminal Information against the Defendant Michael T. Flynn," exhibit 4, May 7, 2020.

79: **Rice gave a different account:** "Read: Declassified Susan Rice Email about January 5, 2017 Oval Office Meeting with Obama," Fox News, May 19, 2020.

80: **the outgoing administration ran its offense:** Evan Perez, Jim Sciutto, Jake Tapper, and Carl Bernstein, "Intel Chiefs Presented Trump with claims of Russian Efforts to Compromise Him," CNN, January 10, 2017.

80: **"FISA derived information…":** US Department of Justice, Office of the Inspector General, "Report of Investigation of Former Bureau of Investigation Director James Comey's Disclosure of Sensitive Investigative Information and Handling of Certain Memoranda," August 2019.

81: **BuzzFeed redacted parts of it:** Katelyn Polantz, "BuzzFeed Outlines in Lawsuit Defense How It Decided to Publish Russia Dossier," CNN, October 1, 2018.

81: **What BuzzFeed redacted from its earlier version:** https://archive.org/stream/TrumpPrivateUKIntelligenceAllegations/Trump%20Private%20UK%20Intelligence%20Allegations_djvu.txt.

82: **Michael Dempsey:** Office of the Director of National Intelligence, Letter from Acting Director Richard Grenell to Sens Charles Grassley and Ron Johnson, May 13, 2020.

82: **Adam Entous was offered the leak:** "Trump Russia Investigations Transcript," Georgetown Law, June 6, 2018.

82: **"take the kill shot…":** Brooke Singman, "FBI Agents Manipulated Flynn File, as Clapper Allegedly Urged 'Kill Shot': Court Filing," Fox News, October 25, 2020.

83: **Vice President Pence said on TV:** *Face the Nation*, CBS News, January 15, 2017, transcript: Pence, Manchin, Gingrich.

83: **"box us in":** "Read the Transcripts of Michael Flynn's Calls with Russian Diplomat," PBS News Hour, May 29, 2020.

83: **deliberated options:** US District Court for the District of Columbia, "Government's Motion to Dismiss the Criminal Information against the Defendant Michael T. Flynn," exhibit 9, May 7, 2020.

84: **didn't think Flynn lied:** House Permanent Select Committee on Intelligence, "Report on Russian Active Measures," March 22, 2018, 5.

84: **Former Obama aides berated:** Philip Gordon, "What's Wrong with Michael Flynn's Bluster on Iran? Plenty," *New York Times*, February 2, 2017.

CHAPTER SEVEN: OUTING SPIES

86: **Intelligence chiefs rushed to Obama's defense:** Jeremy Diamond, "Clapper: 'No Such Wiretap Activity Mounted' on Trump," CNN, March 5, 2017.

86: **Comey wanted the Justice Department:** Michael S. Schmidt and Michael D. Shear, "Comey Asks Justice Dept. to Reject Trump's Wiretapping Claim," *New York Times*, March 5, 2017.

86: **Nunes was precise:** Anna Giaritelli, "Nunes: New Evidence from FBI Continues to Show No Wiretap on Trump," *Washington Examiner*, March 19, 2017.

87: **The left-wing press embraced Nunes:** Chris Cillizza, "Devin Nunes Confirms It: The Evidence of Trump Tower Being Wiretapped Just Doesn't Seem to Exist," *Washington Post*, March 15, 2017.

88: **leaked account of a classified conversation:** Greg Miller and Philip Rucker, "'This Was the Worst Call by Far': Trump Badgered, Bragged, and Abruptly Ended Phone Call with Australian Leader," *Washington Post*, February 2, 2017.

88: **Obama had told Turnbull:** Morgan Winsor, "What We Know about the Refugee Resettlement Deal Obama Forged with Australia," ABC News, February 2, 2017.

92: **Mark Levin broke through:** Joel B. Pollack, "Mark Levin to Congress: Investigate Obama's 'Silent Coup' vs. Trump," Breitbart, March 3, 2017.

93: **We can't let him enact this foreign policy:** Paul Sperry, "Whistleblower Was Overheard in '17 Discussing with Ally How to Remove Trump," RealClear Investigations, January 22, 2020.

95: **Ciaramella emailed Kelly on May 10:** Department of Justice, "Report on the Investigation into Russian Interference in the 2016 Presidential Election" 2:71 n. 468, March 2019.

95: **was Trump acting on behalf of the Russian government:** "Andrew McCabe: The Full Sixty Minutes Interview," CBS News, February 17, 2019.

96: **John Brennan took credit for starting the investigation:** US House of Representatives, Permanent Select Committee on Intelligence, "Transcript: Russian Active Measures During the 2016 Election Campaign. Interview with John Brennan," May 23, 2017.

96: **Intelligence officials told the media:** Jim Sciutto, "Exclusive: US Extracted Top Spy from Inside Russia in 2017," CNN, September 9, 2019.

97: **He may have been recruited:** Alec Luhn, "Alleged US Spy Extracted by CIA Worked in Kremlin, Putin Spokesman Confirms," *Telegraph*, September 10, 2019.

98: **vacation in Montenegro:** Shaun Walker, Julian Borger, and Marc Bennetts, "Oleg Smolenkov: Alleged US Spy Who Gave Russia the Slip," *Guardian*, September 14, 2019.

99: **also spoke of Smolenkov:** David E. Sanger and Matthew Rosenberg, "From the Start, Trump Has Muddied a Clear Message: Putin Interfered," *New York Times*, July 18, 2018.

99: **after Smolenkov was extracted:** DOJ Office of the Inspector General, "Review of Four FISA Applications and Other Aspects of the FBI's Crossfire Hurricane Investigation," December 9, 2019, 192–193.

100: **the Russian government opened up a criminal case:** Sergey Sinegov, "An Employee of the President's Administrative Department Disappeared without a Trace with His Wife and Three Children," Daily Storm, September 12, 2017.

100: **he was living abroad, in Stafford, Virginia:** Todd Prince, "Virginia Residents Question Whether Their Neighbor Was A Russian Informant," Radio Free Europe/Radio Liberty, September 10, 2019.

100: **Reporters walked right up to Smolenkov's front door:** Ken Dalinian and Tatyana Christikova, "Possible Russian Spy for CIA Now Living in Washington Area," NBC News, September 9, 2019.

100: **Smolenkov had worked in the Presidential Administration:** "Kremlin Confirms Smolenkov Worked in Presidential Administration but Was Sacked," TASS, September 10, 2019.

CHAPTER EIGHT: THE SCOPE

102: **Multipronged effort to frame the Trump team:** Lee Smith, "Seven Mysterious Preludes to the FBI's Trump-Russia Probe," *RealClear Investigations*, June 25, 2018.

103: **He wanted to put off the meeting:** US House of Representatives, Permanent Select Committee on Intelligence, "Transcribed Interview of Donald Trump, Jr." December 6, 2017.

103: **Veselnitskaya was part of Moscow's effort:** Lee Smith, "Does US Media Help Russia Destabilize the United States?" *Federalist*, October 10, 2017.

104: **More than a year later, the *New York Times*:** Jo Becker, Matt Apuzzo, and Adam Goldman, "Trump Team Met with Lawyer Linked to Kremlin during Campaign," *New York Times*, July 8, 2017; Jo Becker, Matt Apuzzo, and Adam Goldman, "Trump's Son Met with Russian Lawyer after Being Promised Damaging Information on Clinton," *New York Times*, July 9, 2017; Matt Apuzzo, Jo Becker, Adam Goldman, and Maggie Haberman, "Trump Jr. Was Told in Email of Russian Effort to Aid Campaign," *New York Times*, July 10, 2017; Jo Becker, Matt Apuzzo, and Adam Goldman, "Russian Dirt on Clinton? 'I Love It,' Donald Trump Jr. Said," *New York Times*, July 11, 2017.

104: **the 2018 Pulitzer committee:** The Pulitzer Prizes, "Staffs of the *New York Times* and the *Washington Post*," 2018, https://www.pulitzer.org/winners/staffs-new-york-times-and-washington-post.

105: **the FBI interviewed another figure:** US Department of Justice FBI, "All 302's of Individuals Who Were Questioned/Interviewed by FBI Agents Working for the Office of Special Counsel Robert Mueller," January 17, 2020, http://cdn.cnn.com/cnn/2020/images/01/17/cnn_litigation_4th_release.pdf.

105: **Adam Schiff explained:** Brett Samuels, "Schiff Claims There's Already 'Direct Evidence' of Collusion by Trump Campaign," *The Hill*, March 3, 2019; Tim Hains, "Rep. Adam Schiff: Trump Tower Moscow Deal 'A Different Form of Collusion,'" *RealClear Politics*, February 10, 2019; Madeline Conway, "Schiff: There Is Now 'More than Circumstantial Evidence' of Trump-Russia Collusion," *Politico*, March 22, 2017.

106: **the press already knew what Fusion GPS was:** Jack Gillum and Shawn Boburg, "'Journalism for Rent': Inside the Secretive Firm behind the Trump Dossier," *Washington Post*, December 11, 2017.

106: **The FBI arrested George Papadopoulos:** Lee Smith, "The Maltese Phantom of Russiagate," *RealClear Investigations*, May 29, 2018.

107: **The FBI interviewed Papadopoulos in Chicago:** US Department of Justice FBI, "All 302's of Individuals Who Were Questioned/Interviewed"; http://cdn.cnn.com/cnn/2020/images/01/17/cnn_litigation_4th_release.pdf.

107: **Halper was recording Papadopolous:** DOJ Office of the Inspector General, "Review of Four FISA Applications and Other Aspects of the FBI's Crossfire Hurricane Investigation," December 9, 2019, 329–335; US Department of Justice FBI, "Transcript: Recorded Conversation with Crossfire Typhoon," November 10, 2016.

107: **Jeffrey Wiseman:** Chuck Ross, "After Reviewing Transcripts, George Papadopoulos Says He's Now Positive He Knows Who the FBI Informant in His Case Was," *Daily Caller*, May 6, 2020; US Department of Justice FBI, "Transcript of Papadopoulos's October 31, 2016 conversation with FBI informant," October 31, 2016.

108: **The Maltese-born academic taught diplomats:** Lee Smith, "The Maltese Phantom of Russiagate," *RealClear Investigations*, May 30, 2018.

109: **the FBI prompted him:** US District Court for the District of Columbia, "Government's Sentencing Memorandum for *US v. George Papadopoulos*," August 17, 2018.

110: **statement of offense filed:** US District Court for the District of Columbia, "Statement of the Offense for *US v. George Papadopoulos*," October 5, 2017.

110: **Zelinsky, Rhee, and Goldstein misled the court:** Lee Smith, "Declassified FBI Memos Undercut Mueller Team Claims That Papadopoulos Hindered Russia Probe," *Just the News,* February 25, 2020.

113: **now dissolved Podesta Group:** Nahal Toosi, "Turkey's Coup Attempt a Boon for Lobbyists," *Politico*, July 18, 2016.

114: **former CIA director James Woolsey:** James V. Grimaldi, Dion Nissenbaum, and Margaret Coker, "Ex-CIA Director: Mike Flynn and Turkish Officials Discussed Removal of Erdogan Foe from US," *Wall Street Journal*, March 24, 2017.

115: **SCO was leaking to the press:** Ken Dilanian, "Ex-CIA Director Spoke to Mueller about Flynn's Alleged Turkish Scheme," NBC News, October 27, 2017.

116: **After Michael Flynn left the White House:** US District Court District of Columbia, "Declaration of Michael Flynn," January 29, 2020. Much of the narrative in this section is taken from Flynn's declaration.

118: **they thought Flynn had not lied:** House Permanent Select Committee on Intelligence, Report on Russian Active Measures," March 22, 2018, 5.

118: **rewritten in February:** US District Court District of Columbia, "Government's Motion to Dismiss the Criminal Information against the Defendant Michael T. Flynn," exhibit 7, May 7, 2020.

118: **he pled guilty:** US District Court District of Columbia, "Statement of the Offense for *US v. Michael T. Flynn*," December 1, 2017.

118: **Comey had written a memo to himself:** "James Comey's Memos on His Meetings with Trump," *Washington Post*, 2018.

118: **the obstruction case the SCO was building against Trump:** "The Trump Lawyers' Confidential Memo to Mueller, Explained," *New York Times*, June 2, 2018.

119: **the scope of the special counsel investigation:** US Department of Justice, Office of Legislative Affairs, "Memorandum regarding 'The Scope of Investigation and Definition of Authority,'" May 6, 2020.

CHAPTER NINE: UKRAINE THE MODEL

122: **"raiding Michael Cohen's office…":** Matt Apuzzo, "FBI Raids Office of Trump's Longtime Lawyer Michael Cohen; Trump Calls It 'Disgraceful,'" *New York Times*, April 9, 2018.

125: **Biden first met the future president of Ukraine:** Evan Osnos, "The Biden Agenda," *New Yorker*, July 20, 2014.

126: **Simpson wrote for the *Wall Street Journal*:** Glenn R. Simpson and Mary Jacoby, "How Lobbyists Help Ex-Soviets Woo Washington," *Wall Street Journal*, April 17, 2007.

126: **Manafort's partner Rick Davis:** Mary Jacoby and Glenn R. Simpson, "McCain Consultant Is Tied to Work for Ukraine Party," *Wall Street Journal*, May 14, 2008.

127: **At the outset of Euromaidan:** Katrina Elledge, "Ukraine: Dissident Capabilities in the Cyber Age," in Legatum Institute, *Cyber Propaganda: From How to Start a Revolution to How to Beat ISIS*, November 23, 2015.

128: **Victoria Nuland was in Kiev:** "Top US Official Visits Protestors in Kiev as Obama Admin. Ups Pressure on Ukraine President Yanukovich," CBS News, Decemeber 11, 2013.

128: **"possible to save Ukraine's European future":** "Ashton: Yanukovych Promised Solution within 24 Hours," Radio Free Europe/Radio Liberty, December 11, 2013.

128: **intercept of her conversation:** "Ukraine Crisis: Transcript of Leaked Nuland-Pyatt Call," BBC News, February 7, 2014.

129: **Biden was on the phone constantly:** "Biden, Yanukovych Spoke 9 Times in 3 Months, Source Tells AP," NBC News, February 25, 2014.

129: **White House readout:** The White House, Office of the Vice President, "Readout of Vice President Biden's Call with Ukrainian President Viktor Yanukovych," February 18, 2014.

129: **Biden took the seat at the head of the table:** Evan Osnos, "The Biden Agenda," *New Yorker*, July 20, 2014.

129: **Hunter Biden was named to the Burisma board:** Javier E. David, "Ukraine Gas Producer Appoints Biden's Son to Board," CNBC, May 13, 2014.

130: **paying Hunter Biden more than $80,000 a month:** Brie Stimson, "Hunter Biden Got $83G per Month for Ukraine 'Ceremonial' Gig: Report," Fox News, October 19, 2019.

130: **Ukraine's most wanted list:** Ilya Timtchenko, "Prosecutors Put Zlochevsky, Multimillionaire Ex-Ecology Minister, on Wanted List," *Kyiv Post*, January 18, 2015.

130: **In March, they discussed:** US Embassy in Ukraine, "Readout of the Vice President's Call with Ukrainian President Petro Poroshenko," March 18, 2015.

130: **Biden called Poroshenko again in June, July, and August:** US Embassy in Ukraine, "Readout of the Vice President's Call with Ukrainian President Petro Poroshenko," June 12, 2015; US Embassy in Ukraine, "Readout of the Vice President's Call with Ukrainian President Petro Poroshenko," July 24, 2015; US Embassy in Ukraine, "Readout of the Vice President's Call with Ukrainian President Petro Poroshenko," August 28, 2015. John Solomon published an excellent and detailed timeline: "Timeline of Key Events in Ukraine Scandal That Led to Trump Impeachment," *Just the News*, February 23, 2020.

130: **Obama administration refused to arm Kiev:** Jennifer Steinhauer and David M. Herszenhorn, "Defying Obama, Many in Congress Press to Arm Ukraine," *New York Times*, June 11, 2015.

131: **John Brennan explained:** Ken Dilanian, "Former CIA Director: We Worried Arming Ukraine Would Hand Technology to Russian Spies," NBC News, November 22, 2019.

131: **Obama administration officials seemed to have crossed signals:** "US Ambassador Upbraids Ukrainian Prosecutors over Anticorruption Efforts," Radio Free Europe/Radio Liberty, September 25, 2015.

131: **Four days later, Biden went to Kiev:** US Embassy in Ukraine, "Readout of the Vice President's Meeting with Ukrainian President Petro Poroshenko," September 29, 2015.

132: **He didn't leave the race until the middle of October:** Stephen Collinson, "Joe Biden Won't Run for President," CNN, October 21, 2015.

132: **On December 7, Biden and Poroshenko met:** US Embassy in Ukraine, "Remarks by Vice President Joe Biden and Ukrainian President Petro Poroshenko at a Bilateral Meeting," December 7, 2015.

133: **December 9 speech in Kiev:** The White House, Office of the Vice President, "Remarks by Vice President Joe Biden to The Ukrainian Rada," December 9, 2015.

133: **Obama's NSC invited Ukrainian prosecutors:** US Senate, Committee on Homeland Security and Governmental Affairs, "Johnson, Grassley Request Records from 2016 White House Meetings between Obama Administration and Ukrainian Government, DNC Officials," November 22, 2019.

134: **Victor Pinchuk:** James V. Grimaldi and Rebecca Ballhaus, "Clinton Charity Tapped Foreign Funds," *Wall Street Journal*, March 19, 2015.

134: **Ukrainian prosecutor seized all of the assets:** "Court Seizes Property of Ex-Minister Zlochevksy in Ukraine," Interfax Ukraine, April 2, 2016.

134: **Clinton ally Victoria Nuland:** Victoria Nuland, US Embassy in Ukraine, "Ukrainian Reforms Two Years after the Maidan Revolution and the Russian Invasion," March 15, 2016.

134: **Biden called Poroshenko on March 22:** US Embassy in Ukraine, "Readout of Vice President Biden's Call with President Poroshenko of Ukraine," March 22, 2016.

134: **the Ukrainian parliament voted to dismiss Shokin:** Andrew E. Kramer, "Ukraine Ousts Viktor Shokin, Top Prosecutor, and Political Stability Hangs in the Balance," *New York Times*, March 29, 2016.

134: **$1 billion loan guarantee:** US Embassy in Ukraine, "Readout of Vice President Biden's Meeting with President Petro Poroshenko of Ukraine, March 31, 2016.

134: **three-day period:** Michael Isikoff, "Trump's Campaign Chief Is Questioned about Ties to Russian Billionaire," Yahoo News, April 26, 2016; Steven Mufson and Tom Hamburger, "Inside Trump Adviser Manafort's World of Politics and Global Financial Dealmaking," *Washington Post*, April 26, 2016; Peter Stone, "Trump's New Right-Hand Man Has History of Controversial Clients and Deals," *Guardian*, April 27, 2016; Franklin Foer, "The Quiet American," *Slate*, April 28, 2016.

135: **Alexandra Chalupa:** Kenneth P. Vogel and David Stern, "Ukrainian Efforts to Sabotage Trump Backfire," *Politico*, January 1, 2017.

136: **Andrii Telizhenko:** John Solomon, "Ukrainian Embassy Confirms DNC Contractor Solicited Trump Dirt in 2016," *The Hill*, May 2, 2019.

136: **She consulted frequently with the DNC:** "Emails between Ali Chalupa, Luis Miranda, and Mark Paustenbach," WikiLeaks, May 4, 2016.

136: **Republican National Convention platform's call:** Josh Rogin, "Trump Campaign Guts GOP's Anti-Russia Stance on Ukraine," *Washington Post*, July 18, 2016.

137: **Trump's views on Ukraine had changed:** Michael Crowley, "Trump Changed Views on Ukraine after Hiring Manafort," *Politico*, August 3, 2016.

137: **Ukraine was all over the dossier:** Lee Smith, "It's Not All about the Bidens: Why Trump Has Ukraine on the Brain," *RealClear Investigations*, October 7, 2019.

137: **black ledger:** Rowan Scarborough, "Paul Manafort Russia Conspiracy Rejected by Mueller Report," Associated Press, May 19, 2019.

138: **Serhiy Leshchenko:** US House of Representatives, Executive Session Committee on the Judiciary, Joint with the Committee on Government Reform and Oversight, "Transcript: Interview of Nellie Ohr," October 19, 2018, 115.

138: **Ukrainian officials came out openly:** Valeriy Chaly, "Ukraine's Ambassador: Trump's Comments Send Wrong Message to the World," *The Hill*, August 4, 2016.

138: **senior Ukrainian politicians lined up to attack the GOP candidate:** Roman Olearchyk, "Ukraine's Leaders Campaign against 'Pro-Putin' Trump," *Financial Times*, August 28, 2016.

139: **Joe Biden didn't have to promise Poroshenko anything:** Vladislav Davidzon, "Phone Call from Biden Said to Precipitate Ukraine's UN 'Yes' Vote," *Tablet*, December 27, 2016.

CHAPTER TEN: THE CIARAMELLA DOSSIER

140: **Biden always knew how to make people laugh:** Tim Hains, "Flashback, 2018: Joe Biden Brags at CFR Meeting about Withholding Aid to Ukraine to Force Firing of Prosecutor," *RealClear Politics*, September 27, 2019.

140: **"We're not going to give you the billion dollars":** Council on Foreign Relations, "Foreign Affairs Issue Launch with Former Vice President Joe Biden," January 23, 2018.

141: **money, women, and substance abuse:** Randall Chase, "Estranged Wife: Biden Son Wasted Money on Drugs, Prostitutes," Associated Press, March 2, 2017.

141: **what Joe and Hunter Biden had been up to in Ukraine:** Polina Ivanova, Maria Tsvetkova, Ilyz Zhegulev, and Luke Bager, "What Hunter Biden Did on the Board of Ukrainian Energy Company Burisma," Reuters, October 18, 2019.

143: **"Our country has been through a lot":** White House, "Transcript of Telephone Conversation between President Trump and President Zelenskyy," July 25, 2019.

143: **Fox News's Chris Wallace:** Ian Schwartz, "Chris Wallace: Mueller Hearing Has Been a Disaster for Democrats, Reputation of Robert Mueller," *RealClear Politics*, July 24, 2019.

143: **John Ratcliffe asked Mueller:** Mairead McArdle, "Mueller Says He Cannot Name Another Case Where DOJ Required Proof of Innocence," *National Review*, July 24, 2019.

144: **Durham had already traveled to Italy:** Katie Benner and Adam Goldman, "Justice Dept. Is Said to Open Criminal Inquiry into Its Own Russia Investigation," *New York Times*, October 24, 2019.

145: **Lieutenant Colonel Alexander Vindman:** Ayesha Rascoe, "Who Was on the Trump-Ukraine Call?" National Public Radio, November 7, 2019.

145: **Ciaramella wrote a memo:** Arden Farhi, "Read the Whistleblower's Memo about Trump's Ukraine Call, as Described to CBS News," CBS News, October 9, 2019.

146: **Ciaramella first expressed his concern:** Julian E. Barnes, Michael S. Schmidt, Adam Goldman, and Katie Benner, "White House Knew of Whistle-Blower's Allegations Soon after Trump's Call with Ukraine Leader," *New York Times*, September 26, 2019.

146: **he filed a whistleblower's report:** "Read the Whistleblower Complaint regarding President Trump's Communications with Ukrainian President Volodymyr Zelensky," *Washington Post*, October 16, 2019.

148: **Ciaramella inserted hearsay and secondhand sources into official intelligence channels:** Sean Davis, "Intel Community Admission of Whistleblower Changes Raises Explosive New Questions," *Federalist*, October 1, 2019.

148: **The Justice Department agreed:** "Urgent Concern" Determination by the Inspector General of the Intelligence Community," *Washington Post*, September 24, 2019.

149: **September 5 *Washington Post* editorial:** *Washington Post* Editorial Board, "Trump Tries to Force Ukraine to Meddle in the 2020 Election," *Washington Post*, September 5, 2019.

149: **three of the *Washington Post*'s top collusion conspiracy theory reporters:** Greg Miller, Ellen Nakashima, and Shane Harris, "Trump's Communications with Foreign Leader Are Part of Whistleblower Complaint That Spurred Standoff between Spy Chief and Congress, Former Officials Say," *Washington Post*, September 18, 2019.

150: **"Lawmakers were concerned":** Aaron Blake, "Why Ukraine's Being the Focus of Trump's Whistleblower Complaint Is Particularly Ominous," *Washington Post*, September 20, 2019.

150: **Trump said that he did withhold aid:** "Trump Confirms He Ordered Freeze of Ukraine Aid Ahead of Call under Democratic Scrutiny," Voice of America, September 24, 2019.

150: **March 21, 2016, interview:** *Washington Post* Opinions Staff, "A Transcript of Donald Trump's Meeting with the *Washington Post* Editorial Board," *Washington Post*, March 21, 2016.

151: **"the consensus views of the interagency":** Mark Hemingway, "Donald Trump Versus 'The Interagency Consensus,'" *Federalist*, November 1, 2019.

151: **formal impeachment inquiry:** Nicholas Fandos, "Nancy Pelosi Announces Formal Impeachment Inquiry of Trump," *New York Times*, September 24, 2019.

152: **Patel denied it and brought a defamation case:** Jonathan Swan, "NSC Staffer Denies Having Secret Ukraine Conversations with Trump," *Axios*, November 9, 2019; Howard Kurtz, "White House Official Sues Politico, Targets Schiff's Role in Impeachment," Fox News, November 18, 2019.

155: **"the American people watching at home":** US House of Representatives, Permanent Select Committee on Intelligence, "Impeachment Inquiry: Ms. Jennifer Williams and Lieutenant Colonel Alexander Vindman," November 19, 2019.

157: **Schiff splashed records of Nunes's calls:** The *Wall Street Journal* Editorial Board, "Schiff's Surveillance State," *Wall Street Journal*, December 4, 2019.

157: **CNN's Vicky Ward reported:** Vicky Ward, "Exclusive: Giuliani Associate Willing to Tell Congress Nunes Met with Ex-Ukrainian Official to Get Dirt on Biden," CNN, November 23, 2019.

158: **Libya and Malta:** Deanna Paul and Hannah Knowles, "Devin Nunes Sues CNN for $435 Million, Alleging 'False Hit Piece,'" *Washington Post*, December 4, 2019.

158: **brought a $435 million suit against CNN:** Rowan Scarborough, "Devin Nunes Slaps CNN with $435 Million Defamation Lawsuit," *Washington Times*, December 3, 2019.

158: **he'd brought a case against Fusion GPS:** Kate Irby, "Latest Devin Nunes Lawsuit Targets Fusion GPS, the Firm That Dug Up Dirt on Trump in 2016," *Fresno Bee*, September 4, 2019.

158: **Fusion admitted that it had targeted Nunes:** Glenn Simpson and Peter Fritsch, *Crime in Progress: Inside the Steele Dossier and the Fusion GPS Investigation of Donald Trump* (Random House, 2019), 246.

159: **Horowitz had announced:** US Department of Justice, Office of the Inspector General, "DOJ OIG Announces Initiation of Review," March 28, 2018.

159: **Durham rejected the predication finding:** US Attorney's Office, District of Connecticut, "Statement of US Attorney John H. Durham," December 9, 2019.

160: **Barr agreed with Durham:** United States Department of Justice, "Statement by Attorney General William P. Barr on the Inspector General's Report of the Review of Four FISA Applications and Other Aspects of the FBI's Crossfire Hurricane Investigation," December 9, 2019.

CHAPTER ELEVEN: THE PARTY

167: **Xi Jinping told a Davos audience:** Noah Barkin and Elizabeth Piper, "In Davos, Xi Makes Case for Chinese Leadership Role," Reuters, January 17, 2017.

167: **Wuhan residents left the city:** Erika Kinetz, "Where Did They Go? Millions Left City before Quarantine," Associated Press, February 9, 2020.

167: **let international flights:** Niall Ferguson, "Let's Zoom Xi. He Has Questions to Answer," *Globe and Mail*, April 6, 2020.

167: **wet market:** Sahar Esfandiari, "A New Report Indicates That the Deadly Chinese Coronavirus May Not Actually Have Originated at a Wet Market in Wuhan," *Business Insider*, January 27, 2020.

168: **Hanban, a propaganda arm:** US Department of Education, "US Department of Education Launches Investigation into Foreign Gifts Reporting at Ivy League Universities," February 12, 2020.

168: **Semiconductor Industry Association:** Stephen Nellis and Alexandra Alper, "US Chipmakers Quietly Lobby to Ease Huawei Ban," Reuters, June 16, 2019.

168: **Joe Lieberman:** Daniel Lippman and Steven Overly, "China's ZTE Taps Joe Lieberman for DC Damage Control," *Politico*, December 13, 2018.

168: **ties to the Chinese military and intelligence:** Graham Webster, "China's ZTE Has Long Been on Washington's Radar, for Quite a Few Reasons. Here's the Story," *Washington Post*, May 22, 2018.

169: **chief financial officer of Huawei:** William Sprouse, "Huawei Hit with New Charges; CFO Named as Defendant," *CFO*, February 14, 2020.

169: **Chinese state security:** Kanishka Singh and Nick Macfie, "US Intelligence Says Huawei Funded by Chinese State Security: Report," Reuters, April 19, 2019.

169: **Samir Jain:** Bill Gertz, "Senior Obama Cyber Official Lobbying for China," *Washington Free Beacon*, April 9, 2019.

169: **Trump tweeted:** Dan Strumpf, "Trump Takes Aim at Huawei after Ex-Obama Official Becomes Lobbyist," *Wall Street Journal*, April 15, 2019.

169: **Democratic officials reportedly warned:** Owen Churchill, "In Coronavirus-Gripped Washington, Rhetoric Rises but Anti-China Bills Stall," *South China Morning Post*, April 13, 2020.

170: **Gallagher and Cotton introduced a bill:** Office of Arkansas Senator Tom Cotton, "Cotton, Gallagher Introduce Bill to End US Dependence on Chinese-Manufactured Pharmaceuticals," March 18, 2020.

171: **Henry Kissinger said:** Evelyn Cheng, "Fallout from US-China Trade Conflict Could Be 'Even Worse' than WWI, Kissinger Says," CNBC, November 22, 2019.

172: **"lost" China:** Arthur Waldron, "How China Was 'Lost,'" *Washington Examiner*, January 28, 2013.

173: **post–Cold War era of peace:** "George Bush Sr. in United Nations," OnTheIssues.org, October 1, 1990.

173: **Gephardt described the US ruling class:** Robin Toner, "Gephardt Presses Double Theme: Nationalism and Economic Worry," *New York Times*, March 3, 1988.

174: **xenophobia:** William Saletan and Ben Jacobs, "The Worst of Dick Gephardt," *Slate*, September 3, 2003.

174: **arguing to revoke:** John E. Yang, "Gephardt Bashes US Policy on China," *Washington Post*, May 28, 1997.

174: **"We can't compete with slave labor":** Adam Clymer, "Gephardt Will Denounce Trade Policy toward China," *New York Times*, May 27, 1997.

175: **Obama mocked:** Rebecca Savransky, "Obama to Trump: What Magic Wand Do You Have?" *The Hill*, June 1, 2016.

176: **director's seat:** James T. Areddy, "What We Know about Hunter Biden's Dealings in China," *Wall Street Journal*, October 4, 2019.

176: ***Financial Times:*** Aime Williams, Sun Yu, and Roman Olearchyk, "Hunter Biden's Web of Interests," *Financial Times*, October 8, 2019.

177: **Trump's aggressive China tariffs:** Office of Senator Dianne Feinstein, "Feinstein on Trump Administration's Proposed 25 Percent Tariff on Chinese Imports," June 17, 2019.

177: ***USA Today:*** Samuel Stebbins and John Harrington, "Here Are the Members of Congress with the Highest Estimated Net Worth," *USA Today*, October 25, 2019.

177: ***Los Angeles Times:*** Glenn F. Bunting, "Feinstein, Husband Hold Strong China Connections," *Los Angeles Times*, March 28, 1997.

178: **Shenzhen Development Bank:** "Newbridge Still Has an Eye on China," *South China Morning Post*, October 29, 2003.

178: **rough seas:** "Landmark Deal in China for Newbridge," Private Equity International, August 3, 2004.

178: **two years later:** Henry Sender, "Newbridge Capital Wins Control of Shenzhen Development Bank," *Wall Street Journal*, May 31, 2004.

179: **"good friend:"** "A Conversation with Dianne Feinstein," *Wall Street Journal*, June 6, 2010.

179: **danced together:** Glenn F. Bunting and Dwight Morris, "Husband's Business Ties Pose Dilemma for Feinstein: Politics: She Says His Myriad Investments Do Not Influence Her Votes and She Is Aware of Potential Conflicts," *Los Angeles Times*, October 28, 1994.

179: **Blum was planning:** Bunting and Morris, "Husband's Business Ties Pose Dilemma for Feinstein."

180: **Expressing disapproval of Beijing:** Lance Williams, "Husband Invested in China as Feinstein Pushed Trade," *SFGate*, October 22, 2000.

180: **In a 1996 editorial:** Dianne Feinstein, "Most-Favored Status Is Not a Perk," *Los Angeles Times*, May 19, 1996.

181: **commission of comparative human rights:** Bunting, "Feinstein, Husband Hold Strong China Connections."

181: **"China had no local police":** "A Conversation with Dianne Feinstein," *Wall Street Journal.*

181: **According to reports:** Zach Dorfman, "How Silicon Valley Became a Den of Spies," *Politico,* July 27, 2018.

182: **warned by the FBI:** Robert Pear, "FBI Warned of Donations from China, Senator Says," *New York Times,* March 10, 1997.

182: **never sought to exploit:** Bunting, "Feinstein, Husband Hold Strong China Connections."

183: **John Garnaut:** Bill Bishop, "Engineers of the Soul: Ideology in Xi Jinping's China by John Garnaut," Sinocism, January 16, 2019.

184: **Document No. 9:** Chris Buckley, "China Takes Aim at Western Ideas," *New York Times,* August 19, 2013.

CHAPTER TWELVE: OBAMA'S COUP

185: **Hatfill had been targeted by then FBI director Robert Mueller:** David Freed, "The Wrong Man," *Atlantic,* May 2010.

185: **Hatfill filed for $4.6 million:** Scott Shane and Eric Lichtblau, "Scientist Is Paid Million by US in Anthrax Suit," *New York Times,* June 28, 2008.

187: **another month of stasis:** The White House, "Remarks by President Trump, Vice President Pence, and Members of the Coronavirus Task Force in Press Conference," March 30, 2020.

190: **1,200 public health officials:** Mallory Simon, "Over 1,000 Health Professionals Sign a Letter Saying, Don't Shut Down Protests Using Coronavirus Concerns as an Excuse," CNN, June 5, 2020.

191: **"As tragic as these past few weeks have been":** "WATCH: Obama Holds Virtual Town Hall on Policing and Civil Unrest," PBS, June 3, 2020.

192: **the University of Michigan:** Kim Kozlowski, "Sasha Obama Set to Begin College Career at University of Michigan," *Detroit News,* August 28, 2019.

192: **"You don't have to do this, Joe":** Glenn Thrush, "Obama and Biden's Relationship Looks Rosy. It Wasn't Always That Simple," *New York Times,* August 16, 2019.

195: **Sanders foreign policy team:** National Interest, Matthew Petti, "Bernie Sanders Foreign Policy Advisors Invited to Biden Camp," April 14, 2020.

197: **Brennan was briefing him:** Greg Miller, Ellen Nakashima, and Adam Entous, "Obama's Secret Struggle to Punish Russia for Putin's Election Assault," *Washington Post,* June 23, 2017.

197: **Throughout the preelection period:** Brooke Singman, "Documents Suggest Possible Coordination between CIA, FBI, Obama WH, and Dem Officials Early in Trump-Russia Probe: Investigators," Fox News, March 28, 2018.

197: **Page texted Strzok:** US Senate, Committee on Homeland Security and Governmental Affairs, "The Clinton Email Scandal and the FBI's Investigation of It: An Interim Report," February 7, 2018.

199: **California congresswoman Jane Harman:** Neil A. Lewis and Mark Mazzetti, "Lawmaker Is Said to Have Agreed to Aid Lobbyists," *New York Times,* April 20, 2009.

199: **James Rosen:** Tom McCarthy, "James Rosen: Fox News Reporter Targeted as 'Co-Conspirator' in Spying Case," *Guardian,* May 21, 2013.

199: **Sharyll Attkisson:** John Kruzel, "Journalist Alleging Obama Administration Spied on Her Seeks to Reopen Case," *The Hill*, January 10, 2020.

199: **John Brennan spied on Congress:** Mark Mazetti and Carl Hulse, "Inquiry by C.I.A. Affirms It Spied on Senate Panel," *New York Times*, July 31, 2014.

200: **the Justice Department withdrew its case:** Katelyn Polantz, "Justice Department Drops Criminal Case against Michael Flynn," CNN, May 7, 2020.

200: **amicus brief:** Ronn Blitzer and Bill Mears, "Court-Appointed Attorney Says Judge Should Block DOJ Move to Drop Flynn Case," Fox News, June 10, 2020.

203: **Five police officers were killed in Dallas:** Dave Boyer, "Obama Defends Black Lives Matter Protests at Police Memorial in Dallas," *Washington Times*, July 12, 2016.

203: **Obama hosted BLM officials at the White House:** Jordan Fabian, "Prominent Black Lives Matter Activist to Attend Obama Meeting," *The Hill*, July 13, 2016.

203: **Black Lives Matter website:** https://blacklivesmatter.com.

203: **ActBlue:** Bryan Sldysko, "Democrats Crack $1.5B Raised through Online Portal ActBlue," AP, October 25, 2018.

203: **Defeat Disinfo:** Isaac Stanley-Becker, "Technology Once Used to Combat ISIS Propaganda Is Enlisted by Democratic Group to Counter Trump's Coronavirus Messaging," *Washington Post*, May 2, 2020.

203: **McChrystal had been critical of Trump:** Richard Sisk, "McChrystal Slams Trump over Mattis Resignation, Syria Withdrawal," Military.com, December 30, 2016.

204: **he told Secretary of State Mike Pompeo:** Paul Szoldra, "General McChrystal Told Pompeo to 'Muddle Along' in Afghanistan, Leaked Audio Reveals," *Task and Purpose*, December 6, 2018.

204: **McChrystal teamed up with First Lady Michelle Obama:** Thom Shanker, "McChrystal to Lead Program for Military Families," *New York Times*, April 10, 2011.

204: **Higher Ground Labs:** Peter Hamby, "Can Democrats Win Back the Internet in the Age of Trump?" *Vanity Fair*, June 25, 2019.

205: **Hay-Adams:** NBC Washington Staff and the Associated Press, "17 Arrested, 11 DC Officers Hurt after Killing of George Floyd Sparks Outrage," NBC Washington, May 30, 2020.

206: **James Mattis fired a shot across his bow:** Jeffrey Goldberg, "James Mattis Denounces President Trump, Describes Him as a Threat to the Constitution," *Atlantic*, June 3, 2020.

206: **Governor Pete Wilson called in ten thousand Marines:** Russell Snyder, "Federal Troops Leave Riot-Torn L.A.," UPI, May 10, 1992.

207: **Esper was the first to fall out:** Eric Schmitt, Helene Cooper, Thomas Gibbons-Neff, and Maggie Haberman, "Esper Breaks with Trump on Using Troops against Protesters," *New York Times*, June 3, 2020.

207: **Milley folded the week after:** Ryan Browne, Barbara Starr, and Zachary Cohen, "Top General Apologizes for Appearing in Photo-Op with Trump after Forceful Removal of Protesters," CNN, June 11, 2020.

EPILOGUE: EPILOGUE: JUSTICE AND MICHAEL FLYNN

209: **first openly gay Cabinet secretary:** "Grenell: Trump Told Me Being First Out Gay Cabinet Member Was a 'Big Deal,'" *Washington Blade*, June 2, 2020.

210: **they had cut off the head:** Lee Smith, *The Plot against the President: The True Story of How Congressman Devin Nunes Uncovered the Biggest Political Scandal in US History* (Center Street, 2019), 334.

210: **"Declassifying the transcripts":** Office of the Director of National Intelligence, "53 HPSCI Transcripts." https://www.dni.gov/index.php/features/2753-53-hpsci-transcripts.

211: **"We declassified the footnotes:** Chuck Grassley, "IG Footnotes: Serious Problems with Dossier Sources Didn't Stop FBI's Page Surveillance," April 15, 2020.

211: **Declassification of Rod Rosenstein's memo:** US Department of Justice, Office of Legislative Affairs, "Memorandum regarding 'The Scope of Investigation and Definition of Authority,'" May 6, 2020.

211: **A list of thirty-nine Obama administration officials:** Office of the Director of National Intelligence, Letter from Acting Director Richard Grenell to Sens Charles Grassley and Ron Johnson, May 13, 2020.

211: **transcripts of Flynn's December 23 and 29 conversations:** Brooke Singman, "Flynn-Kislyak Call Transcripts Released, Revealing Fateful Talks over Russia Sanctions," Fox News, May 29, 2020.

211: **memo for the opening of Crossfire Razor:** US District Court for the District of Columbia, "Government's Motion to Dismiss the Criminal Information against the Defendant Michael T. Flynn," Exhibit 2, May 7, 2020.

211: **January 4 memo closing the Flynn investigation:** US District Court for the District of Columbia, "Government's Motion to Dismiss the Criminal Information against the Defendant Michael T. Flynn," Exhibit 1, May 7, 2020.

211: **January 4 text messages:** US District Court for the District of Columbia, "Government's Motion to Dismiss the Criminal Information against the Defendant Michael T. Flynn," Exhibit 7, May 7, 2020.

211: **An FBI interview with Sally Yates:** US District Court for the District of Columbia, "Government's Motion to Dismiss the Criminal Information against the Defendant Michael T. Flynn," Exhibit 4, May 7, 2020.

212: **passage from an email:** "Read: Declassified Susan Rice Email about January 5, 2017, Oval Office Meeting with Obama," Fox News, May 19, 2020.

212: **Handwritten notes of a senior FBI agent:** US District Court for the District of Columbia, "Government's Motion to Dismiss the Criminal Information against the Defendant Michael T. Flynn," Exhibit 10, May 12, 2020.

212: **emails between members:** US District Court for the District of Columbia, "Government's Motion to Dismiss the Criminal Information against the Defendant Michael T. Flynn," Exhibit 9, May 12, 2020.

212: **Strzok's handwritten notes indicate that Obama had not:** Sean Davis and Mollie Hemingway, "Explosive New FBI Notes Confirm Obama Directed Anti-Flynn Operation," Federalist, June 24, 2020.

212: **February 10 text messages:** US District Court for the District of Columbia, "Government's Motion to Dismiss the Criminal Information against the Defendant Michael T. Flynn," Exhibit 7, May 12, 2020.